Games and Sport in Everyday Life

GAMES AND SPORT IN EVERYDAY LIFE

Dialogues and Narratives of the Self

Robert Perinbanayagam

Paradigm Publishers
Boulder • London

Published in the United States by Paradigm Publishers, 3360 Mitchell Lane, Suite E, Boulder, Colorado 80301 USA.

Paradigm Publishers is the trade name of Birkenkamp & Company, LLC, Dean Birkenkamp, President and Publisher.

Library of Congress Cataloging-in-Publication Data

Perinbanayagam, R. S., 1934-
Games and sport in everyday life : dialogues and narratives of the self / Robert Perinbanayagam.
p. cm.
Includes bibliographical references and index.
ISBN 1-59451-108-X
1. Game theory. 2. Political science—Mathematical models. I. Title.
JA72.5.P38 2006
300.1'5193—dc22

2005033051

Printed and bound in the United States of America on acid-free paper that meets the standards of the American National Standard for Permanence of Paper for Printed Library Materials.

Designed and Typeset by Straight Creek Bookmakers.

10 09 08 07 06

5 4 3 2 1

Contents

To Athena, with much love and affection

Preface

Games in general have been studied from a variety of perspectives. They have been studied as forms of activity, as spectacles, as institutions in which class, gender, and race are represented in one way or another, and as instruments for cultural transformation and political domination. Rarely have they been studied as a form of activity that a social agent undertakes in order to interact with an other and construct a system that has meaning to him or her. Games are, after all, played more often by ordinary people in their everyday lives, with little concern for spectators, and played without being paid to do so. Games are not only played voluntarily but are also undertaken by an agent in charge, generally speaking, of all the moves in the game. Games, if played with commitment and dedication, provide a sense of adventure, situate such playing within strictly enforced norms and codes of conduct, and give a modicum of power to the player, to put Simmel, Durkheim, and Marx together into a unified argument. Games become an efficient means of finding surcease from boredom, anomie, and alienation.

Einstein in a famous response to certain implications of quantum theory remarked, "god does not play dice with the universe." In Hindu myth, however, the supreme god Siva does play dice with his consort Parvati and the playing is said to be about time and the universe. In the various myths of Siva and in saivite iconography he is represented as playing dice. The dice that Siva and Parvati use, too, are special ones: each side is said to represent a *yuga,* a measurement of time usually translated as "aeons." Each throw of the dice then represents both the creation of time as well as its fundamental uncertainty: once the dice are thrown the god cannot—or does not choose to—control the unfolding of a temporality. It is truly uncertain and indeterminate and depends on the responses the dice are able to mobilize from the universe of objects they will encounter as they fall. Further, in the mythology of Siva, he is always made to lose the game to his consort. Here then we have an omnipotent and omniscient as well as self-generated god playing dice with Parvati, who herself was created by Siva, managing to lose the game on a continuous basis. One question that arises is why did the myth makers of antiquity create an omnipotent god and then make him lose the dice games to his consort?

There are many theological and philosophical answers to this puzzle—many of them examined brilliantly by Handelman and Shulman

(1997)—but one can nevertheless inquire about the structural and social psychological implications of this arrangement. It seems to me that the mythmakers understood that even omnipotent gods cannot be left alone and isolated. They too need to play, be in the game, and interact with other people. Siva then is made to play dice with his consort and is not allowed to resort to his powers to win. If he is allowed to use his supreme authority to win against Parvati, then there will be no game and no reason for her to play again but an omnipotent god can afford to lose and still want to play insofar as it gives him Parvati's companionship and favors. To make the god lose enables the game to be continued and such interaction as does occur creates various ongoing consequences. Every time Parvati wins the game, the gate is open for conversations: she teases him and cajoles him, demands the payment of his gambling debts, and angers him and later pleases him too. The game then is able to ensure continuous interactions as well as both cognitive and emotional engagement between the two players.

The myths of the god who plays dice enable the confrontation with a number of intellectual problems: Siva, the self-created god, answers the puzzle of the first cause. Once that problem is solved, another is faced: he will need action, movement, and above all interaction. Once Parvati enters the scene, they must have something that they can do together. And insofar as he is god and she is his consort, whatever they do together must have some cosmic significance: so they play with time and the universe, creating and destroying them in ongoing cycles.

This myth captures two of the fundamental features of games: its imbrication with the processes of time and its irrefutably dialogic character. In everyday life, too, as agents play games, they are, in fact, playing with time, their own awareness of the past and the present, and their anticipation of a future that is hoisted on the turn of the dice or the distribution of cards or the movements of a ball that has been hit or driven or thrown or kicked.

Game playing is a structure of activity in which already constituted selves are given play and in which new elements of selves are constructed while old elements are reconstituted or discarded. Insofar as the constitution of selves is an ongoing activity—with the self as both object and subject, constituted and constituting—games, when they occur, are sites and situations in which such constituting activities go on. Such activity is relatively free from the domination and the control of agents that are present in many other arenas of social life. The absence of such domination and control in ordinary game playing provides opportunities for human agents to escape from alienation and seek to achieve some level of creative freedom.

Such freedom is, however, achieved within given structures. These structures both enable and guide these moves of creative action. The structures representing distilled and encapsulated versions of the problems of everyday life have the quality of myths not only in the sense of narratives that have an immutable structure that speaks to certain eternal problems faced by members of the human species, but also as narratives that incorporate current historically specific concerns into their manifestations. In fact, games are myths enacted and performed in situ, in contrast to other myths that are either recounted or performed on stage by actors. Games are narratives, as myths are, but in playing games an agent puts his or her self into play with these narrative structures. Acts, temporality, and emotionality are unified into one process. In these enacted myths, each participant is given the bare structure of the myth which he or she has to use to give play to his or her self while at the same time constructing and reconstructing a self. In putting oneself into the structures of various games, an agent will play hard and play with commitment and work toward a denouement without knowing the denouement in advance. The resolution, in fact, is achieved by the contingent interactions of various forces brought into play by the various players.

In each occasion of game playing, and in each situation within the game, the selves of the players are advanced, challenged, vindicated, and enhanced or defeated and humiliated.These developments in the playing of games will also generate commensurate emotions. For the duration of the game, the player is a hero on a quest, and at the end, he or she is a hero denied or affirmed: he or she has put his or her self at risk and has to live with the consequences. Human agents systematically use the structures of various games to generate meanings for their selves.

Insofar as there are countless numbers of games, it would have been impossible to bring them all under one compass for discussion. Each game has certain unique properties but, as Wittgenstein argued (1958), all the phenomena that are called games have certain "family resemblances" to each other. One can think of all the games as consisting of an extended family or a clan and within this family are smaller units—lineages—in which the resemblances are stronger. I have therefore taken the liberty of classifying the games according to a selected item or resemblance and arrived at the following sets; within each set, I have selected certain games to represent the set for purposes of discussion:

I. Card Games: Bridge and Poker
II. Board Games: Chess
III. Court Games: Tennis
IV. Course Games: Golf
V. Field Games: American Football, Soccer
VI. Hit-and-Run Games: Cricket, Baseball, Stickball

The resemblances or similarities in all the games in the lineage can be studied as the structural properties of games as such. However, each game, while sharing certain features, has its own unique properties, too. Following the logic of classification using the family as a model, one can go a step further and claim that even within a family individual members will have certain features that distinguish them very clearly from each other. For example, all field games and all court games have certain family resemblances as games. But in field games, the distinct characteristic is the placement of players in certain positions as members of a team, while in tennis, the aim of each player is to place a ball within precisely marked spaces. I will call these the fundamental *thematics* of the game: in card games it is *time,* in golf it is the physical *environment,* in tennis it is *space and place,* in cricket and baseball it is a *single player* facing an array of adversaries, and in soccer and American football it is making and managing *networks of positions.* These thematics connect games to other cultural themes and established structures of activity. Games are essentially continuations of certain other themes in the culture within which they were produced.

The work is not in any sense an empirical study. It is rather a structural analysis of games and an investigation of their interactional implications to human agents. I take games as constructed objects, carefully assembled and articulated, albeit by many artists over the years in order to fulfill certain purposes in the everyday life of human agents. Much like a poem or a novel or a myth or a folk tale, games can be studied as objects in themselves as well as in their interconnections to other phenomena in their respective domains. This will enable us to understand the complex significance they have for those who play and the society that sustains them. I suppose my method can be best described as a structural analysis of games and analytical conjectures about their interactional significance.

Acknowledgments

I must thank Ms. Judy Frost for giving me exemplary editorial and research assistance in the preparation of this manuscript. I am also grateful to Ms. Terry McCarthy for transforming my handwriting into typescript with both insight and technical acumen.

I want to acknowledge here, too, the courteous and efficient assistance that I have received from the staff at the Hunter College library during the many years I have been going to them. I want to thank, in particular, Mr. Norman Clarius for obtaining books on interlibrary loan for me, some of them truly esoteric and obscure ones, with dispatch and unfailing courtesy.

Last and not least, I must thank Dean Birkenkamp of Paradigm Press for seeing merit in my work—this one and an earlier one—and deciding to publish it. The staff at Paradigm Publishers—Dianne Ewing and Allison Sullenberger—were not only helpful but were very congenial and wise in the ways of the editorial world and that of publicity, and deserve my heartfelt thanks.

O thou whose cynic sneers express
The censure of our favorite chess
Know that its skill is science's self,
Its play distraction from distress.
It soothes the anxious lover's care;
It weans the drunkard from excess:
It counsels warriors in their art,
When dangers threat and perils press;
And yield us, when we need them most,
Companions in our loneliness.

Ibn ul Mu' taz (1038)

1

Games

The Self in Dialogue and Narrative

Many scholars have worked hard at defining and describing play and games in as specific a manner as possible. In modern times, Johan Huizinga, in a work that is considered a classic, has discussed many specific features of what it is to play a game, focusing particularly on the general concept of play. For him the primary characteristic of play is that it is voluntary. A second characteristic of play is that it is not "ordinary" or "real" life. "It is rather the stepping out of 'real' life into a temporary sphere of activity with a disposition all of its own" (1950: 8). In addition to these two features of play, Huizinga also describes what he calls some "formal characteristics" of play. There is, he notes, the "disinterestedness" of play: "Not being 'ordinary' life, it stands outside the immediate satisfaction of wants and appetites, indeed it tempts the appetitive process." As such it is an "intermezzo in one's life, an interlude in our daily lives." Nevertheless, Huizinga observes, playing as such "adorns life, amplifies it, and is to that extent a necessity, both for the individual—as life function—and for society as by reason of a meaning it contains, its significance, its expressive value, its spiritual and social associations in short, as a cultural function" (1950: 9).

Roger Caillois finds Huizinga's approach "too broad and too narrow" at the same time, and proposes an alternative that is more detailed. He distinguishes the playing of games in terms of "whether in the different games under consideration, the role of competition, chance, simulation or vertigo is dominant ... " He continues, "I shall call them *agôn, alea* and *mimicry* and *ilinx* respectively ... One *plays* football or billiards or chess (*agôn*); roulette or a lottery (*alea*); pirate, Nero or Hamlet (*mimicry*); or one produces in oneself, by rapid whirling or falling movement, a state of dizziness and disorder (*ilinx*)" (1961: 12).

While Huizinga's and Caillois's studies are exemplary and pioneering attempts to define and describe *play,* one is still left in the dark about what exactly a *game* is. In the work of Bernard Suits (1995), however, one comes across a more comprehensive attempt at a definition of games. He writes:

> The elements of a game may now be assembled in the following definition: To play a game is to attempt to achieve a specific state of affairs (prelusory goals), using only means permitted by the rules (lusory means), when the rules prohibit the use of more efficient in favor of less efficient means (constitutive rules), and where such rules are accepted just because they make possible such activity (lusory attitude). I also offer the following, only approximately accurate, but more pretty version: Playing a game is the voluntary attempt to overcome unnecessary obstacles. (1995: 48)

In anthropology, the programmatic essay by J. M. Roberts, M. J. Arth, and R. R. Bush provided a definition of games that many in the field take as a standard one. They argued that a game is "a recreational activity characterized by (1) organized play (2) competition (3) two or more sides (4) criteria for determining the winner (5) agreed upon rules." They further suggested that games can be classified into those involving *physical skill, strategy, and chance,* while in some games these may occur together (1959: 557). This again, like Suits's, is a very parsimonious definition of games. After surveying these approaches to the definition of games and various others, Jasper Juhl gives his own version: "A game is a rule-based formal system with a variable quantified outcome, where different outcomes are assigned different values, the player extends effort in order to influence the outcome and the player feels attached to the outcome and the consequences of the activity are optional and negotiable" (2003: 17).

These various approaches to games, parsimonious and precise as they are, lack the sociological and social psychological dimension of the playing of games. Mihaly Csikszentmihalyi and Stith Bennett, after discussing a variety of games from different cultures, seek to provide this dimension, but they too seem to miss a central point about game playing. They claim:

> The play situation, social reality, is not up for negotiation: the actors are absolutely bound to a limited set of actions; play is a social system with no deviance. Given a manageable number of options for action and an ambiguous symbol system, no viewpoint other than the players' viewpoint is necessary—the social self becomes superfluous and the player can merge with the process of monistic awareness. (1971: 56)

It is impossible to conceive of a human experience—other than a state of comotosity—in which the self becomes "superfluous." The playing of a game is certainly not a "monistic" undertaking. The selves of the participants are far from absent; they are very much present and face a variety of contingencies. Indeed, games must be considered, to begin with, from the standpoint of the player himself or herself, and when one does that it becomes clear that they are fundamentally processes in which agents interact with each other, conduct dialogues of one sort or another, and present and narrate a self. The playing of games then is not another and merely lusory or disinterested series of acts, but rather acts that human agents undertake, as players or spectators, to achieve cognitive involvement and emotional engagement with the other. The playing of games is, in fact, a conversation, a dialogic activity that systematically involves other agents, a continuation of the other processes of everyday life. It is also a means by which a human agent achieves intercourse with the other by using a range of symbols that is broader than language.

The Dialogic Imperative

The fundamental processes in any human agent's life are the acts of addressing another to achieve cognitive involvement, emotional engagement, and at times, physical contact and receiving commensurate responses. It is imperative, therefore, that the full implications of such moves are considered in seeking to understand the human predicament. Marx and Engels expressed this clearly. He wrote:

> Language is as old as consciousness, language is practical consciousness that exists also for other men, and for that reason alone it really exists for me personally as well; language, like consciousness, only arises from the need, the necessity, of *intercourse* with other men. (1970: 51, emphasis added)

Human agents are, indubitably, characterized by a capacity for language. To call this an "instinct" or say that it is "innate" and leave it there is really to evade addressing an important aspect of this capacity for language and engage in a simple-minded reductionism. A human agent does not speak a language as such but a *particular* language such as English or French or Tamil or Swahili that became available to his or her *use* from his or her social circles. *It is not so much that the human animal has language but that he or she uses a particular medium to address others and incorporate them into his or her mind, self, and life and enable the others to do the same that is significant.* Language is intrinsically an *addressive* medium designed to incorporate others into one's existence—real others or presumptive ones. Human agents are complex social creatures because they have a language, and they have a language because they are complex social creatures. Every linguistic articulation is a social act that enmeshes the speaker in an irrevocable relationship with another and allows him or her and the other at least to begin a process of mutual understanding—presumptive or real—and to create the possibility of emotional engagement. Further, if no one addresses a child early in his or her life in such a way, language will never emerge, and however innate or instinctive it may be, there will be no specimens for linguists to study. Once a language has been learned by interacting with others, a human agent is forever trapped in interactions of one sort or another insofar as the language he or she has learned is by definition a public and addressive instrumentation.

A human being, then, is not a mere linguistic animal but a *speaking* and *listening* animal, or an *addressing* and *answering* animal who uses such capacities to good purpose, a *dialogic being* who actively engages the other with a particular language that he or she has mastered. Exchange of talk is not a matter of passing information to each other or undertaking certain formal operations but of engaging the other emotionally and cognitively and constructing the very processes of social existence. While articulate speech is the most common form of such processes of address and answer, they can be undertaken also by other means—for example, with "sign language." *Such cycles of addresses and answers are the essential and ubiquitous feature of the everyday life of the human agents.* They define their being and presence in the world. The selves of such agents—their sense of who they are and what they are—are constituted by ongoing sequences of addresses and responses enabling them to participate in a drama of the self as well as a narrative of the self. And such addresses can be undertaken and responses elicited without using words as such, but tokens thereof. The imperative to talk and enmesh oneself with others, cognitively and emotionally, is so strong that human agents will use a variety of instrumentations to fulfill it.

Conversations and the Self

The moves that an agent makes in the conversation are best described as "social acts" in G. H. Mead's sense of the term. Seeking to develop a social theory of mind and self, he used the concept of the "social act" as the central one in his work. In one form or another, it appears throughout his work, and it became a fundamental element in both his philosophical and social psychological writings. Ethics and morality, conduct and communication, thinking and the social construction of a unique human agent were all addressed through the processes of social action (1938).

Mead gives the following initial description of a social act and then, interestingly enough, uses the notion of a game to illustrate his point. Mead observes:

> In the human organism, the pattern of the whole social act is in some sense initiated in the individual as the pattern of his act. The mechanism of this is the effect which the gesture of the organism has upon itself that is analogous to the effect which it has upon the other ...
>
> The pattern of such a social act in the organism of an individual may be illustrated in a game, in which the gesture of the organism is the stimulus to other players to their appropriate responses. Illustrations may be found in any cooperative process in which each individual indicates by his gestures which belongs to his act what the others have to do. (1938: 446–47)

The ruling concept in the entirety of Mead's work on mind, self, and society is "conversation" as an empirical process and as metaphor. To begin with, he spoke of "the conversation in gestures." Conversations that cannot be translated into articulate speech may be carried on, he observed, and noted, "we are reading the conduct of other people when, perhaps, they are not aware of it. There is something that reveals to us what the purpose is—just the glance of the eye, the attitude of the body which leads to the response" (1934: 14).

From this conversation conducted by nonverbal means, Mead leads to the discussion of what he terms the "vocal gesture." It is through the use of these "vocal gestures" or language that meaning emerges. This claim occurs in many places in his writing, but I will give one citation here:

> Meaning arises and lies within the field of the relationship between the gesture of a given human organism and the subsequent behavior of this organism as indicated to another human organism by that gesture ... The response of one organism to the gesture of another in any given social act is the meaning of that gesture ... (1934: 75, 78)

The social act to which Mead alludes here is really a conversational process: the gesture is addressed to another and it elicits a response. In discussing the emergence of the human agent as a self, Mead ranks the conversational process as the critical one:

> The self ... arises when the conversation of gesture is taken over into the conduct of the individual form. When this conversation of gestures can be taken over into the individual's conduct so that attitude of the other forms can affect the organism, and the organism can reply with its corresponding gesture and thus arouse the attitude of the other in its own process, then a self arises. (Mead, 1934: 167)

In such conversations for Mead, the fundamental process is the need for the human agent to understand and empathize with all the others involved in them. Again, using the game analogy, he notes that in playing a game, an agent:

> must know what everyone is going to do in order to carry out his own play. He has to take all of these roles. They do not have to be present in consciousness at the same time, but at some moments he has to have three or four individuals present in his own attitude, such as the one who is going to throw the ball, the one who is going to catch it, and so on. (1934: 151)

Meaning and self emerge out of these basic processes in which the gesture of one organism, made after due consideration of the role of the other, elicits the same or similar response from the other, who also undertakes a reciprocal consideration of the role of the initial articulator. *The basic processes in a human life are the construction of social acts in which each participant engages the other cognitively and emotionally by taking the role and attitude of the other.* Even private cognitive processes are conceived as such conversations by Mead:

> Thinking or intellectual process—the *internalization* and inner *dramatization,* by the individual, of the external conversation of significant gestures which constitutes this chief mode of interaction with other individuals belonging to the same society—is the earliest experiential phase in the genesis and development of the self. (1934: 173, emphasis added)

In undertaking seemingly solitary tasks, individuals are yet participating in social forms of life. They engage in reflexive activities in which they are able to address their own selves and respond to them, explicitly or implicitly, using a shared language and, indeed, playing a dialogic game. In Mead's words: "It is by means of reflexiveness—the turning back of the experience of the individual upon himself—that the whole social process is brought into the experience of the individual ..." (1934: 134).

From these processes of taking the role of the other and constructing a social act in which one is expected to incorporate the attitude of other into the act, a self arises and becomes an essential element in all conduct. Selves should not be viewed as immanent structures hidden in the head that mysteriously influence the conduct of an individual. Mead argued, "... The essence of the self ... is cognitive: it lies in the *internalized conversation of gestures* which constitute thinking, or in terms of which thought or reflection proceeds" (1934: 173). However, such cognitive processing of the self proceeds to treat it as an "object." The self has the characteristic that is an object to itself and that characteristic distinguishes it from other objects and from the body" (1934: 136). Such a capacity for objectification of self enables an agent to engage in what Mead calls "delayed reaction." He puts it this way: "Delayed reaction is necessary to intelligent conduct. The organization, implicit testing and final selection by the individual of his overt responses or reactions to the social situations which confront him and which present him with the problem of adjustment would be impossible if his overt responses or reactions could not be delayed" (1934: 99).

In engaging in this delayed reaction as well as action, the agent is, in fact, considering the final selection of the act in terms of his or her self. Each act is evaluated in terms of its significance to the self that is already constituted as well as in terms of its likely consequences to the future of the self. Each such act then manifests the self and, indeed, it is in the process of acting that an agent as well as his or her others recognize the presence of self. Once a self has emerged in ordinary life it is subject to revisions and reformulations, based on the responses it receives to the acts it has prosecuted.

Dialogic Processes

Conversations can be conducted between agents on many levels of *complexity* and one of these can be whether they have dialogic properties or not. In his discussion of the uses of language as dialogic processes, Mikhail Bakhtin describes two features: "addressivity" and "answerability." In conversations with dialogic properties, there is the distinct attempt by the parties to infuse their remarks to the other with enough *addressivity* so that the other can provide answers.

He observes that "language enters life through concrete utterances (which manifest language) and life enters language through concrete utterances as well" (1986: 63). He went on to note that in a conversation "when the listener perceives and understands the meaning (the language meaning) of a speech, he simultaneously takes an active responsive attitude toward it" (1986: 68).

In allowing language and life to intermesh with each other, an agent enables himself or herself to participate with another through language—insofar as language is a shared medium—not merely to "respond" to the other, but to actively participate in constructing a response. In order to elicit such an "active response," the initial agent must articulate his or her statements in "anticipation of encountering this response." Bakhtin puts this as follows:

> An essential constituent marker of the utterance is its quality of being directed to someone, its *addressivity* as distinct from signifying units of language—words and sentences—that are impersonal, belonging to nobody, the utterance has both an author ... and an addressee ... Both

> the composition and, particularly, the style of the utterance depend on those to whom the utterance is addressed, how the speaker (or writer) senses and imagines his addressees and the force of their effect on the utterance." (1986: 95)

Each participant in a dialogic conversation is alert to the addressivity that is implicit in his or her contribution. The sum effect of the practice of such addressivity is to elicit the active engagement of the other in the proceedings as he or she provides an answer. Bakhtin observes, "I have to answer with my own life for what I have experienced and understood in art so that everything I have experienced and understood would not remain ineffectual in my life" (1990: 1). An agent is obliged to answer the stimulations he or she receives, from art or elsewhere, in order to be "effectual." One may not have to answer with one's life all the time, but answer one does, as part of the reciprocal foundation of human relationships. Addressivity and answerability became the two pillars of Bakhtin's architectonic of dialogicity with which, in Michael Holquist's words, "a reciprocal simultaneity ... yokes each of the pairings in dialogue not only with each other but with other categories as well" (1990: xxvii).

These processes of addressivity and answerability are strikingly similar to positions advanced by Mead at about the same time as Bakhtin. The processes that Mead calls "taking the role of the other" and the "conversation of gestures" and "taking the attitude of the other" (1934) are akin to Bakhtin's dialogical principles. Indeed, one should consider Mead's work to be parallel to Bakhtin's (Holquist, 1990: 55–57). Mead wrote: "The principle which I have suggested as basic to human social organization is that of communication involving participation in the other. This requires the appearance of the other in the self, the reaching of self-consciousness through the other" (1934: 253).

This "participation in the other" is achieved by an individual who uses gestures to communicate, assuming, Mead argues:

> ... the attitude of the other individual as well as calling it out in the other. He, himself, is in the role of the other whom he is so exciting and influencing. It is through taking this role of the other that he is able to come back on himself and so direct his own process of communication. This taking the role of the other—is not of passing importance. It is not something that just happens as an incidental result of that gesture but is of importance in the development of cooperative activity. (1934: 254)

Mead stresses the importance of these processes: "The very organization of the self-conscious community is dependent upon individuals taking the attitude of the other individuals" (1934: 256). The importance of Mead's argument here, for understanding the workings of human relationships and emergence of social orders, cannot be overemphasized. These processes—taking the role of the other and taking the attitude of the other—are fundamental interpersonal moves in social interactions and relationships, and *whatever else* occurs in interactions occurs within their parameters.

Nevertheless, Mead here elides two different forms of taking the attitude and role of the other into one general description: one in which one takes the role and attitude of the other in order to *cooperate* with him or her and another in which one engages in the same processes in order to *compete* with him or her. In the former, the purposes are sympathetic, loyal, affirming, supportive, and validating; while in the latter, the purpose is to outwit the other, to use him or her for one's own exclusive advantage. One can then distinguish between *sympathetic role taking* which leads to the emergence of interactional solidarity, fulfilling interpersonal relationships and successful enterprises, and *antagonistic role taking,* which leads to conflicts and may lead to further conflicts or at times even a reintegration at a later moment. The exchanges between agents in and through which selves are constituted and meaning is made to emerge are then best described as dialogues or dialogic conversations.

In one work in particular, he has observed, "To be engaged in an occasional activity means to sustain some kind of cognitive and affective engrossment in it, some mobilization of one's psychobiological resources; in short, it means to be *involved* in it" (1963: 36). To the extent that participants in a conversation can manage such "involvement" and "engrossment" and fulfill what Goffman calls "involvement obligations" (1963: 50), they can also sustain significant conversations. In fact, to construct a full dialogic process, a modicum of involvement and engrossment seems mandatory.

The common theme in acting socially, engaging in conversations, and constructing an identity for oneself is this: an agent is continuously engaged in confronting one problem or another and solving it. The acts that compose everyday life involve facing a problem that has been presented to an agent—be it the problem of crossing from one side of the street to another or constructing a self and participating in an interaction with another—and handling it with varying degrees of efficiency. In the latter set of problems, he or she both cooperates with another and contests him or her and seeks to confront him or her. The view of the human agent as a problem-solving creature and his or her acts as moves designed to solve one problem or another is an essential element of the pragmatism of Charles Sanders Peirce and Mead and has recently been given a clear discussion by Hans Joas. He wrote: "Right from its earliest beginnings, pragmatism supplants Cartesianism's guiding notion of the solitary doubting ego with the idea of a co-operative search for truth for the purpose of coping with the real problems encountered in the course of action" (1996: 128).

In such a pragmatic existentialism, the human individual is viewed as an *active agent* who purposefully engages the world around him or her. In Sandra Rosenthal's words, "active agent" indicates "the manner in which one knows the world through structures of the meanings one has created by one's responses to the environment." In addition, there is another meaning involved in the concept of an active agent. Rosenthal (1986: 25) puts it this way: "the active use of knowledge to change society or the environment." Change here does not necessarily mean radical social change, but any kind of alteration, however small or large, in the social and physical environment. *The agent then is an actor whose continued existence in the world is made evident to him or her by the initiation and the reception of various acts by self and others.* Such acts can be external ones: the articulation of signifying speech or the consummation of a physical act like driving a car or mowing a lawn or sowing seed or serving a ball to another in tennis. Or else they can be thinking and debating and cognizing and re-cognizing in the "inner forum" of the mind. Such physical and/or mental activity as well as the responses they mobilize, then, make the agent not only an actor but also a *knowledgeable* actor even if the knowledge that he or she is using is untenable to some others.

The moves that he or she has made in the world in the past and the responses they had elicited are understood and organized into habits of thought and activity that influence subsequent conduct. For such knowledgeable actors, Rosenthal (1986: 31) avers, "Both understanding and imagination are unified and transformed into the creative functioning of habit, as providing a lived or vital intentionality, between knower and known." The use of habit in conduct, "the creative functioning of habit," is really the use of *tacit knowledge* in order to undertake acts of which one becomes aware in their essential properties only when challenged or repudiated by events or others. Further, these acts, both habitual and deliberative, are addressed to an animate or inanimate other and situated within the vital resonances of a fundamental sociality. Life then becomes an ongoing negotiation of tasks, moves *that always incorporate an other into the tasks—positively, negatively, or indifferently.* To put it another way, the ongoing processes of living in the world are problem-solving and dialogic ones that recognize the presence, varied powers, relative concreteness, and articulateness of the other. That is to say, one can address the other and incorporate him or her dialogically into the self, and the other can simultaneously do the same. He or she, just as I and me, are recognized as equally competent dialogic creatures. I can talk to my "me" just as the "me" can talk to my "I." I can talk to the other just as he or she can talk to me as well as to his or her "I" and "me"—and all the other proper nouns and common nouns that these signs represent.

The same can be said, with some qualifications, for the inanimate other. It may be inanimate, but it is never unresponsive. One kicks a stone and feels the hurt in one's foot; one can try to start an automobile and it can start readily or may resist all such attempts and just sit there, and so on. One can try to repair the automobile and succeed at it or fail—eliciting, once again, responses to one's acts that may have a resonance on one's self. There is no doubt that one's relationship to the inanimate environment is a quasi-dialogical one. The inanimate objects may not always "speak" intentionally—unless they are works of art—in return, but their responses do have an impact on the existence of the human agent and his or her conception of self. Works of art by definition embody the intentions of an author, however cryptically, surreptitiously, and confusingly, that a reader or spectator or auditor can either accept or ignore, as recommended by his or her own powers of agency. Nevertheless, there is no doubt that he or she must recognize the presence of such intentionality and take account of it and respond to it in one way or another. The individual, then, is not so much an agent as an *interactive agent.* Such an interactive agency is based on cognitive processes that are oriented to the others in the relationship as they are put into practice.

Every move that he or she undertakes is oriented always to the other and it is the responses that the other makes toward these moves that will define his or her self. The pragmatic acts are reflexive acts that, as they solve an immediate problem presented by the structure of the game in question, also enable an agent to become involved simultaneously with an other in a delimited space and time.

In producing such an act, an agent collapses the past and an anticipated future into the present and produces a move. In such a process of acting, there is a temporal adjustment of the past and future. In such an adjustment, the past is recollected and incorporated into the present act just as the anticipated future is so incorporated. Nevertheless, the fundamental *indeterminacy* of the act, as it evolves, can only be controlled up to a point. An agent may anticipate a particular future as the fruits of his or her current moves, but therein lies the pathos of the human act: the fruits may not be forthcoming, and the agent merely has to wait and see and make preparations to handle whatever contingency eventuates.

In undertaking an act, then, an agent is poised in a discrete present that is continuous with the past and a presumptive future. In other words, social acts are characterized by both *discreteness* and *continuity*: They or their intrinsic units can be separated into distinct processes, just as their connections to each other are evident. Rosenthal, drawing from Charles Sanders Peirce's ruminations, puts this very clearly as follows: "The aspect of discreteness and continuity combined allows for the emergence of the present and, with it, the possibility of the emergence of semiotic and temporal creativity; but this is the case only because of the present creativity, possibilities that are 'there' in the present and stretch into the future" (2000: 123).

It is this complex, intricately related process of action that I call giving play to the self. A conscious, responsible agent selects one act or another and addresses it to a world of others, human or material, and in anticipation of one response or another, receives one and proceeds to the next. This could be called putting a self into play—the selection and articulation of a particularized self or a particularized aspect of the self in a given situation in anticipation of eliciting a particular response. Every act a human agent undertakes objectifying others consciously and deliberately is an act in which he puts a self into play in anticipation of a response. And in the event the response does come, the self gains a presence in the world and often a validation.

The Agonistics of Dialogues

The problematics of the acts that occur in dialogues, however simple or complex they may be, give them an agonistic quality, enabling them to become truly engaging interactions. In reading both Bakhtin and Mead on these conversations and dialogues, however, one gets the impression that such conversational activities are essentially cooperative activities. Mead is aware throughout his work of the complex nature of such intentions in which both cooperation and conflict play a part—witness, for example, his persistent use of the dogfight to illustrate the conversation of gestures. Nevertheless, given his commitment to a general theory of mind, self, and society, he is essentially defining such a conversation as a cooperative process.

There is no doubt a cooperative element in a conversation, *pace* Paul Grice (1989), but all conversations, even the most innocuous-seeming ones, have also an agonistic element in them. And, overtly aggressive conversations may have a number of cooperative elements, too. For example, the roles that Mead claimed each party in conversation plays are typically parts of a system of hierarchies. There is no presumption of equality to them and this will influence the nature of the interaction that will develop and the meanings that will emerge. The form of life in which the conversation emerges is one in which agents have roles that relate to each other in terms of superordination and subordination. This being the case in all relationships between agents in a conversation, it is safe to claim that they have an inherent agonistic element in them.

Huizinga finds the "agonistic factor" of extraordinary importance in all civilizations and traces its presence in a variety of situations. Such situations involve actual contests of physical skill and strength as well as the competitive rituals like the potlatch practiced by various tribes of the

Native Americans, the drinking bouts described in old Norse literature, and so on; Huizinga observes, in the course of his wide-ranging description of such agonistic phenomena:

> The nobleman demonstrates his "virtue" by feats of strength, skill, courage, wit and wisdom, wealth or liberality. For want of these, he may yet excel in a contest of words, that is to say, he may either himself praise the virtues in which he wishes to excel his rivals, or have them praised for him by a poet or a herald. (1950: 65)

Such agonistic exercises through wit and words can be undertaken by promoting one's own virtues or by hiring others to do it. *It is the case, however, the very use of words, with wit or without them, in conversations with others, however ordinary, has a strong agonistic element in them.* To talk to others, to address others is *eo ipso* to present a self, claim an identity that is different from that of the one addressed, thereby creating the structure for an agonistic encounter. Indeed, the agonistic element is present in all encounters and one can see its presence both in the ordinary conversations of everyday life and in those specifically designed as agonistic exercises. Kenneth Burke (1969b: 22) puts this idea succinctly by claiming that since "individuals are at odds with one another" they need rhetoric to deal with each other. This being "at odds with one another" is manifest in all the dealings that agents have with each other, and is found most readily in the conversations in which various rhetorical strategies, some overt and others subtle, are put into practice.

It is, in fact, in this dialogic process of agonistic addresses and responses that a self emerges and is sustained. Consider the following dialogic interaction between members of a book club at one of their meetings:

Judy: *Do we need a contrast to the book we have just read? Something terribly witty, brittle, and civilized?*

With this statement Judy has defined a self and represented it: She has taken the initiative in making a suggestion and then indicated her interest in a work with certain literary qualities. Judy's statement receives a response:

Susan: *Do you know any books like that [laughing]?*

Judy: *[Laughing] Well, we can always read* Emma *or something like that.*

The second installment from Judy continues a theme she initiated with the first one: I know works with certain literary qualities and here is an example—*Emma,* which is a novel by a leading novelist, Jane Austen, one that can be taken as "witty" and "brittle" and "civilized." With this statement, Judy has presented a self that is characterized by judgment, knowledge, literary taste, and perspicacity while the accompanying laughter seeks to diminish any hint of the pompous. The laughter, in fact, undermines to some extent the assertiveness of her comment and indicates that perhaps she is open to a compromise.

Judy's presentation of self receives another response from Mary, who counters Judy's thrust with one of her own:

Mary: *The last one I read was* Outcaste of the Islands *by Joe Conrad—which is great. I have to tell you it was difficult to get into but it was fabulous. I loved reading it. It was just the language and everything. It was just great. I think really great.*

Mary has chosen to ignore Judy's suggestion completely and proffered another great novelist as an alternative to Jane Austen, one who was "difficult" but "just great" and who had a command of "language and everything."

In this exchange, one can see an important element in the presentation of a self to the other: the creation of a distinct identity for the self by establishing *boundaries.* Identity, in fact, must be viewed as the construction of a separate presence for the self by creating a difference with another. This is being undertaken by producing what may be termed agonistic moves. Such moves enable one actor to define himself or herself more clearly and precisely by creating a contrast, however small or large, with the other. These definitional processes enable a binary coding of the participant selves in a dialogue to emerge and give the agent a distinct narrative voice and discursive presence. The aim of such agonistic posturing is not so much to undertake a conflict as to differentiate one's self from the other.

This becomes clearer in a strip of conversation that Harvey Sacks (1974) reported:

Ken: *You wanna hear what muh-eh sister told me a story last night?*

Roger: *I don't wanna hear it. But if you must,*

Al: *What is purple an' an island? Grape-Britain. That's what iz.*

Ken: *No. To stun me she says uh there was these three girls an' they just got married?*

Roger: *Ehhh//hehh hh*

Ken: *An' uh*

Roger: *Hey waita se(h)cond*

Ken: *Heh*

Al: *Heh!*

Roger: *Drag thah by agai(h)n hehh//hehh.*

Ken: *There—there was these three girls and they were all sisters. And they just got married to three brothers.*

Roger: *You better have a long talk with your sis//ter.*

Ken: *Waita—waita min//ute.*

Roger: *Oh// Three brothers.*

Al: *Eh eh*

Ken: *And uh—//*

Al: *Brothers of these sisters*

Ken: *No, they're different—mhh/hh*

Al: *heh*

Ken: *You know different families*

The interaction between Roger, Ken, and Al consists of a series of exchanges, and there are many instances of interruptions and overlaps. Sack's commentary on the long conversation from which this strip is extracted—which he reproduces with great fidelity and an equal commitment to a certain interpretive austerity that is a feature of the school of conversational analysis that he founded—is to describe its structural features. One can nevertheless go beyond Sacks's comments and show some of the interaction's other features. To begin with, there is a persistent tone of bantering and teasing in the exchanges. Every statement by one party is either challenged or ridiculed by sarcastic comments, and subject to various forms of one-upmanship. The teasing and the bantering are themselves indications of these agonistics. The overwhelming feature of this strip is the confrontation between the various participants: they listen, question each other, help the narrative along in various ways, but are also facing off with each other.

Consider the opening gambit between Ken and Roger: Ken opens a line of conversation that is immediately rejected by Roger. Al then enters the conversation and forestalls Ken's story—with a trivial and uninteresting one of his own, thus diminishing Ken in a way. Al and Ken are thus able to claim that they are not the sort of people who will tell such trivial stories. Ken, however, is equal to the task: he begins another story that has the capacity to "stun" him and perhaps the others, too. He then begins a very risqué story—but subject once again to sarcastic interruptions and rejoinders. This conversation—"the course of a joke's telling" as Sacks calls it—represents a very complex dialogic process in which multiple participants present their respective selves and agonistically establish boundaries for themselves.

This strip of conversation, in addition to the rest of the text that Sacks produced, is characterized by agonistic acts of a very distinct sort. The interruptions and overlaps, the sarcasms, and the instructions to each other about how to interpret the various comments are acts in which the aim is to best the other in one way or another. This conversation, besides its being anything else, is a combative encounter among a variety of agents who are able to establish their separate presence in the situation.

The combative elements that are features of ordinary conversations are often idealized and used to put the selves of various agents into play.

These are deliberate language games. The forms of interaction that are called variously "playing the dozens," "joning," "signifying," or "sounding" are occasions in which agents confront each other verbally. In such contests, the object is to produce insults to the other that are characterized by wit and force as well as bite. Roger Abrahams describes the playing as follows:

> "Sounding" occurs only in crowds of boys. One insults a member of another's family; others in the group make disapproving sounds to spur on the coming exchange. The one who has been insulted feels at this point that he must reply, with a slur on the protagonist's family which is clever enough to defend his honor ... This, of course, leads the other to make further jabs. (1962: 309–10)

The practice of sounding then is a direct verbal attack on the other's "honor"—that is, an aspect of his self—and thereby presents an assertive self while at the same time constructing a narrative of his self as one who will stand up to defend his honor. The differentiating element here is the verbal dexterity and metaphorical inventiveness of the author's presentations. "Joning" or "sounding" are verbal contests in which an agent tests the limits of the other's capacity for tolerance by invading the boundaries—frontiers—of the other's self and esteem while maintaining his own emotions under control.

Joning is obviously a game played with words where the agonistic element is very strong. The agonistics of conversations are also revealed in an idealized, and, indeed, a perfect form, in the practice of *riddling*—a universal form of verbal gaming found in many cultures. Students of folklore and myth have produced a large number of collections of riddles and subjected them to analysis. Such analyses have also resulted in a number of theories about their structure, about their structures in context, and their processes, and so on, including the usual Freudian interpretations. However, none of them, as far as I am aware, considered riddles as forms of conversation between agents who live in dialogic relationships with each other in given societies. Riddles are, to begin with, practiced by human agents coming together and facing each other and undertaking verbal performances. Unlike other conversations, riddles have one party to the conversation confronting the other with a puzzle and asking him or her to solve it. It is overtly agonistic, a contest in fact, and if the respondent returns an acceptable answer, he or she wins points or "credits." And if he or she cannot produce such an answer, the opener has to provide an answer. In mythology, in any case, the answering of a riddle can provide rewards, sometimes rewards of doubtful long-term value, as happened to Oedipus.

It is not riddles as such that are of interest here but the act of riddling and the context of riddling. In a comprehensive examination of the riddling act, Thomas Burns identifies four elements: I. Initiation: *It is daddy's turn to tell a riddle,* or *Come on, Sue, you ask a riddle.* II. The riddle statement or question: *What is it that walks on four legs in the morning, two at noon, and three in the evening*? III. Period of contemplation: *The time given for the riddlee to answer the question.* IV. The answer: *"Man,"* Oedipus said, but today he might have said "Human." If the riddlee gives the answer, he or she wins, but if the riddler has to give the answer, he or she has won.

These acts of riddling occur on various "occasions," avers Burns, and he describes several such occasions—as components of rituals, as an element in courtship sequences, as a pedagogic instrument in teaching, as a greeting when meeting someone, as features of songs and narratives, and finally, he concludes, as leisure-time riddling, which is the most complex and the focus of most of the literature on riddling (1976: 144–45).

David Evans insists, however, that these structural studies of riddles are incomplete and that one should study riddling as it occurs in given "structures of context" (1976). He describes various such contexts from his own studies: an old man telling riddles to boys, for example. The various contexts Evans describes are really exchanges: the old man tells a riddle and then the young man tells one and so it goes. In between the riddling and the answering, there are explanations and occasional taunting and teasing between the parties:

Old man:	*All right. Well, I am reaching for another one coming through, through, a riddle. Okay, well, tell me, what is this then? Long black slim fellow. Pull his cock and let him bellow. I got you now. I got you now.*
Young man:	*Long black slim fellow. Pull his cock and let him bellow.*
Old man:	*And you used him too.*
Young man:	*Wait a minute. A long black slim fellow?*
Middle aged man:	*Shotgun.*
Old man:	*Shotgun is right.*
Young man:	*Shotgun.*
Old man:	*You sure have to cock him before you shoot him, don't you?*
Young man:	*Sure do.*
Old man:	*Ha, ha, ha.*
Young man:	*I wasn't thinking about no gun though ha, ha ha. Sure wasn't.*

The sexual innuendo that is contained in the riddle misdirects the young man and he goes looking for an answer in the wrong place, but the other man gets it. This misdirection is an essential element of riddling and is, in fact, reproduced in various games: the "googly" ball that a bowler delivers in cricket and the curve ball in baseball, for example. The occasions for these riddling contests are convivial and sociable occasions and there is much laughter and affectionate teasing. Nevertheless, the agonistic element is present in strong measure—indeed, without this element, there is no riddling.

By presenting the riddle, the agent presents a wise and knowledgeable self, one that is alert to the shades and nuances of the riddle's significance and meaning perceived by others. He narrates it into being. In the end, the riddle presents a solution that would be given by either party to the transaction. If the riddlee provides the solution, he or she enjoys a moment of victory, and if he or she cannot produce the solution, the riddler does so. Either outcome differentiates the self and establishes its boundaries.

Buber claimed in his influential work that "all actual life is encounter" (1970: 62)—but there is more in these encounters than he, with his religious orientations, was disposed to acknowledge. All real life, it appears, is a confrontation with the other, in varying intensities, in which selves are presented and given play by each party to the encounter. In such encounters one can always find plays by an agent and counterplays by another—however muted it may be on many occasions. Indeed, when human agents come together, their respective selves are *fronts* that are put forward to face the other with each participant seeking to defend its frontiers with varying degrees of force and subtlety.

Dialogues and interactions have agonistic properties, whether they are designed as such or not. The agonistic features of interactions confer validation of the other's self by indicating that the other is a worthy contender with whom one can test will, wit, skill, poise, decorum, honor, prestige, and claims to competence, intelligence, and insight.

Narratives and the Self

In putting the self into play, an agent undertakes two simultaneous operations: one participates in *dialogic* processes with another person and engages him or her in the moment and in the situation where he or she finds himself or herself. Also, one develops a *narrative* of the self, consisting of ongoing sequences of logically and causally related acts of dialogue. It is through narratives that an agent is able to apprehend time and conceive his or her self as a temporal process—in the short run or long run. In other words, selves are given presence in two ways: as discrete interactional events and as continuous processes in which the significance of the events is assembled into a coherence. It is not, however, just a dialogue with the other but a complex dialogue in which the self as an other and the other as a self are both actively involved as situated presences and as recollected presences in each other's memory. An agent then performs a self to himself or herself as to the other with various modalities at his or her disposal and does so on a continuous basis.

The self of a human agent, then, emerges in and through processes that are both *discrete* as performances and *continuous* as narratives—and are similarly maintained and sustained. The objectified self is both discrete and continuous. That is, it is situated in moments and occasions and places as well as having a continuity over time. It is in this perspective on the self and agent that a dramaturgical social psychology and a narrative social psychology can be reconciled: the former captures situated activities of agents described in the classic studies of Erving Goffman (1959; 1967); the latter captures the self as an ongoing process in which an agent remembers a past and anticipates a future, as do his or her others. There is then a *drama of the self* as well as a *narrative of the self* and the two are truly inseparable in practice: dramas contain narratives and narratives are successive enactments of little dramas.

Narratives are integrations of disparate elements—of various characters, incidents, and interactions—into logically coherent and causally related structures. Agents use these structures not only to make sense of their lives but also to operate in the dialogic routines of their everyday lives. Indeed, they *cast* their selves into selected narratives and seek to take them to their logical conclusions. These narrative structures are made available to members by the cultural system of the society in which they live—though in reality each agent typically takes one or more of these structures and runs on his or her own with them. David Maines puts their essential qualities nicely as follows:

> Narratives are frameworks of meaning within which lives are configured; they are frameworks of meaning that can be told but mostly are simply tacitly believed and routinely enacted; they set limits to ordinary imaginations of the possible; and they define boundaries of normalcy and acceptability. (2001: 177)

The selves of given agents are articulated in terms of these narratives and will manifest themselves in the trajectories specified by these narratives. These narrative structures are cognitive instruments with which an individual is enabled to control, order, and give form and significance to the temporal and behavioral abyss that lies ahead in his or her life. Every moment of a person's conscious existence (I will leave aside the unconscious for the time being) is understood, and every move he or she makes in it is performed and seen as parts of developmental series: I eat a meal and it is without doubt part of a series in which earlier meals and later meals have a part, parts that the actor, however vaguely, must acknowledge. I am slighted by another and I experience the slight, indeed the very definition of it, as a slight by its place in the narrative of my life: I am a young man, full of vim and vigor, status and prestige, and the young woman I seek to court laughs at me and rejects me. The narrative imagination of being a "young man" does typically involve such moves. To the extent that the agent casts his life in the narrative of honor and prestige and manhood, with its attendant acts, this becomes a slight. If he had been cast in the narrative of a servant and had been slighted by a mistress of the household, the slight would not injure too deeply, if at all. Once the young man has been slighted by the young woman, he has to act the further sequence of the narrative in which he has cast himself. Among the sequences available to him, mention could be made of two extremes: he can say that is the way life is, win some and lose some, and move to courting another woman; or he can cast himself in the role of one who does not take insults lightly, one who is an avenger, goes home, finds a gun, and kills the young woman.

The narrative options society makes available to individuals are legion. They are given as objective narrative structures and take many forms. To begin with, as he or she is socialized, the individual is *cast* into already existing narrative structures by his or her others; a child who is born with a penis and testicles is cast into the narrative of "boyhood"; he has to undertake various typical acts that cohere into plots, which eventually become the narrative of "manhood" and so on. The very act of naming a child puts him or her into a particular narrative category: a boy child named John and a girl child named Sandra are compelled to follow the narrative line of typical boyhood and girlhood, and are implicitly being encouraged to do so. In addition to these narratives of gender—with detailed variations within particular cultures and subcultures—a child will find himself or herself given various other narratives within which he or she has to articulate his or her acts: jobs, careers, causes, and religions, which become attached to identities, responsibilities, and commitments. Some of these may be negotiated between the individual and others, and it is possible for the child to reject one narrative given by the others and select one on its own. A boy child given the narrative line of manhood—acts of courage and aggressiveness, physical dexterity, and domination—can transform it into the path of marriage or committed relationship and possibly fatherhood; become a responsible household partner, breadwinner, and so on; or may remain single. Manhood as a narrative, for example, implies a particular set of prescribed acts rather than another: the child plays with bat, balls, guns; he is assertive, aggressive, emotionally controlled, and domineering. He performs various acts that exemplify these characteristics and anticipates performing them in the future. Further, these narratives develop various plots: being aggressive and assertive means that in one's relationship with others he must deal with them in ways that conform to the demands of this particular plot. He does not back down, does not run away from a fight, and deals with others in a proper "manly" way—even if he is a child at this stage. Emotions, too, are given play according to the logic of the narrative of manhood: he holds back his tears, never complains, and if provoked to anger resorts to violence.

In fact, every identity that is selected or thrust upon one automatically casts one into a given narrative for one's entire life. Once an individual becomes a self-conscious entity, he or she can cast himself or herself into a narrative and enact the moves that are mandated by it. If at any point in time—whether time is conceived by him or her as a linear structure or a circular structure—it is the individual's capacity for reflexivity that enables him or her to enter the narrative and use it. It is the method by which the time of the self is conceived and handled. The narrative structure, in fact, becomes the sign-system with which the individual handles his or her place in time, its unfolding trajectory of anticipation and recollection. Manhood, womanhood, gunfighter, doctor, lawyer become dynamic signs that a culture provides for the emerging individual with which he or she can temporize his or her self, conceive time concretely, and anticipate, however imperfectly and tentatively, the trajectory of his or her life. Narratives, in other words, allow a reflexive situating of the self in constructed time. Such a time is sometimes conceived as linear from a point stretching into the future or as a circle, without beginning or end. From the point of view of a reflexive individual, this makes no real difference: the circle is, after all, only an endless line and at any point in it an individual can conceive the next step in his or her life, wherever he or she happens to be on the line.

These narratives in which a self gets articulated in his or her life may be termed *primary narratives*. These narratives of manhood, womanhood, husband, father, wife, mother, lawyer, doctor, dockworker, candlestick maker, and so forth are after all the primary processes through which human beings articulate their selves and the acts of their lives. The agencies that human individuals manifest through their social acts are conceived as elements of these narratives. It is, indeed, the inevitable predicament of a human agent, symbolically minded as he or she is, to be immersed in narratives of one kind or another, either directly as a protagonist or vicariously by identifying with others.

Agency, Alienation, and Narratives

The idea of alienation has been the subject of many definitions and classifications and has lead to many controversies. There is said to be, for example, a "historical-materialist" version of alienation at one extreme, and an "existentialist" one at the other (Ollman, 1971; Schaff, 1963).

Instead of taking a position on these controversies, I will use Marx's commentary for my purposes. After discussing the many facets of alienation, Marx observed: "Just as alienated labor separates man from nature and from himself—his own active functions and life activity—so, too, it alienates him from the species, from other men. It degrades all the life of the species and makes some cold and abstract notion of individual life and toil into the goal of the entire species, whose common life also becomes abstract and alienated" (in Josephson and Josephson, 1962: 99). He expands on this further:

> In the real world of practice, this self-alienation can only be expressed in the real, practical relation of man to his fellow men. This medium through which alienation occurs is itself a practical one. Through alienated labor, therefore, man not only produces his relation to the object and to the process of production as alien and hostile to men; he also produces the relation of other men to his production and his produce. (in Bottomore, 1956: 169)

The upshot of this process of alienation from the product of one's labor and from his or her fellow workers is described as follows:

> What constitutes the alienation of labor? First that the work is external to the worker, that it is not part of his nature; and that consequently, he does not fulfill himself in his work, but denies himself, has a feeling of misery rather than well-being, does not develop freely his mental and physical energies, but is physically exhausted and mentally debased ... This work is not voluntary but imposed, *forced labor*. (in Bottomore, 1963: 124-25)

This "labor power" that Marx uses as the basis of relationships between human beings "in the real world of practice," the exercise of which is the basic social act, is really the "powers of agency" in modern terminology. In early work Marx and Engels argued that

> men can be distinguished from animals by consciousness, by religion or anything else you like. They themselves begin to distinguish themselves from animals as soon as they begin to produce their means of subsistence, a step which is conditioned by their physical organization. By producing their means of subsistence, men are indirectly producing their actual material life. (1970: 42)

In another essay, he puts this very well: "The object of labor is, therefore, the *objectification of man's species-life*; for he no longer reproduces himself merely intellectually, as in consciousness, but actively, and in a real sense, he sees his own reflection in a world which he had constructed" (in Bottomore, 1963: 128).

The "physical organization" of human beings predisposes them to produce their means of subsistence in individual and social activity in general—that is, predisposes them to activity and agency. When labor is not "external" to human beings, one is able to "develop freely" and it does not "mortify" one's body or "ruin" his or her mind. In other words, a person is able to cast his or her self into the activity of production, of being an agent—be it production of objects, gestures, or words.

However, the productive relations that occur within certain societies not only alienate an individual from the products of his or her own labor but also poison his or her relationship with fellow humans. And this alienation, Marx notes, "draws itself not merely in the result, but also in the process of productions, within productive activity itself" (in Bottomore, 1956: 169). *In other words, the individual is alienated from himself or herself; his or her capacity for creative actions, for the exercise of agency, is thwarted and he or she feels powerless, unable to control either his or her creativity vis-à-vis his or her relation to the "object" of his or her productivity.* Further, he or she is alienated from others because they are competitors in the productive process, "hostile men." Their relation to him or her also then has the potential to thwart his or her freedom and creativity and agency. The upshot of this is that the "worker therefore feels himself at home only during his leisure, whereas at work he feels homeless" (in Bottomore, 1963: 125).

What happens to him or her in his or her leisure, however? In his home, in his leisure, too, he or she may feel alienation because of poverty, poor housing, too many children to nurture, and so forth.

For the man there is no guarantee that his home would prove a real home. The relations that obtain in the home may be alienating as well. Indeed, in many cases the alienation the worker is subject to at work is transferred to the home: the low wages, the long hours of work, and the sense of defeat that are engendered in many places of work are likely to thwart the individual from being a full-fledged and robust agent at home, too. The woman in this home may not feel at home either because she will suffer domination from the man and feel herself thwarted from exercising her agentic powers. She may experience a rage and a frustration that she is forced to suppress.

While members of certain ethnic groups or social classes are more likely to experience this alienation than others, there is no doubt that alienation as an interactional process can afflict anyone. *That is to say, in the life of every human being the likelihood of his or her sense of agency being thwarted, and his or her commitment to being an agent truncated, cannot be overlooked.* Indeed, to the extent that human beings live and work with other human beings the opportunity for these relationships to be characterized, not only by love and affection and lust but also by malice, envy, jealousy and spite, officiousness, insensitivity, lust for power, and hunger for status are ever present.

Faced then with situations in life in which their primary narratives leave them with a sense of alienation and inadequacy and above all bereft of agentic opportunities, many individuals seek to capture a sense of agency and the identity of being an agent by immersing themselves in what may be termed *secondary narratives.* Such narratives are constituted by individual authors or by a collective tradition and given to individual actors in a variety of ways. These narratives present characters, conflicts, dilemmas, and resolutions that a reader can selectively distill and use to live a narratively inebriated life. One can see what one wants to see, remember what one wants to remember, anticipate what one wants to anticipate, and attain a sort of cauterized bliss by immersing oneself in such narratives. One can experience extreme suffering, misfortune, and betrayal and yet *narrativize* his or her life along the theme of he or she who suffers, goes to heaven, reaches God.

Marx's own analysis of religion can be interpreted as an alienated individual immersing himself or herself in secondary narratives as an alternative to the sufferings of this worldly life. He wrote:

> Man makes religion, religion does not make man. Religion is indeed man's self-consciousness and self-awareness as long as he had not found his feet in the universe. But man is not an abstract being squatting outside the world. Man is in the world of men, state and society. The state, the society produces religion which is an inverted world-consciousness, because they are an inverted world. Religion is the general theory of this world, its encyclopedic compendium, its logic, its popular form, its spiritual point d'honoeur, its enthusiasm, its moral sanction, its solemn compliment, its general basis of consolation and justification. (in Bottomore, 1956: 26)

This "encyclopedic compendium, its logic in popular form," is provided to the populace in narrative forms. The religious system becomes available to the devotees as stories with characters, their interactions as plots, and their developments and denouements.

Kenneth Burke wrote that theology is "words about God" (1966: 1). Not only is theology words about God, however, but words that are often organized into stories into which an individual can cast himself or herself in one way or another and make sense of his or her experiences. Burke himself has detailed the processes by which "an old poet, libertarian and regicide, blind, fallen on evil days, in sullen warlike verse celebrates Samson" (1969b: 3). In doing so John Milton is not just writing about Samson, but *identifying* with him. "In saying, with fervor, that the blind Biblical hero *did* conquer, the poet is 'substantially' saying that he in his blindness *will* conquer" (1969b: 5). Others can encounter the narrative of Jesus, and claim: If the only begotten son of God can suffer so, can experience beatings and a crown of thorns and a cruel death, then why should I be exempt from suffering of one kind or another? In any case, I, too, will rise from death and find life everlasting. The plot line of my life and its denouement will parallel that of Jesus. Any suffering and any alienation will become tolerable by such "substantialized" identification.

These secondary narratives, made available in a variety of forms to the populace, enable the believers to identify, however partially and incompletely, with the protagonists and see a parallel to their own lives. They become an instrument for handling one form of alienation by providing a narrative about the suffering in this world, only to be given powers of agency in the next life—in heaven, sitting on the right side of God, where those who are last in this world become first, or in being reincarnated after death to a higher station, where there will be greater powers of agency.

The significant feature of secondary narratives is that there is the quality of "as if" to them, and furthermore, an individual has a choice as to which character in the narrative with whom he or she would want to identify. Encountering these secondary narratives, an individual interacts and gets involved with the values that are deployed and the denouements the narrative creates. In developing his or her complex relationship with these narratives, then, a spectator will become an agent, however indirectly, of the actions that are depicted in a text or are being enacted in front of him or her. In such narratives, an actor is able to reconstitute the identity of an agent and exercise a certain degree of control and power by participating in a narrative in which one is a protagonist. In other words, these narratives are able to elicit cognitive engagement and emotional involvement. The former is achieved by engaging the mind in the issues, problems, and confabulations that the plot provides, and the latter is cultivated by identifying with one or more of the characters that inhabit the narrative and with their aims and interests (Burke, 1969b).

Games as Dialogues and Narratives

In games, one finds all these characteristics of dialogues and narratives represented in very concrete forms. Games are, in fact, mimeses of the interactional life of human agents who live in organized societies. They are instrumentations with which agents seek to engage the other cognitively and emotionally. To engage the other cognitively, emotionally, and the world, physically, is after all the fundamental activity of the human agent. He or she is always engaging a real or imaginary other in cognitive relationships and emotional ones and dealing with the objects in the world by touching them, manipulating them, maneuvering oneself around them, trying to shape them, or use them in myriad other ways. And this is exactly what games allow a human agent to undertake—but in a very concentrated and surefire way. *It is not, then, that interactions and conversations are games; it is rather that games are conversations*

with which an agent engages the social and material other with great intensity and commitment. In such games the problematics that agents have to face and handle, interactionally and dialogically, are built into the very structure of the game. Mead and Bahktin both stressed the linguistic aspect of communicative process, although Mead did pay some attention to the broader processes of gestural and bodily communication. Games are, in fact, a structure of activity in which dialogic processes are put into operation without too many words. These acts are characterized by a complex interplay of rationality, emotionality, and pragmatism in and through which a human agent is able to put his or her self into a dialogue and cast the self into a narrative that is significantly different from the primary narratives in which he or she may be enmeshed.

The moves that a player makes in games demand calculation, anticipation of the likely consequences of the moves, and a significant plan about the manner of dealing with these consequences when and if they manifest themselves. In other words, the moves a player makes in playing games are *rational acts.* Stephen Kalberg has pointed out that Weber used four types of rationality in his works: practical rationality, theoretical rationality, substantive rationality, and formal rationality. Games are one of the rare structures of activity in which all four of these types of rationality are manifest concurrently. Kalberg writes that practical rationality is "... every way of life that views and judges worldly activity in relation to the individual's purely pragmatic and egotistic interests" (1980: 151). In playing a game, an agent makes moves that are of this sort. In making a move in tennis or chess, such an agent is interested purely in its impact on the interests of the player. Even in a team game like soccer or baseball, the player no doubt makes moves that will aid the team, but they are still practical, rational moves insofar as repeated successes in such moves will accrue benefits to the player just as repeated failures will deny these benefits.

Theoretical rationality is clearly central to the playing of games insofar as it involves various cognitive processes such as an understanding of logical relationships, attribution of causality, and a general comprehension of phenomena in one's immediate world. The playing of games demands all these forms of cognition both in the mastery of the rules of the game and its conventions and the application of these rules in specific situations. Substantive rationality controls actions by relating them to "values." Values are the ultimate basis of human actions and in undertaking actions in games, all the moves, by and large, are made under the influence of one fundamental value or the other: grit, determination, grace and decorum, sportsmanship and "fair play," for example. Putting these values into practice is calculated to elicit both admiration and membership in a values-oriented moral community. Further, it is not an exaggeration to say that every move made in games is fraught with formal rationality. One serves along the centerline or to the sideline in tennis or one sacrifices the queen in chess or bends the ball toward the goal in soccer in order to reach certain ends, fulfill certain calculated purposes. They are not unthought-out, habitual acts, nor are they typically undertaken without examining the deeper ends of the move. Once the decision is made to execute them, a player must systematically anticipate not only the return move the adversary will make but also one's own further moves as well. All moves in games have anticipated answers to which a player must be ready to make his or her own answer as well as unanticipated ones to which he or she must be prepared to answer.

The acts that players execute in games are also characterized by a definite *emotionality*—indeed, it could be said that emotions limn all social acts to varying degrees. Emotions bring color to them and enrich them and eventually help in defining the social acts in their own terms. To introduce emotions into the playing of a game is also to bring commitment and dedication to the goals of the playing, as well as to master the techniques of playing it well. Once the skills have been acquired, various emotions are parlayed in the execution of the acts and in recollecting them afterward—pride and satisfaction, dejection and sorrow. In the execution of the act, however, emotions enhance the strength of the act and become a progressive presence in the interaction. As Norman Denzin observes, "As social acts, emotions have phases including beginnings, middles and ends ... Emotional acts may be inhibited, blunted, checked or redefined" (1984: 58).

Denzin's description refers to the process of emotions in the acts of everyday life, but they apply, in a nicely concentrated way, to the playing of games. Emotions may be mild or strong at the beginning of a game and will become stronger as the game proceeds, or else they may become inhibited and blunted as the game proceeds, too. For example, if the opposition is too weak, players may not get their "blood up" to contest them or if they feel that they are being cheated by the umpire, they may well "tank" the game, as they say in tennis, in despair and frustration. Joe Maguire (1992: 105), examining the relationship between sports and emotions, notes that the playing of games allows a "socially permitted self-centeredness" in which excitement is elicited by the creation of tensions: this can involve imaginary or "real" danger, mimetic fear and/or pleasure, sadness and/or joy. Citing the work of Elias and Dunning, Maguire also calls attention to the need to maintain a "tension-balance" in the game: Too much or too little will make the game unplayable or uninteresting.

One can extend this argument to claim that too much of any emotion in the execution of the social acts in a game would make it unplayable: too much anger or hostility, too much love for the opponent, too much resentment and envy and jealousy would interfere with the controlled and well-aimed and well-timed rationality that are necessary for the successful execution of game-acts. To get too angry in a boxing match, for instance, can lead to a loss of control of one's moves, just as to be emotionally overwrought at a bad line call in tennis is to be underinvolved or overinvolved in the current act. Emotionality, yes, but neither too little nor too much. Nevertheless, there is no gainsaying the claim that in playing games—as one faces problems and seeks to solve them, engages the other and proceeds on a trajectory of sequential actions—he or she is, in fact, *escaping from affectlessness* by giving play to a variety of emotions.

The acts that agents deploy in games, besides being rational and emotional acts, are also *pragmatic acts.* Games are objective structures that provide an agent with problems to face and overcome in an ongoing process. These problems are both cognitive and practical that an agent has to handle with his or her voluntary action and are characterized by what Hans Joas has called "situated creativity." These acts do not consist in following rules in a mechanical way to overcome obstacles nor are they directed toward clear-cut goals. Rather, he notes, "every situation contains a horizon of possibilities which in a crisis of action has to be rediscovered. Hypotheses are put forward: supposition about new ways of creating bridges between the impulses to action and the given circumstances of a situation" (1996: 133).

Games are, in fact, *pragmatic machines* artfully constructed to provide challenges and resistances that an agent can face and with which he or she can put his or her self into play and garner new graces to it, notes, tones, and pitches, that can be assembled to form a whole. In playing games, a player becomes the supreme manifestation of an interactive agent who undertakes acts in terms of their conceivable effects on another agent and his or her responsive acts. They are directed toward the other in anticipation of certain consequences and if these effects eventuate, further acts will follow along the same lines. Or else, if the effects are not realized, then changes have to be made according to the effects desired in the second stage. And so such acts go on, in a series of first moves and responsive second moves.

In putting one's self into play through these machines, an agent allows a subtle and intricate interplay between rationality and emotionality to guide his or her actions without yielding completely and unreservedly to one or another. Such moves, which are creative responses to the situation as well as subject to a disciplining by the rules of the game, are used to advance to the goals of the game. Neither a fully rational approach nor a totally emotional one, and neither a hidebound rule-following nor an anarchic indifference to rules, will enable a gaming situation to occur and prosper.

Games are variations on the processes of existence in which the dialogic animal that the human agent is sustains himself or herself. They are another method for cultivating the human beingness in dialogue. They enable agents to engage with each other and develop ongoing dramas of the self with performances and presentations. And because each of these games presents a series of moves that are *sequentially and causally* related to each other with an agent (or a set of agents) as protagonists, they also enable him or her to narrate a self and obtain a sense of agency and control.

While religious stories, myths, novels, and movies as secondary narratives provide relatively easy ways of capturing *vicariously* a sense of power and agency, games—playing them and watching them—are very fertile areas as well. They, too, represent the "logic" of the relevant world in "popular form" in Marx's words. They give a sense of immediacy and presence, a feeling of getting one's hands and feet dirty, the body sweaty, the mind engaged, emotionally and cognitively. One can then conceive of games as narrative structures that represent the societal and the interactional and the temporal orders of a human life and provide opportunities for participants to enjoy a sense of power and control by casting themselves into the proceedings. They achieve this sense of agency by manipulating, directly or vicariously, various tokens: balls, pucks, cards, chess-pieces, checker-pieces in games, just as they do by identifying with characters and their moves in other narratives.

The acts and moves made by gaming agents are elements with which a narrative of the self is constructed. As a secondary narrative, the structures of games are unique in allowing an agent to cast his or her self into them, imaginatively, actively, and, in many cases, physically, and experience emotions in a direct and participatory way. It is into these structures of action that become narratives that an individual casts his or her self and seeks various degrees of performative freedom and control and the instrumentation for the manifestation of self. One can box, wrestle, kick, dribble, pass, hit, drive, carry, throw, or even just run and give expression to a self that is relatively free from domination and control and write a story about it—albeit a short story.

These moves enable an agent to engage with the other cognitively, emotionally, and—in constructing narratives of the self in relation to the other or others—socially, and materially. In undertaking such conversations using bats, balls, cards, chess-pieces, and so forth, agents are also able to immerse themselves in various narratives as well as actively participate in constructing them, however mundane and lackluster some of them may become. Nevertheless, with these moves, agents are able to find avenues out of anomie, alienation, and aloneness as well as toward cathartic moments and heroic narratives, at times even rapture, by making use of the structures and processes of games.

2

The Structures of Games

The games that human cultures have devised over the centuries have intricate and complex structures. To begin with, they are narrative forms. They are comparable to other narrative forms that are able to engross human beings and are more readily available to most people. And they have an added advantage over the other forms: agents can participate actively in them rather than merely watch them or read them. As narrative forms in which agents are able to be active participants, they represent fundamental social processes in *miniaturized* structures.

People throughout history have used stories to reduce complex, confusing, and unresolvable social and conceptual problems into neat patterns, giving them clear lines of development and resolution (Lévi-Strauss, 1967). In such narratives, characters drawn from everyday life are idealized to a small or large degree, put into the experiencing of various events, and then allowed to move forward according to their character and the logic of the events. The problems that the characters face, the decisions they have to make, the fortunes and misfortunes they have to experience and their resolutions are idealized and exaggerated in various ways but are not so far-fetched as to prevent audiences from understanding or identifying with the characters. Stories and dramas are then really representations of events of everyday life depicted in various levels of condensation. In dealing with such stories and dramas, individuals in given cultures have the choice of listening to them or watching them or performing them. Dramas on stages are then not radically different from everyday dramas in which human beings participate routinely and habitually. They are, in fact, idealized mimeses of such a life that constructs vehicles in which the deepest emotional, social, and political theories of everyday life are represented for study or contemplation or action.

The most ubiquitous of these narratives are the myths that all human cultures have devised over the centuries. Philosophers and social scientists have sought, over the years, to unravel the connection between myths, legends, folktales, and the societies that produced and used them. Among the many who have written on this relationship one could mention James

Fraser, Bronislaw Malinowski, Sigmund Freud, Bruno Bethelheim, Claude Lévi-Strauss, and Joseph Campbell. Each of these scholars has taken strikingly different approaches to the study of the relationship between what may be called symbolic forms and society. Still, one must accept Burke's claim that literature must be considered as "equipment for living" (1957) as the most parsimonious approach: not just literature but all symbolically articulated narratives are indeed used to live and endure life's infinite vicissitudes.

These many approaches have undoubtedly paid great theoretical dividends. It has been shown that there are coded and "buried" structures within myths and tales, and they do perform various functions for the societies that constituted them, nurtured them, and transmitted them to succeeding generations. That is, myths and folktales and imaginative literature, too, can be examined as a whole, in their total manifestation, as representations of certain central concerns of the society that allowed them to be constituted and that sustained them. They can, in other words, be considered as *mimetic* structures constituted to represent certain themes and to use them recursively to inform, edify, and control an attentive populace.

The concept of mimesis has been discussed by many authors. Starting with the classic study by Erich Auerbach, many recent authors—Roland Barthes, Jacques Derrida, and Paul Ricoeur—have made important contributions toward our understanding of both the processes of mimesis and their implications. Among these, it is Ricoeur's work that seems most useful for the study of games insofar as he focuses on the temporality of human experience and the realization of such experiences in narratives by means of emplotment. Ricoeur describes his project as follows:

> What is ultimately at stake in the case of the structural identity of the narrative function as well as in that of the truth claim of every narrative work, is the temporal character of human experience—time becomes human time to the extent that it is organized after the manner of a narrative; narrative, in turn, is meaningful to the extent that it portrays the features of temporal existence. (1984: 3)

The mimetic work of art is an attempt to complete in idealized form what is incomplete or incoherent in nature; a move to give it symmetry, shape, and form and to depict potentialities and possibilities. This is achieved by converting characters and incidents and events into textual forms and embedding them in structures of temporality.

The composition of these works of narrative art and the reading of them are mediated by the practices of *emplotment*, according to Ricoeur: "... the dynamics of emplotment is the key to the problem of the relation between time and narrative." By means of constructing plots that necessarily embody the three modes of experiencing time and peopling such plots with characters, a composer as well as reader can follow "the destiny of a prefigured time that becomes a prefigured time through the mediation of a configured time" (Ricoeur, 1984: 54). This emplotment and the figuration of time it involves result in the mimesis of experience—that is, the "imitating or representation of activities—produces something, namely, the organization of events by *emplotment*" (1984: 34).

Human agents then respond to these emplotments in direct encounters. Myths, tales, novels, and poems may exist as texts, may reproduce certain basic structures in their manifestations, and may share these structures with each other; but for all that, they are read or heard or seen on specific occasions and situations. In other words, individuals, either in groups or alone, confront these narratives and decode them and respond to them on an immediate or current basis. The degree of such participation may vary; but there is no doubt that the reader gets actively involved with the text. Further, the text that is presented to the reader is not a passive text. It is organized and arranged in such a way, according to its own discipline and logic, that a reader can take the text to have its own intentionalities structured to elicit particular responses from the reader, rather than others.

These acts of dialogic reading are occasions in which an individual is able to engage his or her capacity for agency. The reader is able to cast his or her self into the narrative as an agent and participate vicariously in its developments and denouements, emotionalities and conflicts and tensions. In such acts of agentic reading, unlike the acts in which real others participate, there is little chance of being thwarted or frustrated and the reader is able to engage his or her imaginative and interpretive skills to the fill. These acts, in fact, become the secondary narratives of the life of the individual: ones in which he or she can immerse himself or herself and participate indirectly in exercising a sense of agency and emotional play, the story of his or her own life being the primary narrative.

Games as Myths

The games that human cultures have constructed over the centuries are essentially mimetic forms in and through which human agents undertake the experiencing of time, emotion, and action. In fact, games must be considered as myths made active and practical; mimeses of action, attitude, and emotionality; metaphors that aid cognition and communication. In Joseph Gusfield's words, "sports events replay, in mythical fashion, a spectrum of common experiences, dilemmas and conflicts with which audiences who watch them can identify" (2000: 12). While one reads or listens to myths in one form or another, games are myths that are not only watched but are put into forms that various players can *enact.* In doing so, they put body, mind, and self into actions that cohere into a narrative and enable the participants to experience both interaction with the social and physical environment, to feel their respective forces and resistances, and to lead them all to a definitive resolution. In playing a game, an agent is in fact participating in an emplotment of his or her self just as he or she may be following an already constituted plot of the game.

Games are more particularly myths of combat made flesh. Joseph Fontenrose (1959) discusses many myths of combat from all over the ancient world and he observes: "Every god has his enemy whom he must vanquish and destroy. Zeus and Baal, Coyote and Ahura Mazda, Thor and the Lord of the Hosts are all alike in this: that each must face a dreadful antagonist. Apollo's enemy was the great Python whom he had to fight and kill before he could establish his temple and oracle at Delphi" (1959: 1).

Fontenrose's study enables him to summarize his findings about such myths as follows in terms of what he calls "themes" (1959: 9–11):

1. The enemy was of divine origin.
2. The enemy had a distinctive habitation.
3. The enemy had an extraordinary appearance and properties.
4. The enemy was vicious and greedy.
5. The enemy conspired against heaven.
6. A divine champion appeared to face him.
7. The champion fought the enemy.
8. The champion nearly lost the battle.
9. The enemy was finally destroyed after being outwitted, deceived or bewitched.
10. The champion disposed of the enemy and celebrated his victory.

Each of these ten themes can be transformed into their essential properties and made to apply to games as follows:

1a. The antagonist was of extraordinary skill, talent, or charisma. Gamesters typically come with a reputation for skill and talent. In fact, there are formal and informal rules by which only people of matched skill and reputations are allowed to play against each other.

2a. The antagonist has a distinctive locus of identity—membership in a club, or an ethnic group, religion, region, nation. Each player is identified with specific group labels.

3a. The antagonist has extraordinary strength, height, dexterity, speed, cunning, tactical sense, and so forth. Each player is granted, if not truly extraordinary skills, a measure of skill and talent—to be allowed or invited to play.

4a. The antagonist is mean, greedy, vicious, a "dirty fighter"; a cheat; or from a "wrong" club, ethnicity, nation.

5a. The antagonist conspired against or spoke against authority or ridiculed the team, player, coach or club, region, ethnic group, nation.
6a. A gifted, charismatic champion came to face him or her.
7a. The champion faced the challenger.
8a. The champion nearly lost the struggles several times—or lost it finally.
9a. The antagonist was defeated after being outplayed.
10a. The champion vanquished the antagonist and celebrated his or her victory.

In combat myths—perhaps all myths—then, one has two antagonists or two sets of antagonists, facing each other with the audience given the cues, by one narrative technique or other, to read who the champion is and who the villain is. These structures of conflict are translated into the formal aspects of all the secondary narratives that members of societies embrace. Myths, legends, plays, novels, short stories, films, and the like are *always* organized in terms of self or other structures, constructing the protagonist and the enemy as alien, outsider, the evil one, the dark one, the deformed one, morally or physically, and so on. This latter may be termed the *narrative other* and is drawn from a wide variety of sources. In the story of Odysseus, it is the variety of others whom he and his companions hunt and fight, along with various other enemies that they confront along the way. In the Hindu myth of the *Mahabharata,* it is the divine Krishna and his companions, the Pandavas, and their enemy Kauravas who, among other transgressions, refuse to acknowledge the divinity of Krishna. In the Oedipus myths, it is the proud human being, afflicted with *hubris,* against powerful gods who are always seeking to humble the proud and the arrogant.

In many modern American works of fiction and movies, there are two kinds of narrative others: the alien, the savage, the foreigner, the national outsider for one, and the local people who have sought to violate the law and become savages in the form of the gangster, the crook, and the generally lawless people. This usually follows current national concerns and policies: During the early years of the European settlement of the Americas, the narrative other was the native people. Countless novels were produced during this period, and later when movies came along, these novels provided a ready supply of narrative. The Native Americans became the reviled savages, unruly, violent, and incapable of fighting according to the European rules of war or of being "tamed."

Once the United States began to look outward, the alien nation became the narrative other: Russians for a while, and when the Soviet Union became an ally during the war, Germans became the narrative other, and after the war they were replaced by the Russians all over again. Mexicans have been, for some reason, a cause of concern for Americans. Often they have been depicted as evil and unpredictable. The American moviemakers often took the burden of *narrativizing* the other of the British Empire and depicted peoples of India and Africa as savages to whom the English had brought the light, reason, and the railways.

Representation of this principle of the narrative other that we find in myths, novels, and movies is found in games. Here, however, for the players at least, each is a narrative other to the self. Each player constructs the other as the "enemy," "alien," antagonist, and the self as the "friend," "insider," or "native"; the protagonist undertakes his or her moves accordingly. He or she will bring a passion and a dedication to the moves he or she will make in the game; often such a passion itself will become a cause to ensure victory and avoid defeat. The defeat will remain a major event in the immediate life of the player and may continue to haunt him or her for a long time.

The Arrow of Time

A game—with the *passage* of a ball, puck, or chess- and checker-pieces across a field of play or the movement of a pair of dice or the development of a trick in card games, managed and maneuvered by the players—becomes, in fact, a machine to experience the "arrow of time." Time may not be absolute, but it seems to move always in one direction as far as human beings are concerned. Stephen Hawking argues that there are "at least three different arrows of time. First, there is the thermodynamic arrow of time, the direction of time in which disorder or entropy increases. Then, there is the psychological arrow of time. This is the direction in which we feel time passes, the direction in which we remember the past, but not the future. Finally, there is the cosmological arrow of time. This is the direction of time in which the universe is expanding rather than contracting" (1988: 145).

In playing a game or watching it as a spectator, one is participating in constructing the arrows of time—the thermodynamic one and the psychological one. The game begins in an ordered state, with players standing in their positions, and then dissolves into a mass of distorted movements that are oriented to the future. Every movement in the game is just one moment that leads immediately to the next one—the earlier moment gone forever without possibility of recovery.

The actions of the agents in a game occur irrevocably in the present. These actions are not told and retold stories that happened once upon a time. Rather, they occur and are recounted at the same time and are events in the present tense. As one watches, one sees the story constituted. Different from dramas and movies, they were not assembled at an earlier time, except in very general terms, by a playwright or director but emerge as the game is played, with the denouement dependent on a series of contingent circumstances and not on the dramatic or psychological theories of a sentient author, removed from the readers and spectators. The moves the players make on the field or court, table or board, express what may be termed narrative intention right then and there. Each move is an element in the emerging narrative and each player, in fact, is constructing a narrative, the development and completion of which depends on the collaboration of the other players.

The arrow of time is reconstituted in structures of narrative in which an agent is able to experience it as, more or less, in his or her control. Games, as narrative structures, have a distinct temporal structure to them. Paul Ricoeur's discussion of narrative captures neatly the elements of narrativity that undergirds games. Time, Ricoeur notes, consisting as it does of three "moments" that a human mind is able to cognize simultaneously—remembrance, attention, and anticipation—can create an "existential burden of discordance." Ricoeur notes that one can remember a distant or immediate past, with various points in between, one can attend to many moments in the present, itself, and can anticipate the near future or distant one, including "eternity." Such an existential discordance, however, can be mediated by poetic composition. "Aristotle," says Ricoeur, "discerns in the poetic act par excellence—the composing of a tragic poem—the triumph of concordance over discordance" (1984: 31). It is not the composing alone that gives a concordance to the experiencing of time but also the act of reading a composition: "The reader is that operator par excellence who takes up through doing something"—an act of reading—"the experiencing of the various modes of time" (1984: 50).

These modes of experiencing time are available as mimetic structures. As one participates, directly or vicariously, in the temporalizing moves of the narrative, in the short duration or the long one, he or she cannot help but apprehend the mimesis of the shortness of the moments of one's life, the importance of experience, and the transience of life itself.

The representation of temporality—and provisioning of metaphors with which a mind can conceive temporality—is achieved by constructing episodes that are narratively related and become plots for Ricoeur. The narrative conceptualization of time is opposed to the Husserlian notion of time consciousness. "In this regard," he notes, "Husserl's analysis and discussion in his lectures on the phenomenology of internal time consciousness will constitute the major counter example to my thesis about the definitely aporetic character of the phenomenology of time ... the aporetic poetics of narrativity responds and corresponds to the aporetics of temporality" (1984: 83–84).

That is to say, before one can experience an "internal time consciousness," he or she must have a priori "signs, rules and norms," in Ricoeur's words, with which to experience it. Time cannot be experienced as "inner durée" or as an "inner consciousness" except as it occurs as mimesis in signs. These signs, rules, and norms are available to humans in many forms whose fundamental feature is narrativity. Ricoeur's thesis, in fact, is that "speculation on time is an inconclusive rumination to which narrative activity alone can respond" (1984: 6). Narratives allow a reader or a participant or a spectator to experience time with an immediacy and a nowness. Reading a novel, watching a play or movie, or even writing a novel are narrative or poetic structures through which a human mind is able to conceive time as well as experience it.

Playing a game or watching it being played is similar to these more conventional narratives. *Indeed, games are poetic and narrative structures that enable a human being to conceive time and experience it.* Watching games or playing them, a "reader" experiences time in its three-dimensional complexity—attending, remembering, and anticipating. What Ricoeur calls "poetic structures" are sign-systems or numeric structures that allow readers to conceive of time and experience it.

That is to say, the mimesis of action and its embeddedness in plot and narrative, in an imaginary form, eventually—or simultaneously as the case may be—face the audience of readers and listeners and spectators and participants who live in a practical world of their own, allowing the narrated world of the text and their own world to interact and speak to each other. The texts that are constructed along these three mimetic stages are now, however, self-contained linguistic and symbolic units, but refer, in one way or another, to the real world in which the readers are living.

Games as narratives not only occur in specified time frames but they also define the use of time and space for a person playing the game. While time in everyday life structures indefinitely into a future—with an agent's anticipating various stages in it, including his or her demise—in games, time has a refreshing finality to it. A game begins, runs an appointed course, and ends at a particular moment. It is all final, cut and dried, neat, and not subject to doubts, debates, and reruns.

Games are played in a temporal framework that is set apart from the other activities of everyday life. One leaves a set of activities, reconstitutes himself or herself in various ways, and then enters the new frame. This often will involve a change of costume and demeanor, an alteration in attitude, and changed bodily postures and languages. During the course of the game, these changes will be maintained, and once the game is over, they are sloughed off and the standard identity resumed. If the game involved physical activity, the player will take a shower afterward—no doubt to clean himself or herself of the sweat, but as a ritual bath signaling a return to the status quo ante.

Further, many games occur within specified time frameworks. Football, soccer, cricket, baseball, and hockey have to begin at a particular time and end after a specified number of minutes have elapsed. Sometimes there are "overtime" plays if there was no decision during "regulation" time—but again, it is specified beforehand. The games have a beginning and an end and at the end, typically, there is a winner and a loser and within the time frame of a game are encapsulated not only the semblances of the acts of everyday life but the temporality of a life, too. In life one is born, performs various acts in a series, assembles the meanings and consequences of these acts into a self, and then sooner or later faces an ending. Often these acts distinguish the actor in some way from the other, and he or she may claim either the status of a hero or villain and may even end his or her day heroically. However, most lives are mundane ones, but heroic, villainous, or mundane, they end. In games, the beginnings of life are mimicked: the beginning of the game is the beginning insofar as prior games and their scores are discounted, and each player or side starts afresh. The game is played, and then both winners and losers find an ending, a consummation, devoutly wished or not, but a death nevertheless. Games are not just a mimesis of life, but of the routines of a life, its moves and countermoves, its joys and sorrows, its victories and defeats, its successes and failures, its sense of control and loss of control and anticipations of one's ending, and provide a "sense of an ending" to use Frank Kermode's (2000) phrase at the finish. Games, like other narratives, have very precise endings, giving a firm closure to the proceedings as well as a dependable sense of closure to the players and spectators.

From the beginning of a game to the end, the players in a typical game do not know how it will turn out. The games and players are arranged and selected in such a way that there is always an element of uncertainty of outcome. If there is no such uncertainty, there is no game. Furthermore, each player is expected to give his or her "best" to the game, display a fighting spirit, have "game" as the saying goes. The uncertainty of human life, how it will turn out, what fate is waiting to unfold, what the "hand of god" has written as its destiny, whether god had "elected" a person or not are mimified and captured in games. One plays with the time of one's life—in games and in everyday life.

Within the broad outlines of an uncertain ending is nested another series of uncertainties. During the course of play, between the beginnings and the endings, the agents undertake acts—variously called "moves," "plays," and so on—and engage the other in an interaction. Each of these moves once again brings time into play; at any moment in the transaction, the moves may turn out to be positive ones for a given player or negative ones, and between the beginning of the move and its own ending, there is experienced an uncertainty. Each move is a gamble, each act fraught with either positive or negative consequences. The uncertainty of outcome of the final ending is really a summation of the small uncertainties that characterize the separate moves of a game: a pass in football can be caught or intercepted and eventually the outcome of this event will influence the final outcome; so with bridge—a finesse may or may not work and the determination of the winner of the game will be influenced by the outcome of this move. Little nested uncertainties develop into a pattern that defines the game and leads to the ultimate determination of a winner and the obviation of the final uncertainty.

In games, this sense of temporality, uncertainty, and *peripeteia* is represented in well-organized structures. One who plays the game, as the one who watches it, is trapped into the sensing of temporality. Indeed, one may say that games are machines with which temporality is articulated on the one hand and experienced on the other.

The Dialectic of Games

Actions that a human being undertakes meet with various forms of *resistance*. The resistance may be from the physical environment: the ground may be too icy to walk without care and caution; the mountain one may want to climb may be too steep and rough; the car one wants to drive may be too old and dilapidated, and so on. Besides this, the human other with whom one has to interact *always* will give some kind of resistance—sometimes mild and at other times heavy. *Every human act will meet with resistance from the material environment and the social other to some degree or other.* Every interaction, then, between actors, however overtly friendly it may be, is a combat between agents and selves with different biographies and destinations, each marked in different moments in the trajectories of their respective lives. In such encounters, each may seek to know the mind of the other and such knowledge will bring the actors in concert with each other. Such knowledge, however, is obtained by the revelations and concealment that each provides the other and is never either full or complete.

This condition and circumstance is reproduced with great fidelity, and perhaps some exaggeration, in the games that human cultures have devised. The entire structure of games is arranged to offer disciplined resistance to the player. Bernard Suits has argued that games are structures in which one is made to choose the most difficult and/or circuitous route of reaching a goal (1967). This is so because the very organization of the game incorporates resistances into them. Even in a simple footrace from point A to point B, one is obliged to run around the track rather than crossing it diagonally. The rule that one should run around the perimeter is a built-in resistance that the runner has to overcome to complete the race. Even in games of solitaire, the rules of the game provide the resistance though no human other is involved.

It is, however, in the interactional games that one meets with the phenomenon of resistance full-blown. In them, every player has to meet with three forms of resistance: one from the environment—the playing arena and the equipment. The playing arena may be wet and sodden as in football and soccer, the "wicket" may be "sticky"; the ball, too, may be wet or worn down, "lost its shine" and so on. The bats and racquets may not be perfectly tuned or turned out. The cards may be dirty, or marked or otherwise difficult to handle. The arena of play may be too noisy and distracting and the watching fans may be too boisterous or obstreperous. The weather may be too hot or too cold or too wet.

The second form of resistance a player has to confront is from the structure of the game itself. Every game has its negative and positive elements that are described in the rules of the game. Every move must be made in accordance with these rules. These rules, in other words, deny a player the freedom to do as he or she pleases and forces him or her to control his or her impulses and conform to a strict pattern of behavior.

And finally, the third type of resistance is the opposing player or players. It is this structure of moves and countermoves that defines the game. Without the full-hearted and committed resistance that each player or each side offers to the other, there is no game—in every sense of the latter word. However, these resistances are offered by one to the other according to the strict rule structure of the game itself. While this is true of all dialogic games, one can see this most clearly in American football because rough and violent tackling is an essential ingredient of the game. The game begins with a kickoff of the ball by one side and the ball is picked up by one from the other side and carried forward. He will be interrupted by the player of the opposing side by a series of physical tackles, the object of which is to bring him down to the ground. In all these moves, often there is a great deal of violence—and often players are hurt—but it is nevertheless *disciplined violence.* Many times, in the course of these proceedings, the referee will call "foul" for "unnecessary roughness" and other offenses that exceed permitted violence and other moves that transcend the rules of appropriate conduct.

The dialectic of action and resistance is neatly articulated by constructing games as binary structures. The great variety of games that human cultures have devised over the centuries has one feature in common: they are all organized as a binary system. In every game two antagonists as individuals facing each other, or partners or teams facing each other, play to win against the other. In board games, the contest is either with two partners facing each other or two players doing so. In card games, too, there can be face-to-face encounters between two players or a player and a partner facing another such pair. In such games, there are two kinds of relationships: one between members of a pair where they collaborate with each other, but even here some agonistic element can creep in, and the other between the two pairs who are by definition antagonistic. In some games—card games like poker, for example—several players at a table play for themselves and without partners, and in this case, too, a binarism manifests itself: it is one player on one side against the others who all constitute the antagonists.

In court games like tennis, badminton, squash, and table tennis, again there are contests between two individual antagonists and two pairs of antagonists. Here, too, there are two kinds of relationships: a simple one between the two antagonists and a more complex one between the two partners in a pair and the opposing partners of a pair. One must play with one's partner and against the others and one must also take full account of one's partner's weaknesses and strengths and coordinate his or her moves accordingly. Various complex emotional resonances, defined by these binarisms, are created in the playing of the game.

Even in games that are contests between two teams, the execution of the various moves that constitute the game are binary encounters. In baseball, the initial move is a confrontation between the pitcher and the batter as it is in cricket, though here the actors are called bowler and batsman. Once the ball is hit, the encounter is between the fielder and the batter/batsman. In such binary encounters, the other members do play their roles but essentially as supporting players.

In football—the American version, which is principally played with hands, and the English version, which is played with feet and at times with the head—the essential moves with the ball are binary encounters. In American football, the initial move is a pass from the quarterback to the receiver from his or her own team and then the receiver is challenged by a defender from the other team. These structures change with great rapidity—a pass from one teammate suddenly becomes a structure between the receiver and an opponent. The moves by a quarterback himself or herself are challenged by players from the adversary team, once again creating an opposition between two protagonists. In soccer again, the contest is between two players who "mark" each other or support each other. The game begins with a pass from the striker in the center of the attacking phalanx to a teammate and soon he or she is challenged by one from the other side, both establishing a set of binary structures.

Binary structures then define the contests in games, with the team games permitting a variety and complexity of structures. The structures also change with great rapidity—a pass from one to a teammate suddenly becomes a structure between him and an opponent that, too, can change, with a pass to a friendly interaction with a teammate. This is more often the case in soccer, hockey, and rugby than in American football. The changing relationships from antagonism to protagonism enable complex emotions to be given play and selves are given form and substance in rapid succession. The game itself—its moves and countermoves, the rules and regulations—provide themes for the ensuing interactions. In football and soccer, while there are turn-taking procedures in operation on certain aspects of the playing, in others the very object of the game is to interrupt the other's moves. A quarterback in football initiates a move by throwing the ball to one of his players, but a player from the other side can "intercept" it and sabotage the move.

As the playing proceeds, a very subtle differentiated procedure of interaction will emerge. Strict adherence to the rules of turn taking are expected in certain aspects of the game while *sanctioned interruptions* are permitted in others. In bridge, for example, each player bids in turn and plays a card in turn and also deals in turn to begin the game and no exceptions are permitted. But once the card is played—the opening move in a conversation of gestures—the opposing players, fulfilling their agonistic mission, will seek to interrupt the ongoing move of the card toward fulfillment of its *telos* in a successful trick for the initial player by "trumping it"—that is, interrupting its onward progress. In chess, too, each player has to adhere strictly to an initial set of rules about turn taking. The player who has opted for the white pieces plays first and then the other responds and this goes on in alternate moves. Within the game, however, the aim of each player would be to interrupt the onward progress of the other's moves by forestalling the moving of a piece from one position to another or by "capturing" it. In soccer, too, the same phenomenon can be seen: A ball is passed from one player to the other but an antagonist can interrupt it and take it over. Henceforth, both the intercepted passes become initiatives in the hands or feet of the interceptor and he or she makes his or her moves. These interruptions, however, are not arbitrary and willful moves by one player but are strictly regulated and are built into the game, emphasizing the agonistic element of the game.

These moves and interruptions proceed apace and eventually the game has to end. In many games, time is used to end a game: soccer and football are played according to a prescribed time schedule. However, in certain important games, if the game is "tied," at the end of the allotted period, further time is allocated until a victor is determined. If that doesn't provide a victor, special procedures—like the penalty "shoot-out" in soccer—are prescribed.

The Dialogic of Games

In all games, a player faces another player or one side faces another and by means of various tokens—like pucks, balls, "men," or cards—tries to beat the other by undertaking an act that is termed a "move." In order to do this successfully, he or she has to put into practice the two elements of what Bakhtin called a dialogic process: addressivity and answerability. Each player's moves are fraught with addressivity: he or she must take the role of the other and attitude of the other, to use G. H. Mead's phrasing, in as specific and as minute a manner as possible and issue his or her acts. In playing bridge, for example, each player gets a chance to "lead" a card—that is, to play it first. The response from the other players will be based on this lead and, consequently, the leader is able to control, to some extent, the nature of this response. In leading a card, a player has to choose a suit to lead and a particular card as well. It is, of course, never a random or haphazard act. He or she must take account of the bidding that went before the game opened, the relative strengths and weaknesses of the opponents as well as one's partner and the cards that have been played before this move, and then make his or her move. Further, he must also take notice that once the card is played, others, including his or her partner will use it as evidence of the player's intention as well as a clue to the contents of the rest of his or her hand. All these features are present in one move and they are addressed to self and other in the course of the play. If these addressive features of play are not countenanced, then the game will be an impoverished one, or may not be a game at all.

While this kind of dialogism is present in all games, it is very pronounced in tennis. In the beginning of a game of tennis, a player has to serve the ball. To the extent that it has to be served and served in a particular manner (both feet outside the back line of the court, for example) and into a particular part of the other side of the net, both players are in one mind: each can take the role of the other on this score. However, the server is intent not only in playing the game but also on thwarting the other from returning the serve or making an effective one.

In games in which there are only four players as in bridge, or two as in "singles" tennis, the dialogic processes are rather simple while in team games like soccer and football, they are much more complicated. Each player has to address not only one player on the side but several, just as he or she has to countenance several of his or her own teammates. These players on one's own side as well as those on the other side have various minutely differentiated roles assigned to them and the player with the ball in his or her control is obliged to consider them all, as far as is practicable, and address the move accordingly. In field games, the answers are not as easily anticipated and readily fulfilled because there are so many players who can change the course of play—lending them opportunities for reversal of fortune.

The process of addressing a move toward another and the consequent arrival of answers are achieved by the giving and taking of "turns." The most momentous event in social life is, in fact, the taking of a turn in a conversation and the giving of a turn to another. This allows the other to enter one's mind and life, or life and mind, just as one's earlier articulation did the same for the other. It recognizes that the other has certain rights to participate in the ongoing processes just as it creates the opportunities for common viewpoints and shared perspectives to emerge—or in the alternative, to discover that there are viewpoints that are different from one's own that one should take into account. These moves, taking a turn in a conversation and enabling another to have to go, form the foundation of society. How is society possible? Society is possible because agents take a turn in a conversation—using the word in the widest possible sense—and allowing others to do so, too. In fact, the procedure of turn taking is the machinery by which dialogism is made to emerge in conversations as in games.

Sacks, Schegloff, and Jefferson write that the results of their "examination suggest that, at least, a model for turn taking in conversation will be characterized as locally managed, party-administered, interactionally controlled, and sensitive to recipient design" (1974: 696). This is no doubt true but the system of turn taking in games has certain variations. They are certainly "locally managed" but the management is administered by "parties" other than the conversationalists. They are, in fact, administered by referees and umpires and they typically enforce rules of turn taking made elsewhere. Typically, exceptions are not tolerated: to change the rules is, in fact, to change the nature of the game. Nevertheless, it is no doubt true that in amateur games there is a very strict adherence to local management and self-administration. In the turn-taking processes that occur in games, there is both systematicity and predictability, and each turn is used by one party to address the other and elicit a particular response. The players thereby construct what Sacks et al. (1974) called "an adjacency pair." These are, in one commentator's words, "sequences that are two utterances long and are adjacently placed . . ." and he continues, "they are 'relatively ordered' because one goes before the other. They are also discriminatively related in that the first part defines the character (or discriminates between) an appropriate second part" (Silverman 1998: 105). In a game of tennis, for example, the "service" functions as the first part of the adjacency pair and the return, the second part. Its quality—speed, placement, and pace—will be to a great extent determined by the quality of the first part. If this is obviously the case in two-party games, it is also true of multiple-party games. In bridge, for instance, there are four players, but each pair of them constitutes a team and the game becomes a two-party game. However, at the bidding stage, there are four individuals initiating bids and responding to the bids of others in sequence, with each such move eliciting a response from the other and constituting a series of adjacency pairs. In poker, there are no partners as such, but each move by a player elicits a commensurate response from the others and thereby constitutes, again, a series of pairs.

Once an initial turn is taken in a game and a response elicited constituting adjacency pairs, the process continues in a very strictly ordered and disciplined manner. In everyday conversation, participants can disrupt and violate the various elements of the "device" of turn taking with varying consequences. For instance, egomaniacs, prima donnas, and heads of organizations can dominate a conversation and be miserly in the offering of turns to the others. Or else, the other may be uninterested in the niceties of conversational politeness and etiquette and interrupt the other and forestall his or her presentation of his or her turn. Further, in ordinary conversations, one party can change the topic, with warrant or without, and change the course of the next series of exchanges.

In games, none of these contingencies is likely to occur. No interruptions or overlaps are permitted, no change of topics, no domination of the other by controlling turns. Indeed, in some games like tennis, badminton, volleyball, and table tennis, special steps are taken to ensure that the principle of alternative turns is followed strictly. For instance, in tennis, the nested scoring system—points, games, and sets—with each player getting to serve alternately, enables a certain equalization of the advantages that accrue to the one who initiates the first part of the adjacency pair—the serve.

The turn-taking structure of games enables players to address each other and answer the other. In such addresses and answers, selves are presented and either validated or repudiated, emotions generated and given play, and a sense of catharsis achieved. The dialogic structure of human relations demands the use of various "devices" for their efficient functioning and the device of turn taking is one of the most important ones. In games, this device is presented in an idealized and encapsulated form—indeed as a mimesis of everyday phenomena.

Structures of Place

Human beings live in spatial environments that have very specific characteristics: seashores; jungles and forests; deserts; rivers, streams, and lakes; frozen and snow-ridden terrains; farmland and pastureland; mountainous areas; cities and towns.

The people who live in each of these environments need to learn the terrain of the land and how to read the marks left on it by nature as well as those marks made on it by themselves. In each such environment, the agents have to learn to manage the limitations that the features of the environment visit on those who live there as well as to utilize the strengths and opportunities it provides.

In addition to the practical and utilitarian ways in which they handle the limitations and use the opportunities, the people who live there construct certain structures of activity that constitute the play-form of such relationships with the environment. In mountainous regions, the inhabitants have to deal with their special features on a routine basis, on the one hand, and devise games and challenges in which the features of the mountain become a significant element.

Mountain climbing as an activity and a competitive endeavor between actors becomes a favored game though this will be later taken up by others as well. On the flatland, grazing cattle and managing them in efficient and parsimonious ways are very important for survival; "rodeo" becomes the play-form of the routine activities of everyday life. Kicking a ball on the flat ground—as well as moving it along and trying to keep it from being captured by another player, too—is a game that evolved in places where there is free land for such activity. Even in this form of activity, the players become one with the land they use for their living and measure it with their activities as well as take its measure. Is it soft and yielding? Then run and walk and dribble with caution. Is it hard and resistant? Move and play accordingly.

Living in frozen landscapes where there is ice for most of the year demands particular agility and control of one's body to keep from falling. Such moves are idealized, focused, and concentrated in the playing of various "winter games." Skiing, skating, and the like, are indulged in by the ice-people with enthusiasm. Instead of staying indoors and enjoying the warmth of the fireplace, hibernating after a fashion, they go on the ice and convert a problem and a nuisance into an opportunity and a challenge. Ice hockey is a nice apotheosis of this tendency where speed, control, and the management of body and limbs on a slippery and unsure surface become the essence of the game.

The human being makes accommodations to the physical environment—the *immediate landscape* of his or her life—and will seek to make it familiar, come to terms with it, take its measure, and learn to live in it and with it and sometimes around it. It is safe to say that ontogenetically, the human species has sought to control its spatial environment by converting the wilderness into gardens and fields; caves into marked dwellings; open spaces into huts and houses, arenas, stadiums, and stages; breaks in the forest into pathways; rivers into passageways with sluices and gates; and seashores into harbors and havens. *These moves were essentially ones that enclosed space into manageable units by the construction of boundaries.* These boundaries are constructed in a manner that is different from those marked by animals and varies across cultures—but mark the space they do and convert space into places that can be named, identified, and experienced in one way or another. The style and manner of doing this involves two levels: the collective, historically derived and culturally specific way and the pivotal manner in which an agent as a self learns to handle it, live in it, and create and participate in its significance and meaning.

Insofar as all human beings have to live in a world of space rendered meaningful, they construct various systems by which it can be conceptualized and managed for everyday life. Among these, one can mention the Hindu and Buddhist system called *Tantrism* in which a mimesis of the universe and its relation to the human agent is constructed in the *mandala.*

Tantrism is a variation on Buddhist and Hindu themes that stresses meditation and ritual practices. Agehananda Bharati, the noted Tantric scholar writes:

> There is decidedly such a thing as a common Hindu and Buddhist tantric ideology, and I believe that the real difference between tantric and non-tantric traditions is methodological: tantra is the psycho-experimental interpretation of non-tantric lore. By 'psycho-experimental', I mean given to experimenting with one's mind, not in the manner of the speculative philosopher or poet, but rather in the fashion of a would be psycho-analyst who is himself being analyzed by some senior man in the trade. (1970: 20)

These psycho-experimental practices, called *sadana,* are considered to be more important and fulfilling than speculative philosophizing and abstract theologic indulgences and are conducted with various aids and instruments. One such instrument is the minimalized and artistically executed representation of space into bounded and internally segmented units. A practicing tantric, for example, would trace a mandala with rice powder or other materials like *cinnabar* or *sesamum* seed and invoke the four great "seats" of the soul that are common to the Hindus and the Buddhists (Bharati, 1970: 254). These seats are polarized positions within an enclosed space and the practitioner focuses on the mandala and its internal features as he recites a *mantra,* a magical formula.

By tracing a mandala on the ground, the tantric practitioner is truly enmeshing his or her self into the bounded space and allowing it both to wander in it as well as feel contained by it. This entry of the self into the mandala, or at least, a participation in it, is achieved by the chanting of the mantra. Such a chanting creates a somewhat complex feeling tone in the practicing person, says Bharati, who talks also of "an emotive numinous effect" (1970: 102–03). The mantra is a very personal and individualized formula and can be identified as a summary of the ritual self as well as the instrument of its expression.

One of the many ways in which the mandala principle was realized was in architecture. In temple architecture as well as in the constructing of palaces and even dwellings, some version of the mandala principle was put into practice. *In other words, the mandala systematics was essentially a way of dealing with space: defining and reducing it to human proportions so that a human mind and human body can handle it.* It is a form of the mimesis of space, of converting immensities into miniatures, of converting space into place by giving it a logic of relations. In doing this, the dangers and threats of an "outside" world are diminished, if not eliminated, by creating an "inside" that is different from an "outside" world of untamed demonical forces. Thus, a jungle and a forest are excluded by making a garden, a farm, and a paddock; wild open spaces are made into dwellings and yards with inner and outer boundaries. Tucci observes:

> First and foremost, a mandala delineates a consecrated superficies and protects it from invasion by disintegrating forces synchronized in a demoniacal cycle. But a mandala is much more than just a consecrated area ... It is, above all, a map of the cosmos. It is the whole universe in its essential plan, in its process of emanation and of reabsorption. (1970: 23)

A universe is expressed in a minimalized form in the mandala, an imagined cosmos with order and shape, and is rendered conceptually manageable and related to act and self. *In spite of all the esoterica associated with the* mandala *concept, the use of the* mandala *principle is truly ubiquitous in the secular as well as in the religious life.* Indeed, one can say that there is nothing special about this principle except for its sacred claims. It is essentially a way of marking out space, enclosing it with boundaries and investing it with special significance. The vast expanse of space is measured and marked so that an agent can place himself or herself in it.

One space is thus measured with boundaries, symmetries, harmonies, parallels, connections, entrances, and exits; an agent can handle it *conceptually and practically*. It is home now—familiar and bounded space. It is just another case of converting space, empty, vast, unbounded and untamed, sometimes even wild and dangerous, into place, marked with whatever significance can be given to it collectively and individually. It was a way of marking out space, enclosing it with boundaries, and investing it with significance. Such places can be used to aid one's contemplation and meditation, to engage, that is, in psycho-experimentation, as well as to live and act within it—which may also be a form of psycho-experimentation. To circumnavigate a temple, to move into a constructed dwelling, to wander in one's farm, ranch, or garden, to perhaps even practice the "art of walking in the city," are ways of handling and managing space, of getting a sense of place and the selves in it, taking its measure and the measure of one's own self in relation to it.

The marked space gives a sense of boundedness, each such differentiated place demanding different attitudes and acts. In these exercises of perception, contact, and manipulation of space as an object, the neutral space is, in fact, turned into a place that has a specialized meaning to the actor. The sidewalk and road are not mere spaces, but are named and categorized entities, to wit a place just as one's own home and the stranger's home: they are significant places; they have been transformed into places. They have become significant to the self and any act performed within them and with them will be undertaken with reference to the self.

The Places of Play

If the mandala—and its many variations—are an instrumentation with which space is conceptualized and rendered into a logic of relationships, the games that human agents have devised is another. The conversion and management of space is indeed one of the central features of many games.

Johan Huizinga, discussing the relationship between ritual and play, notes that "marking out of some sacred spot is the primary characteristic of every sacred act," just as in play "a closed space is marked out for it, either materially or ideally hedged off from the everyday surrounding." Huizinga concludes that "formally speaking, there is no distinction whatever between marking out a space for sacred purposes and marking it out for purposes of sheer play" (1950: 19-20).

Human beings live in space, but they take this space, its vastness, openness, and limitlessness, and transform it by *marking* it in various ways and putting bounds on it. Space thus becomes smaller, bounded, limited, and intimately known and experienced. It is reduced to human proportions. Indeed Yi-Fu Tuan, in a pioneering study of space and place, has argued that in spatial consideration "man is the measure." He writes, "in a literal sense, the human body is the measure of direction, location, and distance ... Spatial propositions are anthropocentric, whether they are nouns derived from parts of the human body or not" (1977: 44-45). He later concludes, "Certain spatial divisions and values owe their existence and meaning to the human body and also that distance—a spatial term—is closely tied to terms expressive of interpersonal relationships" (1977: 50).

Using the human being—his or her self and body—as a location point, human agents can speak of left and right, front and behind, up and down, to discuss the space in which they find themselves. Further, they are able to demarcate space and define it as "mine," "yours," "his," "hers," and so on. In Tuan's words, "What began as undifferentiated *space* becomes *place* as we get to know it better and endow it with value" (1977: 6) (emphasis added). Eventually, one invests emotions into these places and if one becomes positive about them, he or she is subject to *topophilia,* Tuan notes (1974). Or else, he or she can [view] spaces as "landscapes of fear" (1981) and experience *topophobia.* While Tuan applies these concepts to large historical and mythological arenas, they can apply to smaller scapes, too. A good description of such a "feeling for place" is given by the fan of a soccer stadium: "There is a rush of adrenaline every time I go through the gate. It is home away from home. I feel more at home there than I do in my home ...This piece of land is wrapped up into my Saturday, you know, in the sense that it is consistent with how I conduct my Saturday—where I go before the game, who I meet up with, what time I leave" (McKay, 1995, cited in Bale, 1996).

This transformation of space into place personalizes it and renders it into a meaningful symbol for the relevant human beings. It ceases to be abstract and evanescent and becomes a concrete and permanent entity readily identified and associated with the relevant actor. It becomes an aspect of the self of the actor, an essential element of its conception of its own boundaries, worth, and value. It is not "territory" that a human actor craves "imperatively," but a socially meaningful extension of his or her self. To own property is not to claim it in the same way an animal claims its territory, but to be able to use it to define and extend one's self. He or she can do this by using it to claim power over others, by gifting it or selling it or bequeathing it to one's descendants—in fact, using it as a semiotic of the self in all its being and transactions. The transformation of space into place is accomplished by an agent or structures of agents, observing and defining and then living in it. In places thus transformed and defined by human intervention, social relations of a particular sort are conducted. The playing of games is, in fact, the conduct of a social relation of an idealized form in a miniaturized representation of social space. If the Hindu and Buddhist converted certain spaces into sacred ones as mandalas, the playing arenas of modern games are not that different in having a charged emotional and cognitive significance for the devotees of the games.

To experience this sense of place, to personalize space, one does not have to actually own the space. Attachments to place can occur even when the space is public or shared with others and such places can be put to various uses. One of the uses to which space is put is converting it to a place for games. In games, ordinary space is transformed into place—valued cognitively and emotionally, invested with meaning, and featured in conversations and memories. For example, a football field, to begin with, is demarcated from the surrounding territory and made to stand apart. Within outer boundaries there are further marks indicating "yards" of space and at each end, there are marks indicating "end zones," and there are upright posts with crossbars at the far end. These markings are signs that are easily read by the players as well as the spectators who thereby convert the space into a place where certain disciplined and meaningful activity is to take place. Similar observations can be made about other games played in space. Tennis, for example, has rather simple markings but they too signify the conversion of space into meaningful place where certain moves will be made.

In cricket and baseball again, a wild space is transformed into a place with significance. There is a "diamond" with four points in baseball and a mound in the middle of the field. In cricket, a circular field is marked out with string mounted on spikes with a "pitch" in the middle. On either end of the pitch is a wicket with three stumps with a heading called the "bails," which are loosely hoisted on top of the stumps. Here the major conversion of space into place is the distance between the bases in baseball and between the wickets in cricket. The "run" between these points is the object of the game. This simple distance of 77 feet in baseball and 22 yards in cricket becomes an object of contest and the measure of success and failure. Again, an ordinary space is converted into place in many ways: the diamond and the pitch, the space between bases and wickets, and the whole field in which the diamond and the pitch are situated.

These "markings" on the ground in field games are aids that enable the players to perform and indicate fundamental human proportions. The space can be read as "left and right," "front and back," "in" and "out," "forward" and "backward," "our side" and "their side," and such readings enable the action in the field to flow smoothly and intelligibly to all and sundry. For the players, these markings indicate their own place, give them a sense of familiarity, even perhaps ownership, and certainly a sense of being at home: I belong here; I can handle the intricacies of being in this place and can even perform satisfactorily here. These markings, in fact, convert space into a place—a field, or court, into home.

In board games, the space is miniaturized and converted into place: A white square in a chess board is not just a white space but a meaningful place that one must protect and defend—just as one would a place in the outside world. The spaces are marked to be constructed into meaningful places to which emotional and cognitive significance can be adduced. Once such conversions have occurred, these places on the board will be treated with deference and commitment and often one's life and destiny and self-esteem and honor are determined by the success or failure of the relevant moves. In any case, space and place are significant in these games as well as in football and cricket.

In field games, court games, and board games, the players handle space that, mercifully, has a *finite* character. It is not the endlessness of the plains or the roads or the sea and the sky. Not only does it have boundaries, it has all manner of internal marks that guide one's actions, circumscribe them, and give a sense of order and discipline, and an assurance of how one should act in them.

Once the player is situated in the space, whole or miniaturized, and begins to understand his or her location and its demands and responsibilities, he or she is not only in a place, but knows how to *use* it in a variety of ways. If one takes field games to start with, the player has to move within the parameters of the field in certain ways and use the space in front of him or her or behind or to the left and to the right and above his or her head to achieve certain goals. Indeed, in many games, to achieve a goal, he or she takes possession of the space, his or her place in fact and moves the ball or puck in a variety of directions, but directions that are determined by the objective of the game. ***The ball and the puck, in fact, are instruments for the measurement of space and its relation to self and within the scheme of the game.*** The move toward the goal of the opponent undertaken by one player gives him or her status and honor. In these moves, the movements across the space of an object by an agent become both a measure of the game's winners as well as the estimation of the player's self.

These observations are true for chess, checkers, and backgammon, too. The space is small and the moves are made by hand rather than with hands, feet, or sticks, but the spaces are significant for self. One is there, in the space, and the uses he or she makes of the marked places will grant him or her esteem or obloquy. The chess pieces, variegated in complex ways from each other, as opposed to those in checkers, are once again units used to transverse complexly marked spaces and meet other pieces and engage them in combat or evasion. The winners and losers are determined by the number of pieces that are removed from the spaces of the board and the number remaining.

The transformation of space into place also means that it becomes endowed with a special sanctity. In sacrificial rites, again space is converted into a scared place in which specially qualified objects are brought and offered to the gods. In other words, space itself is an object that an agent has to perceive, construe, and manipulate as he or she acts: the space in which he or she is standing, the space surrounding where he or she may happen to be standing, and the one to which he or she may want to move to next. For instance, he or she may be standing on the edge of the sidewalk, about to cross the street and move to the other side. These spaces are perceived, construed, and manipulated in the act of crossing the street—a series of moves that reflect a self as well as construct elements of it. For instance, he or she may cross against the light of the traffic regulator or may wait as an obedient, law-abiding, disciplined Boy Scout and cross only when the light turns green.

Or else the space may be in his or her home and it has several significances in terms of rights, duties, and obligations, all of which have to be construed as one perceives the space and manipulates his or her acts. Conversely, the space may belong to someone else. He or she may be trespassing, which will demand a different set of constraints and manipulations.

In games, it is not so much that the field of play is rendered into "sacred space"; rather the rendering of any space into place, including a sacred one, is an act of humanizing space, making it familiar, friendly, and easily negotiable to conduct a life and the acts thereof. Taking a wild field and marking it in various ways renders it into a familiar and friendly place in which orderly life can be conducted, just as marking a blackboard with squares and rectangles makes it into a disciplined system in which systematic moves can be made.

Object Relations

The fundamental feature of the playing of games is that the human agent is made to use an object external to him or her to undertake various acts that are addressed to another. These objects are invested with a special significance and used to prosecute acts, present selves, and construct interactions.

In addition to a theory of the self developing out of a series of interactions that a human agent has with his or her fellow human being, G. H. Mead developed also a theory about the relationship of such a self to the physical and spatial world. This theory is canvassed in many of his essays—indeed, in far too many to be noticed in detail here. Fortunately, Doyle McCarthy has produced an admirable summary of his theory as well as an insightful discussion of its significance for social psychology. Four topics, she argues, constitute the main themes of Mead's commentary, and these are:

> The function of the object in the definition of the bodily self and its environment; the phenomena of the resistance and interiorization in the self's contact with physical things; the self's identification with the world of physical objects; the perceptual and manipulatory phases of acts. (1984: 106)

Developing these ideas, McCarthy observes that, for Mead, the human hand and its functional capacity to touch, to grasp, and to hold objects is of vital importance in the building up of the environment (1984: 107).

This capacity to relate to objects in this manual way enables us to feel both their *resistance* as well as their *pliancy* and relate to them. "It is only man who has entered into a social relation with his environment" (Mead, 1938: 110). This allows a human agent to undertake cooperative activities with objects and conduct a life by systematically and transformatively taking account of them. That is to say, we never see objects and deal with them as isolated and alienated entities, but always as parts of larger systems with both a single significance and a collective meaning. A tree is a tree by itself, but it is also a part of a class of trees that may belong to the agent in relation to it or may not—and so on.

Objects, however, can exist, Mead argues, only within the stages of an act: objects have to be *perceived* to begin with and then *manipulated.* Again, McCarthy's commentary on this is illuminating:

> At the perceptual stage, the object is a "distant object." Even objects which are close are "distant" in the sense that their outline and position are perceived with reference to an organized environment and their distance becoming reality can only be experienced "by an act reaching into the future." (1984: 110)

Once the "distant" object is perceived in that phase of the act, it is brought into the manipulatory phase. In this phase, the object is "contacted" and, with such contact, allows the agent to determine if his or her perceptions were in error (Mead, 1938: 141). Contact also enables an agent to elicit the object's response to the manipulation, observes McCarthy (1984: 110), quoting Mead: "Out of this experience arises the physical thing in its reality. For it implies that the individual has called out in himself the sort of resistance that he is seeking in the physical thing with the sense of effort which accompanies his own response" (1938: 187).

It is in this responsive resistance between the manipulatory phase of the act and the object that a self becomes involved with it. The agent is able, as a consequence of his or her complex relationship with the object in question, to incorporate its features and his or her relationship to them into his or her self. An agent encounters a boulder in his or her peregrinations on a road. He or she perceives it as a distant object and then, when he or she comes into contact with it, he or she is able to touch it and participate in the manipulatory phase of an act. He or she is able to feel its texture to begin with, but he or she is also able to relate to it as follows: It is too heavy for a person like me to move all by myself. In any case, it is not my responsibility to move it out of the way. I will call the relevant authorities and report the obstruction. He or she, in other words, has estimated a relationship between his or her strength and the boulder as well as the responsibilities his or her self bears in the situation.

Take another example: John perceives an automobile in his driveway. He is able to identify it as his own vehicle, the importance it has in his life, the significance of its character, and the cost to his self-esteem, and so on. He moves toward it, enters its driver's seat, and starts and drives it away. The latter steps, too, have significance to his self: the car did not stall and act like an old jalopy; he was able to drive it and display his mastery over an important craft that defines the modern American self. In this case, both possession of the object and his ability to manipulate it successfully, reflected on his self. Conversely, the absence of these two features or failures in the latter one may reflect on the self, too. In any case, the relationship between object and self is a complex one, involving not only perception but the particular relationship one has to the object in question and his or her skill and capacity in manipulating, after the initial contact experience. The contact experience brings the body into a relationship with the object and then the features of the object, and one's manner of dealing with it becomes elements of one's self. One can deal with it successfully or one can be defeated by it or one can merely use it to take the measure of one's self: I cannot handle this object satisfactorily—I am that kind of a person; or I can handle this object satisfactorily.

The object that the agent has to perceive and manipulate in the acts that he or she will produce is to be found in spaces of some kind or another. It is this spatial perception and constraint that become relevant in the handling of objects that are distant from the agent—that are removed appreciably from the agent in question. It is the object that he or she can perceive and construe, but cannot touch. As such, it is an object, the features of which the agent has to construct imaginatively and conjecturally. Space separates the object from the agent and he or she has to imagine, to begin with, the distance to the object, its characteristics and qualities, and finally, and very significantly, the nature of the relationship that he or she can have with it. Here again, the meaning of the distant object becomes referred to the self.

In giving presence to selves in games, there is also the need to handle material objects. In board games, there are boards and the pieces that are played on them, while in the other games, there are more complicated instruments, the uses of which must be mastered—bats, rackets, clubs, balls, pucks, shuttlecocks. In field games and court games and golf, the understanding and mastery of these objects becomes of great importance. Recalling Lev Vygotsky's (in Luria and Vygotsky: 1992) claim that the habitual use of tools—including sign-systems—was the instrumentation through which human beings construct and transform themselves, one can conclude that the various objects used in playing games are truly analogues of tools with which a human agent transforms himself or herself and either constructs or refurbishes his or her self and consciousness (Vygotsky, 1978). Consider here a description of tool use by one of Vygotsksy's associates, R. E. Levina, that will recall forcefully a golfer at play: A four-and-a-half-year-old girl was asked to get candy from a cupboard, with a stool and a stick as possible tools. Lavina's description reads as follows:

> (Stands on a stool, quietly looking, feeling along a shelf with stick.) "On the stool." (Gances at experimenter. Puts stick in other hand.) "Is that really the candy?" (Hesitates.) "I can get it from that other stool, stand and get it." (Gets second stool.) "No, that doesn't get it. I could use the stick." (Takes stick, knocks at the candy.) "It will move now." (Knocks candy.) "It moved, I couldn't get it with the stool, but the, but the, stick worked." (Vygotsky, 1978: 25)

One only has to substitute "clubs" for stick and stool to get the picture of a golfer getting ready to putt.

In the places of play, the instruments of play become the means by which the objectives of the games are reached. Indeed, the very objective of these games is to transverse and transcend a defined place using one "tool" and relating the selves of the players with each other by the resistance that is faced from other players, and from the instruments of play and the places of play.

Society in Games

Games as mimetic structures represent, simultaneously, two fundamental features of society—the orderliness of societies and the orderliness of interactions, on one hand, and the persistence of societies on the other hand. In spite of the obvious presence of conflict, dissonance, and disarray in human societies as in human interactions, it is easy to see that there is not only an underlying orderliness to them but also that most members of society seek to maintain such order.

In the work of Talcott Parsons, one finds a nice distillation of the work of a variety of scholars who have discussed the issue of social order over the years. Games can be considered "social systems" in the Parsonian sense. Parsons sought to argue that society had strict systemic properties, but no known society can be shown to be systemic in his sense while, ironically, games can be shown to have these features. In fact, Parsons reaches to a game as an analogue for his claim that even two-person interactions are considered social systems:

> The essential starting point is the conception of two (or more) individuals interacting in such a way as to constitute an interdependent system ... The essentials of the interaction situation can be illustrated by any two-player game such as chess. Each player is presumed to have some motivation to participate in the game including a "desire to win," hence, he has a goal and relative to this some conception of effective strategies. (1961: 40–41)

Parsons, in fact, is able to find nearly all the elements of the social system in this game. The rules of the game—or what Talcott Parsons calls "normative patterns" (1961: 38)—have, according to him, two aspects. The first concerns the character of the normative pattern itself; the second concerns the state of "institutionalization." The normative patterns of society function, Parsons argues, to maintain "at the cultural level the stability of the institutionalized values through the processes which articulate values with the belief system, namely, religious beliefs, ideology and the like." Individuals in given societies are socialized into these normative patterns and to the extent they continue to observe them, they can be said to be institutionalized and their "patterns" maintained over time. Parsons derives this theory of socialization from Freud. The child is born with various institutional drives and is subjected to a social discipline in the family system through which these drives are suppressed, and certain culturally acceptable conduct, as "norms," is internalized in the child. Other sociologists and philosophers have variously called this "learning" or the "emergence of the self." G. H Mead, in fact, observes, "The unity of the complete self reflects the unity and structure of the social process as a whole; and each of the elementary selves of which it is composed reflects the unity and structure of one of the various aspects of that process in which the individual is implicated" (1934: 44). In another essay, discussing the relationship between an individual and social control, he writes: "Social control then will depend upon the degree to which the individual does assume the attitudes of those in the group who are involved with him in his social activities" (1962: 290). These social processes and the activities Mead is alluding to here can be a small circle of individuals as participants or a society as a whole of which one is a member.

Mead and Parsons are calling attention to the ordered ways in which individuals relate to each other and form their own "selves" or personalities. Parsons extends such membership to include not only sharing certain "goals," but the incorporation of the desire to attain these goals in the individual's personality. Such "normative patterns" and the "attitudes of the other" that an individual is expected to take are reinscribed in the games that human cultures have devised.

Parsons further advances the notion that societies,in order to function effectively and persist over time, must fulfill certain requirements.These "functional imperatives," they described as follows: 1. adaptation; 2. goal attainment; 3. integration; 4. latency.

Adaptation refers to the optimum utilization of the available resources and facilities in the face of a plurality of goals. Parsons put it this way: "It is on this basis that an analytical distinction must be made between the function of effective goal attainment and that of providing disposable facilities independent of their relevance to any particular goal. The adaptive function is described as the provision of facilities" (1961: 40).

In games, the adaptability is constantly being put into practice. Environmental conditions may change from situation to situation—from dry weather and hard ground to rain, snow, and perhaps hail and ice and mushy ground, but the players have to soldier on. The composition of the antagonists, their social character, and cultural ethos may change and the play proceedings—a casual game, a championship game, a "friendly" game, a game with deeply hated antagonists—need adaptations. Players often have to change their roles as their particular strategies change. For example, in field games, if one player is exiled or injured, the other players must change their playing strategies and cover the position of the absent player—that is, change their own roles. In card games and board games and in cricket, the players may be proceeding to win the main goal and, finding along the way that it is unreachable, may adapt their game to reach a lesser goal: a draw, rather than a win, a less humiliating defeat; and so on. Parsons describes the "functions of goal attainment" as follows:

> For the social system as such, the focus of its goal-orientation lies in its relation as a system to the personalities of the participating individuals. It concerns, therefore, not commitment to the values of the society, but motivation to contribute to what is necessary for the functioning of the system; these contributions "vary according to particular exigencies." (1961: 39)

In games, goals are more precisely defined than in social systems as each individual player has to perform in very specific ways to attain these goals. Nevertheless, just as in the social system, a game may have subsidiary goals as well, which in a crunch, must be sacrificed in order to work toward reaching the main goal. In a football game, a player's goal of individual success and glory may be sacrificed if his or her physical condition makes the individual less than fully competent in order for the team to win the game. Both main goals and subsidiary ones, however, are realized in social circumstances. The "expectations" of others, and their actions, become, in fact, the "conditions" under which a player may move toward his or her goal.

The next element of social orderliness and continuity, according to Parsons is the imperative to "integrate." This imperative applies to many levels of the social system. Parsons is primarily referring to the interdependence of the various roles and role-systems in given societies. Parsons argues as follows:

> Our recognition of the significance of integration implies that all social systems except for a limiting case, are differentiated and segmented into relatively independent units, i.e. must be treated as boundary maintaining systems within an environment of other systems, which in this case are other subsystems of the same more inclusive system. (1961: 40)

Parsons here is addressing an issue originally found in the work of Henry Sumner Maine, Adam Smith, and Max Weber, among others, and more particularly and productively, in the work of Emile Durkheim—the division of labor in society. Distinguishing between societies characterized by the "likeness of conscience" and those characterized by the "division of labor"—the former creates "mechanical solidarity" and the latter "organic solidarity"—Durkheim argues that though labor is *divided* in modern societies and performed by distinct occupational groups, at the societal level an *integration* is achieved because each such group becomes dependent on the fruits of the other's labor (1964). "Division," in other words, creates "interdependence" and integration. This view can be applied to whole societies as well as to small groups like the family.

In team games, there is a very strict division of labor. Each player in American football and soccer, for example, is assigned to a "position" with well-defined "expectations." Each player makes his or her unique contribution to the collective effort to reach the goals of the team. Each player's performance is circumscribed by the rules, though some degree of role switching is permitted in certain games. In any case, in these games one finds the perfect example of integration achieved through dividing the labor of the participants. No doubt, in team games, stars do emerge but the star could not have achieved his or her brilliance without participating in an integrated and functioning unit of several actors performing differentiated roles according to strict rules.

The final functional imperative has been variously called "latency" and "pattern maintenance" and is described as follows: "The function of pattern-maintenance refers to the imperative of maintaining the stability of institutionalized culture defining the structure of the system" (Parsons 1961: 38).

Games have this function fulfilled in two ways: first, the informal systems by which fans and aficionados of the respective games discuss and debate and transmit the rules of the game and keep them alive and, indeed, functional; second, modern games have established various governing bodies to administer the games and interpret the rules authoritatively whenever it becomes necessary and change them if need be. In this way the integrity and stability of the game is ensured.

It is the case that, as many have noticed, Parsons's depiction of social order does not describe any known empirical society with any fidelity. However, it describes the social structure of games with great precision because his theory of social systems and the systematicity one can find in games are both idealizations, epic renderings of order as such.

The Gaming Order

The dialogic processes and the binary systems that operate in games are articulated by the agents engaging in direct, face-to-face interactions—with the exception of modern "virtual games." In such interactions, in addition to doing the basic mechanics of the relevant games, the players have to sustain the demands of what Erving Goffman called "the interaction order." In this revolutionary recasting of the focus of sociological inquiry, he has shown that such an interaction order is a "substantive domain in its own right," and even claimed that "isolating the interaction order provides the means and a reason to examine other societies comparatively and our own historically" (1983: 2). In fact, a game is the quintessential representation of an interaction order.

To describe such an order, Goffman begins by arguing that such orders are generated because for "all kinds of unsentimental and uninherited reasons ... individuals everywhere—strangers and intimates—find it expedient to spend time in each other's company" (1983: 3). Indeed, but there are also good sentimental reasons why they find themselves in each other's company. Further, insofar as human beings are speaking creatures and the language they speak is inevitably addressed to another, there is an imperative to be in someone's company often so that the language and the linguistic mind can be experienced and exercised. After all, human beings do not so much learn a language as learn to address others with organized words and in so doing will seek to find opportunities to do so. The playing of games enables the agents to be in each other's company, engage in both sentimental and unsentimental activities and at the same time engage their speech and speechlike acts with each other and sustain their respective minds. These goals are served very efficiently in the playing of games.

Once such a process of being in each other's company by means of games is initiated, the players will have to maintain both "engrossment" and "involvement" in the ongoing proceedings, "and these cognitive states cannot be sustained over extended periods of time" (1983: 3). In games engrossment and involvement are fundamental to their initiation and continuation. However, they have to be maintained only for limited durations.

In interaction orders, "emotions, moods, cognitive bodily orientations and muscular effort are intrinsically involved," as Goffman observes (1983: 3), and this is certainly the case in games. In playing games, again, as in all interaction orders, "ease and uneasiness, unself-consciousness and wariness are central ..." Once an agent has mastered the craft of the game, he or she achieves a sense of ease, but in given instances of play uneasiness and wariness intrude themselves. This wariness is manifested in everyday life in the "visual regard," that we visit on each other. Each such participant uses such visual attention to "glean the other's immediate intent and purpose" (1983: 3). In playing games, too,

> Individuals are admirably placed to share a joint focus of attention, and to perceive that they are doing so, and perceive this perceiving. This, in conjunction with the capacity to indicate a joint course of physical action and to rapidly convey reactions to such indications from others, provides the preconditions for something crucial: sustained intimate coordination of action, whether in support of closely collaborative tasks or as means of accommodating closely adjacent others." (1983: 3)

In conducting such exercises within games, agents also conduct "strategic interactions," which Goffman describes as follows:

> Two or more parties [find] themselves in a well structured situation of mutual impingement where each party must make a move, where every possible move carries fateful implications for all parties. In this situation, each player must influence his own decisions by his knowing that the other players are likely to dope out his decision in advance and may even appreciate that he knows that this is likely. (1969: 137)

In undertaking such strategic interactions in games an agent takes actions that consist of chancy tasks undertaken "for their own sake," Goffman notes. He continues, "During occasions of this kind of action, not only will character be at stake, mutual fatefulness will prevail in this regard. Each person will be at least incidentally concerned with establishing evidence of strong character and conditions will be such as to allow this only at the expense of the character of the other participants" (1967: 240).

In such moves within the interaction order of games, agents also have to present selves appropriate to the situation, maintain the proper demeanor, and show the relevant deference and do face-work when necessary (1967). In dealing with each other, individuals are obliged to give due deference and maintain proper demeanor. In Goffman's words: "By deference, I shall refer to that component of activity which functions as a symbolic means by which appreciation is regularly conveyed *to a recipient of this recipient* or of something of which this recipient is taken as a symbol, extension or agent" (1967: 56).

To the extent this is done according to the demands of the participants involved in the interaction, order in it will be maintained. One of the most ubiquitous ways of showing the appropriate deference is to pay attention to the remarks or the moves that each is making. The absence of such deference in interactions would lead to the withdrawal of the person, who feels sufficient attention is not being paid to him or her, from the interaction—either physically or cognitively or emotionally. Goffman continues:

> Proper demeanor too is a feature of orderly interactions: "Demeanor is: that element of the individual's ceremonial behavior typically conveyed through deportment, dress and bearing which selves express to those in his immediate presence that he is a person of desirable or undesirable qualities." (Goffman, 1967: 76)

These encounters in which orderly interactions are maintained as in games give presence to the selves of the participants, enabling them to pulsate into an existential awareness and fulfillment insofar as order is maintained in the game interaction.

The Rules of the Game

The order that exists in the interactions of everyday life, as in gaming ones, is maintained by the observance of various rules. All games are constituted by rules, and without them there is no such thing as a game. Indeed, one can even say that when one is playing a game, he or she is, in fact, putting various rules into play. Even when one speaks or writes a language, it could be said that rules are being put into play. Ludwig Wittgenstein, writing in the middle of the last century, resorted to the game analogy to explicate two features of the use of language and the construction of meaning through it. Christopher Cherry puts this very succinctly:

> The first Wittgensteinian doctrine is "that language-using and games-playing share one common feature of being rule-governed activities ... The second doctrine affirms as its point of analogy between language and games not simply a common rule-governed nature, but a rule-*constituted* nature. It affirms that the rules of games and language alike constitute and do not (or do not merely) regulate activities of game-playing and language using." (1975: 532)

Wittgenstein himself put it this way:

> Consider, for example, the proceedings that we call "games." I mean board games, card-games, ball games, Olympic games, and so on. What is common to them all?—Don't say: There *must* be something common, or they would not be called "games"—but *look* and *see* whether there is anything common to all—And the result of this examination is: we see a complicated network of similarities overlapping and criss-crossing: sometimes overall similarities, sometimes similarities of detail . . . I can think of no better expression to characterize these similarities than "family resemblances," or the various resemblances between members of a family: build, features, color of eyes, gait, temperament, etc. etc. overlap and crisscross in the same way—And shall I say: "games form a family." (1958: par. 66 and 67)

There is something in common among these phenomena that are called games and the common feature is that they all exist and are functional because they put into practice certain delimited sets of rules.

Cherry's article is a probing examination of Wittgenstein's doctrines, and in order to solve certain problems in them, he advances various additional doctrines. This need not detain us here insofar as my interest is not in language per se but in games and the way they are constituted and how regulations of ordinary conduct affect the actual playing of the game.

Bernard Suits, seeking to define games as such, observes that the rules of a game "seem to stand in a peculiar relationship to ends. The end in poker is not simply to gain money, nor the end in golf simply to get the ball into a hole, but to do these things in prescribed ... ways; that is to do them in accordance with certain rules" (1967: 149). For him, the ends of a game and the rules of the game are "inseparable."

It is, however, not only games, but all human activities that are enabled and constrained by rules of one kind or another. This is acknowledged very forcefully in John Searle's study of "speech acts." He, once again, is interested not in games as such, but in explicating the construction or emergence of meaning in the speech acts of human agents. Nevertheless, he, too, resorts to games as a resource to solve his problems. He distinguishes between what he calls "constitutive rules" and "regulative rules." The former "create or define new forms of behavior and the latter regulate antecedently or independently existing behavior (1969: 33). The rules of football, for example, bring into being the game as such. These rules may be changed as the situation warrants, as the game continues to be played, but the rules nevertheless define the details and parameters of the game.

The Searlian position on rules—"constitutive rules" and "regulative rules"—is a formal distinction that does have certain uses in the philosophy of language use. In understanding social life, the separation seems too formal to explain actually occurring processes. Searle observes: "In baseball, after hitting the ball fair, the batter runs in the direction of first base, not in the direction of say third base or the left field grand stand ... My knowledge is based on knowing how to play baseball which is *inter alia* having internalized a set of rules" (1969: 14).

These are the "constitutive rules," but they can be put into practice only if there are accompanying regulative rules. These latter rules control the way a player must comport and disport himself or herself as he or she puts the other rules into effect. This involves rules of etiquette certainly, but also rules of demeanor and deference, of civility and decorum insofar as the game is an inescapably interactional activity. Players must address and speak to each other as well as to the coaches, managers, and even adversaries with acceptable levels of etiquette and decorum. This creates the illusion of the players engaging in a cooperative activity and the sense of a team. Clearly, if there is systematic rudeness and incivility on an ongoing basis, it would be difficult to play the game. A certain minimum of deference toward the star players of the game and particularly toward umpires, managers, and coaches, too, is mandatory for successful game playing. Proper demeanor, too, in terms of attire and presentation of the self in nonverbal forms of conduct—like distance between interactants and tone-usage—must be maintained for the game to proceed. Once the game is begun, the rules of constitution must be observed as scrupulously as possible. It is at this juncture that constitutive rules and regulative rules come into contact with each other. The issue is this: who is to enforce the constitutive rules? In the vast majority of games played throughout the world—chess, checkers, snakes-and-ladders, scrabble, backgammon, tennis, badminton, touch football, pick-up basketball and sandlot baseball, stick-ball, boys' cricket—there are no referees or umpires. The players themselves enforce the rules. It is here that the regulative rules become operational. Players have to accept the judgments of other players that an infraction has occurred, a foul has been committed, an "out" has occurred, a score has been made, a point has been won or lost, a move has been made, and so on. The acceptance of these judgments is an instance of the constitutive rules being in operation, and their maintenance is also an instance of deference and demeanor of decorum and trust occurring in the playing of games. Just as in language games, game playing involves a self-enforcement of the rules by two or more agents acting in concert with each other.

The regulative rules apply even after the game is over. When the game is won or lost, one must win with decorum and courtesy and lose with poise and dignity. A handbook on cricket (in Williams, 1999: 75) put some of these prescriptions for a "sportsman" and a "gentleman" very well as follows:

I. Plays the game for the game's sake.
II. Plays for his side and not for himself.
III. Is a good winner and good loser.
IV. Accepts all decisions in a proper spirit.
V. Is chivalrous toward an opponent.
VI. Is unselfish and always ready to help others to become proficient.

It is not, however, the case that these rules of a regulative nature are the property of a particular social class or civilization nor are they merely adventitious to the constitutive rules. Rather the playing of games as a constant and continuing activity among a set of players would be impossible without the regulative rules within which the constitutive rules are framed. In the face of persistent violation of the regulative rules, the teams would collapse, the adversarial players would not be willing to play again, and all forms of interaction, of which gaming is a subset, would become impossible. In other words, the regulative rules are functionally necessary for the playing of games. Games are not one-shot affairs: there is a move and a countermove and other moves after that, as well as other games to be played on later occasions. Games are, after all, played in social contexts. If the regulative rules are not in operation, no game would start, and if started, allowed to continue, and if continued, would not be resumed on another occasion. The game system would come to an end, sooner or later.

These rules, then, constitutive rules and regulative rules, operate contingently in the playing of games. Nevertheless, a question remains: who operates them? Wittgenstein's answer to this issue when he considered the use of language as analogous to the playing of games was that it was a self-correcting system. In other words, the speakers themselves—or players, one should say—operate the rules of language usage. This has two aspects to it: insofar as one is trained in the use of language, the speaker himself or herself will use its elements in such a way that they conform to the rules of the game; if one user makes a mistake, the other or others in his or her presence will correct the mistake(s), if they occur, thereby enforcing the rules. Summarizing Wittgenstein's position on this, David Pears observes:

> One way of appreciating his position is to ask how language-games operate as self-correcting systems. The obvious part of the answer is that we correct one another and conformity is enforced by the need to communicate. This is our first resource. But we also have a second resource: our shared language is itself continually but more unobtrusively tested against the world. (1987: 458)

These rules allow human agents to establish successful communication and in order to achieve this and to undertake it with sufficient efficiency, we are correcting our selves and others as well as modifying it if they fail the test against the world—for example, experientially. In games, conformity to the rules is established by the desire to play—and continue to play.

In the actual playing of games, this seems to be the case. To be able to play a game, one must be trained in it and such training involves the acquisition of the rules of the game. Further, once the rules have been acquired, they are enforced in the playing itself, with each player taking care to observe them on the one hand and correcting infractions thereof as they occur. If these conditions are not met, the game cannot be played. The second resource that Pears describes is, however, not relevant in the playing of games: the rules of tennis, for example, are not "tested against the world," though if certain rules prove inefficient, they will be replaced by other rules.

The issue is ultimately not one of just playing a game—language game or nonlanguage game—but of maintaining the dialogic relationship that is the game. If one violates the constitutive and regulative rules of either game on a continuing and systematic basis, other people will refuse to play anymore. The rule breaker will be excluded or abandoned or exiled. This is the case with the rules of the language game, too: if an agent systematically violates the rules of this game, he or she will be deemed to be mentally ill or retarded or *agrammatic* or *aphasic* and kept out of the conversation.

A game, in its structural and interactional aspects, is a wondrous instrument. It is a structure in which social acts can be undertaken—but within certain boundaries, and within these boundaries, an agent has to produce his or her creative acts, redeeming moves, and heroic gestures.

One may find an idealized version of the principles of social order in the Parsonian scheme in games, but a game is also an "interaction order" in Goffman's happy phrase. Within its form, games permit conversations to emerge and to be conducted, with words and without them, selves and emotions to be given presence and play, a narrative of the self with a swift denouement constructed, and an existence in time and place affirmed. Act, interaction and self, temporality and social structure and social order are unified and encapsulated neatly in the structure of games, making them one of the most universal of cultural artifacts in history. In such orders of interaction, agents are able to present their selves to each other, have them tested and validated, give play to their emotions, and enjoy a sense of vital presence in the world of others, social and material.

3

The Self at Play

The Self in Time, Place, and Position

In playing a game an agent, in fact, is putting the structures of games into play—that is, converting these structures into active and situated moves with varying degrees of awareness and intent. In playing a game, an actor is almost entirely the master or mistress of the acts that he or she is expected to produce. There may be others like captains, coaches, and partners who may seek to control the act, but this control is minimal. At the moment of execution—kicking, hitting, or throwing a ball or playing a card or moving a chess piece, the actor is in charge. This is one fundamental difference between work arenas and play arenas of the amateurs: in the work arena, the actor is subject to minute forms of control and management from a variety of others, with consequential diminishment of the self and the emergence of stress and hierarchical anxieties and tensions. In the play arena, he or she becomes an agent in the full sense of the term: he or she executes a move in accordance with his or her judgment of the situation and faces the consequences. In some games like tennis and even field games like soccer and hockey, such control is larger than in American football since in it the coaches exercise a great deal of control—nevertheless, at the moment of execution the player is in charge.

Further, the structures of the games are organized to elicit *active participation* as well as to provide opportunities for the *assertion* of self and its redemption. Consider the structure of any game in detail: it consists of a series of small moves and minor steps, each of which can be scored in terms of a minus or a plus that accumulate into a total, which ultimately defines a winner and a loser.

The playing of a game, in fact, is the construction and experiencing of a dialogic relationship and a narrative of the self by *situating* it in time, place, and positions in social relationships, all the while giving expression to one myth or another. The game is built up from small units to constitute larger units in a nested and sequenced system. Each of these units allows a particular form of emotional structure to emerge. Games, as opposed to other narrative forms, are unique in providing a framework in which emotions associated with winning or losing come in quick succession, each such moment leading cumulatively to a resounding climax. In such interactions, an actor engages the other emotionally and cognitively and achieves intersubjective communion, even if the exchange has been one characterized by contests and disagreements, thus obviating his or her sense of aloneness in the world.

The Cards of Time: Bridge and Poker

One of the essential experiences of the human agent is the awareness of the unpredictability of the future. One can remember the past, however selectively, and observe the present, however incompletely, but the future is uncertain and unpredictable. Nevertheless, many religions attempt to give some means by which an agent can control it to some extent and anticipate a particular future. Further, religions also attempt to instruct agents as to how they may control the future by managing the present in a certain way and, conversely, explain the present by claiming that particular series of acts and events in the past caused the current predicament. Nevertheless, the human agent anticipates the future, but also expects to be disappointed if the events do not turn out as anticipated.

These ideas have also been represented in games. Indeed, it can be claimed that all games are played in anticipation of a future that the players attempt to control by their current actions.This is the case in various card games that have been devised over the years as in games played with dice.

Playing games with cards to which various values were attributed has been a popular form of recreation for a long time. It is generally believed that card games originated in the Islamic world and were brought to Europe in the fourteenth century.The original pack of cards consisted of fifty-two pieces divided into four suits.Various games were played with them and it is out of these original cards that the tarot cards themselves were derived. The tarot cards originated as a game in Italy near the end of the fifteenth century, and not as an instrument for divination.The tarot pack was devised by adding twenty-two new picture cards as additions to the normal pack.These twenty-two cards had greater power in a game and were known as *triomfi* in Italian, from which we get today's "trump" in bridge.These twenty-two cards consisted of a card called the *matto* or fool—not to be confused with the "joker"—and a sequence of twenty-one trumps.These cards were used to play various games on a table, but other interactional games were also played. For example, there is a minor verse form in Italian known as the *tarochi appropriate,* which are verses composed about individuals to whom a tarot card was assigned. A poet would select twenty-two people and assign them one of the twenty-two *triomfi* cards and write verses describing each person with the card assigned to him or her as a major *motif* of the verse (Decker, Depaulis, and Dummett, 1996: 33).

Decker, Depaulis, and Dummett argue that originally *triomfi* had some esoteric meanings known only to the initiated, but that it was soon forgotten and only the symbolism that was obvious to everyone playing the game was used to interpret the significance of the cards (1996: 34). Nevertheless, the esoteric symbolism was retained, developed, and used to predict a future—either by shuffling the cards oneself and interpreting the configurations that resulted from a deal or by consulting a specialist who did the same. The interpretation was accomplished by using the syntactic meaning of the cards that are opened to construct a narrative of one's life—with or without the help of an official narratologist. The life that is narrated—or at least certain episodes of the plot—typically begins with a past and is oriented toward the future.

Dummett, an Oxford philosopher who wrote, along with Decker, a history of the tarot as a game (Decker and Dummett, 2002) and who, with Depaulis as his collaborator (1996), produced an account of its emergence as an occult practice is no doubt *historically* correct in claiming that the use of the tarot cards for reading the future—divination—was a later development. Even here Alice Hutton disagrees with this conclusion and states categorically, "Fortune-telling aspect was the original function" (1979: 12). *Structurally, however, every game of cards is an attempt not only to read the future but to actively control it as well as one may.* In other words, even without the esoteric symbolism that occultists assign to the tarot and use to devine the future, every time a card pack is shuffled and dealt to players and a game played with the resulting distribution, fortunes are being told and read into them. The difference between fortune-telling with tarot cards and ordinary games is that, in the former, there is an attention to the more fundamental issues of life—like death, fortune, marriage,—whereas, in the latter, the only question is how one's self is going to fare in the immediate future.

In playing a hand that is dealt to one in a card game, one is trapped in two narratives, one in which he or she is the protagonist and another in which he or she is the narrator: as a protagonist, he or she is casting his or her self—esteem, honor, skill, and identity as an individual or as a representative of a club or country—into the role of a player against another. In the game itself, the player has to construct plausible narratives with the cards dealt to him or her and arrive at workable syntactical relationships between them.

In playing card games, it is the case that the pattern created by the distributed cards that are in the hands of given players indicate the immediate status, esteem, and emotionality of the self, as well as its destiny in the immediate future. If the distribution is satisfactory and if the cards are deployed and played well and a win obtained, the status and esteem of the self is enhanced and often its economic standing. The win will enable the player to stay in the game and continue to play, and if the player succeeds in future plays, the self is defined in enhanced terms; or, on the other hand, one may lose and lose continuously and heavily and leave with loss of esteem and status—and even fortune. Every time then, when one is dealt a hand, it is possible to read one's future in it and if one reads it right and plays accordingly, he or she may be able to control it—up to a point. In both cases, it is the combination of *skillful play* and the chancy distribution of cards that determines the fate of the self.

The players, as they participate in these proceedings of the game, become the authors of these moves and jointly construct a narrative of their selves. Each player, as the author of his or her own narrative, is not just playing cards, but rather with the help of the cards, he or she is constructing narratives so that he or she can play with time. The narrative that one constructs as he or she plays a hand contains episodes in a plot that reproduce a life that is lived. With each move in the game, an agent puts his or her self forward into the future by using the control he or she has over the tokens, allows them to interact with the selves of the other players, and envisages consequential development of the plot.

These sequences of moves are not only articulated as narratives of temporality but are truly attempts to both experience time and handle its vicissitudes. Insofar as one cannot ever be certain whether an anticipated result will transpire, a human is always conscious of what may be termed the *chanciness* of life's developments. This chanciness is represented in all its fullness in games of cards. Card games are mimeses of human interaction with time, which is experienced narratively.

Every move a player makes anticipates a particular future, just as he or she remembers the immediate past. The "past" in this case contains the information that was conveyed during the bidding and the data revealed by earlier moves in the game. The bidding enables each player to gauge the strength of each hand and the moves made in the game will enable the player to estimate the strength of each suit in the player's hands. At every point the player's past is used to attend to the card being led at the moment and to anticipate not only the effect that particular card will have, but often how the rest of the playing is going to proceed. Every move in the game is fraught with memory and anticipation, a freight that is used to organize the attentive moments of the act of play. For a human being, reflexive minded, memoried, and prospective minded, the fact of playing with cards is a direct encounter with the limitless uncertainty of time and its essential character.

All the various games of cards—whether solitaire or interactional games—make for a confrontation with this uncertain future at the point of the deal. Once such a confrontation is experienced and the fruits come into one's hands, the player will seek to *control* the future by taking charge of the bidding and the playing. Every word he or she utters, as every card he or she plays, is an attempt to both control the consequences of the fruits that the deal provided as well as control the interaction of the fruits that were delivered to others. The various games of cards are then really playing with time and its uncertainty and seeking to control that uncertainty. It is in this experience of uncertainty and anticipation of one future or another that one can find the excitement and ecstasy of card playing.

It is this property of card games—their capacity to enmesh individuals in time through their ability to construct plots, articulated as varied distributions that agents can obtain by shuffling the cards—that enabled the tarot, originally a mere game, to be adapted to apprehend a past, focus on the present, and prognosticate a future for an individual who submits himself or herself to its vagaries. The cards in tarot are given not only a symbolic significance but also a narrative role. The card with the hanged man has the significance, for instance, of indicating ill fortune if it turns up after a deal, but this significance is given a further twist if it is found in conjunction with cards with other significations. If, for instance, it turns up with the card for death, it will acquire a particular meaning as opposed to when it occurs with the card for lovers. The two cards can now be syntactically joined to constitute the narrative: "Your love is doomed; it will not fructify; it will end like a hanged man before it reaches fulfillment." Fundamentally, then, games with cards enable agents to construct narratives that enmesh them in a remembered past, a focused present, and an anticipated future.

Time and the Self in Bridge

The enmeshing of the self in a remembered past and an anticipated future that are focused in a single moment is nicely articulated in bridge. The complex dialogic of bridge, constructed between *two teams* as well as between *two partners,* is undertaken within a strict narrative structure. The very organization of the cards portends a temporal process articulated as a narrative structure. In ordinary card games, the instruments of play are complexly and intricately related to each other. There are fifty-two cards, each of them with a face value—king, queen, jack, or a numerical value, one through ten. These fifty-two cards are further divided by color into two subsuites: red and black, and then divided by sign—spades, hearts, diamonds, and clubs. The ruling principle in the organization of the pack of cards is *hierarchy*: king, queen, jack, ten, and onward to one, represented by the ace. They are divided this way only so that they can be symbolically combined in actual play to constitute episodes in a plot and narrative sequences.The rules of each card game provide the framework by which such narrative sequences are to be constructed. Once they are played, there can always be analyses of how well some of these sequences may have been assembled.

The game can be divided into three movements (four, if one were to count the postmortems of each game): the deal, the bidding, and the playing. In the interactions that are manifested in the playing of card games, two perennial processes that emerge in an agent's relationship to the other are confronted: how do I know the mind of the other and how do I deal with it? Wittgenstein argued that our knowledge of other minds is achieved by evaluating the *criteria* that others provide about their minding processes. For the purposes of bridge, in any case, the philosophical conundrum that Wittgenstein considered at some length is solved by the existence of a nonprivate language—the rules and conventions of bidding in bridge—and its use by a player to indicate, conversationally, what is in his or her hand/mind. How does one come to have "knowledge of other minds," to use Norman Malcolm's (1966: 371-83) phrase? In explaining this issue, he puts it this way: "The circumstances, behavior and utterances of others actually are his *criteria* (not merely his evidence) for the existence of their mental states" (1966: 380-81).

In playing bridge—as in all card games—the fundamental quest is to look for the criteria by which what is in the mind of the other can be assessed. The game of bridge begins with the establishment of two-person teams, and one of them is selected to deal. He or she shuffles the cards in the pack in full view of the other players and then gives the pack to one member of the opposing team for a "cut." He or she divides the pack into two and then puts the top portion at the bottom and gives it back to the dealer. That is, every step is taken to ensure the random and arbitrary nature of the distribution that each player gets. Once the cards are dealt and each player has received thirteen cards, he or she arranges them and evaluates their significance for the conduct of bidding and play. The deal recreates one of the fundamental features of social life: the arbitrary manner in which the essential *assets* with which life is lived are distributed and the consequent *differences* in the power and advantage each individual enjoys. These assets can be hereditary privilege, wealth, health, intelligence, strength, beauty, and so on. Once these assets are distributed, one must deploy them as well as one can and get on with his or her life. The card game becomes a mimesis of the facts of social life. In life, as in card games, one begins the play with unequal assets distributed by various arbitrary practices.

The Bidding

Once the cards are distributed to each player, he or she studies and evaluates them. The interpreted meaning of these structures is now used to arrive at a contract to win a certain number of tricks in the playing by "bidding."This constitutes the second move of the game. Since each player has a hand that displays relative strengths and weaknesses, the bidding becomes an occasion for the assumption of control and the display of agentic powers. Every move in the bidding phase is about control—though often one has to cede the control to others and wait for the next deal.

The bidding leads to the emergence of a "contract" to win a certain number of tricks. The entire structure of bidding and contracting represents *interdependence* of social beings in everyday activities and eloquently exemplifies Durkheim's thesis about contracts (1964). Contracts are instances of social relations and interpersonal obligations that are entered into by those who are already committed to certain rules and customs—indeed, to interactional selves and interactional orders. In the playing of bridge, three dimensions of self and interactional order are simultaneously manifested: in one's relationship with a partner, he or she works *with* him or her, thereby achieving both sociability and interdependence; in one's relationship with the opposing side, one enacts the very precisely articulated rules of bridge and the general principles of the social interaction of civility, decorum, deference, and demeanor. And finally, the bidding and eventually the playing recreate one of the most fundamental processes of the interactional life: how to deal with the other without having ready access to his or her mind. In the interactional encounter, the other is always something of a mystery to the self, which is looking for dramaturgically presented information to reduce the mystery. In bridge—and other card games—each party reveals and conceals information and challenges the other to handle the consequences.

Once people sit down to play cards, they enter a world that is radically different from the ones in which each usually lives. To begin with, it is a rigidly ordered world in which the rules of conduct are clearly and unambiguously laid out and are enforced right then and there. It is a world in which each player is in charge of his or her actions and is able to exert control over them. Further, it is a world in which he or she is able to interact with the others on a basis of presumptive equality. Typically, each player is well versed in the game and is able to join a universe of discourse and participate in a significant communication. The game demands active participation and a committed series of acts—acts that define the players' self and become instruments of its presence in a world of interaction. As the bidding and the playing proceed, each player becomes conscious of his or her powers of agency.

The person sitting to the left of the dealer opens the bidding after studying his or her cards. His or her remarks are addressed to the other three players with particular indications to his or her partner. In this address is coded information that the others have to interpret and use to make their own remarks. This code has a special quality to it: it cannot contain any secret signals that only the partner can understand. It is, in other words, an open code that both his or her partner and the opponents can use to read one's hand and use to construct their own bids and play. In a championship game, for example, the bidding went as follows:

Peter: One diamond
Sharif: Pass
Alan: One spade
Forquet: Pass
Peter: Two no trumps
Sharif: Pass
Alan: Three no trumps

> The bid to "Two no trumps" was unusual in two ways: there was a jump to two instead of starting with "one no trump." Secondly, instead of investigating the possibility of playing in another suit if the spade that was bid was unsuitable, there was a switch to "two no trumps." This could have been based on a private code, and Omar Sharif promptly challenges it: "What does 'two no trump' mean?" He is given an explanation, though as it turned out not a very satisfactory one. The game proceeded anyway. (Sontag, 1977: 22)

Any variation in this code introduced by one player in collusion with his or her partner is tantamount to cheating and will be punished with varying degrees of severity. Sometimes, game officials analyze bidding procedures and the distribution of different hands to see whether a team has cheated in championship games. Even in club bridge, those who violate the open coding scheme of bidding in bridge meet with disapproval and the lowering of prestige. In a study of a bridge club, Bonnie Erickson and T. A. Nosanchuk (1984) report the following as some of the offenses against the code:

1. Taking your partner's tone of voice or long pauses into account when making your own bids.
2. Failing to alert your opponents to the fine details of your bidding or carding that may not be clear from your convention card.
3. Giving your partner unasked-for criticism at the table between hands.
4. Trying to distract or disconcert your opponents.

The game of bridge, then, has codes of conduct besides the ordinary rules of the game. They define the game as not only a contest but as a cooperative process in which information is revealed to others, as well as concealed, according to certain principles. There is no attempt to systematically mislead or bluff as in poker, no attempt at willful aggrandizement and combative posturings. Rather, players use an open code that both one's partner and one's opponents can understand and use to construct their own answers and moves in the game.

The addresses that each player makes are clues or criteria that will enable the other players to know what is in his or her mind/in his or her hand. He or she gets this knowledge by the evidence presented in the bid. The bidder, for example, says, "One heart." The other three players, including his or her partners, will know that he or she has a minimum of five heart cards, including some high cards as well as other cards that indicate a range of strength. The player who is to bid next will reassess his or her hand in the light of this bid by taking into consideration its significance. He or she will now reject his or her original intention to bid "one trump," since the original bidder seems to have both suit strength and supporting strength, and will bid "one spade." At this stage, both the original bidder as well as his or her partners and the second bidder as well as the partners will have information about what is in the minds of their respective partners as well as that of the opposing player. The third player now must introduce into his or her calculations the knowledge that his or her partner wants to play in hearts unless dissuaded by him or her and that the opposition has strength in spades. If the third player has a secondary strength in spades and has supportive strength in hearts, he or she will use this information to support his or her partner's bid of hearts and say, "Two hearts."

At this stage of the bidding, the third bidder has an advantage that the second bidder—the opponent—does not have: he or she knows his or her own controlling strength in spades as well as his or her supportive strength in hearts and is able to endorse his or her partner's bid of hearts. The fourth player will use the information available and study his or her hand to decide whether to support his or her partner's bid in spades. Insofar as the third bidder has a strength in spades, it is unlikely that he or she will have enough spades to support his or her partner. He or she can indicate his or her strength in diamonds, if he or she has the necessary cards, or he or she can pass.

In this stage of the bidding conversation, then, we have examples of what may be strategic revelation and concealment. The opening bidding revealed strength in hearts as well as overall strength in the other cards—indicating a "biddable" and, with support from the partner, a "playable" hand. Everyone's subsequent action was influenced by the information this revealed. The second bidder took this into account and revealed his or her strength in spades as in other cards. The third player, however, was able to conceal his or her control over the opponent's spades and revealed his or her strength in hearts. The "pass" from the fourth player revealed his weakness in spades as well as in the other suits. It is now up to the original bidder to carry the bidding forward by providing the information available to him or her. The fact that the opponent's bid in spades was not supported by his or her partner revealed to the opening bidder the possibility that his or her own partner may have some strength in spades that can be used to "check" the other's strength in spades. He or she can now raise the bid to "four hearts," which is enough to make a "game." His or her partner now has the chance to use all the information that has been revealed as well as all that he or she has concealed and decide whether to go for a "slam" or not.

The bidding was not, however, about arriving at a contract alone. Rather, a certain amount of information about each hand was conveyed to all the players that they will take into account in the actual playing of the cards. In announcing a bid, an opener, one indicates to his or her partner as well as to one's adversaries something about his or her hand. However, one also indicates these matters to the others while retaining the ability to control the next move one will have to make. Let us say one has the following: Diamonds: J, 4; Clubs: Q, 10, 3; Hearts: A, Q, 6; Spades: A, Q, 5, 3, 2.

Here the stronger suit in the hand is spades—it has two high cards and three in minor cards. Nevertheless, one can open with the weakest suit and bid "one club." This will enable the partner to indicate his or her strength and when the turn comes back to the original bidder, he or she can take the information given by the partner and rebid his or her strong suit by going to spades. The partner could have rejected clubs by saying "one diamond," or may even have said "one spade." The opening bid of "one club," it turns out, was a ploy to elicit relevant information from the partner and to use it to control the outcome.

The bids in these specialized forms are, in fact, signs used with specialized and esoteric significations. Perhaps the most obviously coded sign in bridge is the "two clubs" one. If one opens with a suit bid of two, it indicates strength in the suit and in the hand in general. However, a "two club" opening is a "forcing" one and indicates a general strength in the hand, but not necessarily in clubs. For example, one can open with a "two clubs" with the following hand: Spades: A, K, Q, 10, 6, 5; Hearts: A, K, 9, 3; Diamonds: A, 8; Clubs: 3. The player has a very weak suit in clubs—indeed a singleton—yet he or she bids clubs. The coded signification of this bid to the partner is "I have a very strong hand; please indicate your strength so that we can go for a high contract." The partner can respond, again in code, as follows: "Two diamonds—0-3 high card points; two hearts—4-6 high card points; two spades—7-9 high card points; two no trumps—10 or more high card points" (Jacoby, 1987: 49).

The mind as an *ongoing social emergent* cannot be illustrated with a better example than the proceedings in the playing of bridge. By the systematics of ongoing addresses and answers, a shared universe of discourse—an interactional concert—has been constructed, with each player making his or her contribution. Further, each of these moves are presentations, if not of self, then of the worth of one's self in the immediate interactional environment. For all current purposes of the game, all other claims to worth, value, and esteem are sidelined and only the worth of the hand that the player is holding is held to be relevant.

The Playing

The third movement of the narrative begins with the one who began the accepted bid becoming the declarer and taking charge of the actual playing. He or she becomes the narrative center while his or her partner becomes a silent one and his or her adversaries become the narrative antagonists and the source of conflict and contradiction.The former proposes an act and the latter two will resist as strongly as they can, recreating the themes of the myth of combat. In taking turns at play, the players will follow a strict narrative logic. Each trick in the game contains a narrative order within it—ace of spaces, three of spades, eight of diamonds, and the four of spades, for instance—with each card signifying a meaning to the players. Further, each card that is played indicates its membership in the order of the suits and in the structure of the players' hands—that is, it, too, is part of an implicit narrative order that all players have to construct, if they are to play satisfactorily.This implicit narrative in the hand of the player is really a variation on the hierarchic ordering of the cards: If the second player plays the king of spades to an ace of spades played by the first player, then the narrative order in the hand of the second player becomes clear: he or she must have only one spade and he or she may be short and/or long in the other suits. Systematically then, the playing allows an agent to enmesh his or her mind and self in narratives—their own and that of others including fictional ones: the ace of spades and the king and the queen, not to speak of the knave.

Once the play begins, then an actor is able to experience the controlling of a situation in two ways: one, in an assertive way by leading powerful and winning cards and expecting the others to submit; two, by seeking to thwart the other's operations by defensive maneuvers.

In the playing, the sense of agency and control become more pronounced. Every time a player enters a card into the game and allows the others to react to it, it is an exercise that tests the limits of the power and control that he or she has vis-à-vis that of the others. Each play is, in fact, an exercise in control, the seeking of control, the validation or refutation of the claim of power and control—indeed a mimesis of every relationship, conversation, interaction in everyday life. In the actual playing, the narrative structure is achieved in combination with the cards in the hands of the four players.

In this subtle and intricately organized combat, each card that is led or given as a response carries information that each player will try to use to his or her advantage. Errors of judgment will be made as well as excellent moves, and the conversation proceeds along this route. Each move will involve memory—the cards that have already been played; attention—the cards that are being played; and anticipation—what cards are still left to play. A skillful player will remember the cards that have been played, coordinate this with the memory of the bidding, and attend and anticipate what is to come next.

And so it goes until the end of the game. Such games are, then, not only conversations but also significant ones—complex, intricately organized, and disciplined. The game is also an idealized version of the rules of conversation: there is a consensually accepted topic, a strict observance of the rules of turn taking, a specialized language of conversation, which each party understands more or less completely, and the enforcement of an obligation to respond, to participate, or to leave the table. The game is a site in which the rules of decorum and demeanor are put into play and interactional offenses are rare. Indeed, in a game of bridge as it is usually played, the rituals of interaction are realized to the fullest possible extent.

It is at the bidding stage of the game that the player begins to get a sense of agency over his or her actions, a feeling of control over his or her destiny, in the short run at least, and begins the construction of a narrative of the self. If he or she has a strong hand, this can lead to a number of maneuvers in which this sense of agency and control are exerted by outbidding the other on the one hand and collaborating with the partner on the other. Even in the collaboration, there can be a contest as to who has the stronger hand and a playable hand and, therefore, who should become the declarer.

Even those who have weak hands and do not expect to become the declarer-side have opportunities to manifest their agency and control. They can seek to thwart the other side at the bidding stage itself and communicate with each other their respective strengths so as to be able to defend themselves.This move and countermove of agency and control eventually lead to a "contract"—the claim that they can win a given number of tricks.

The game of bridge is, then, a focused and significant conversation with precise turn-taking procedures, a tightly organized and coordinated coding system by which selves can be presented to others for attention and validation, and a structure of activity in which various agents can obtain both cognitive involvement and emotional engagement.

Poker as Dialogue and Narrative

Poker is the quintessential gambling game. In it, various commodities, or their value in various tokens, are staked and one may lose them or win somebody else's commodity. It, too, is a significant dialogue in which selves are narrated, and in this narration, money as a flexible token of value becomes an important instrumentation in the narrative.

In this game, too, each player seeks to engage in an antagonistic dialogue with the other by watching for the criteria by which the mind of the other can be read. Poker, like most forms of gambling, is a social and sociable activity. It involves interactions with other people—fellow players as well as dealers. In playing poker one cognitively engages the other in a very systematic way. It is possible to conduct the ordinary interactions of everyday life with a minimum of such engagement; but in playing poker, or for that matter any game, each party to the transaction that is the game must simultaneously read the other as well as face the reluctance of the other to be read correctly, just as one is seeking to prevent the other from reading one's own mind. This creates a complex interactional structure through which one will seek to put the self into active play. This form of an active and engaged self, of the self in cognitive and emotional engagement and at times of turmoil, gives it a sense of a strong and passionate presence in the social world.

The game of poker is, in fact, a mimesis of the fundamental process of the social and interactional life: taking the role and attitude of the other. In the game of poker, each player takes the role and attitude of the other and addresses significant moves toward him or her with the aid of a scare resource as the token of the self.

In one form of this game called "straight poker," a number of players gather around a card table with a dealer distributing the cards. Once the cards are in the hands of the players, the player on the left of the dealer begins the game by putting up an agreed-upon amount of money—or tokens thereof—called the "ante" and then the player to the left of him or her puts up a higher value of tokens known as the "straddle." Hamlyn's book of card games gives an admirably parsimonious description of the ensuing play:

> The dealer now deals, face downwards, five cards to each player. After looking at his cards, the player on the left of the straddle has the option of playing or not. If he decides not to play, he throws his cards face downwards and takes no further interest in the deal in progress. (2001: 178)

The game proceeds along these lines with each player left in the game getting more cards from the dealer, discarding some of his own, and putting tokens on the table to claim the right to continue in the game. Hamlyn's book observes:

> Poker falls naturally into two parts: staking and betting. The staking is the easier part of the game because it is open to a precise arithmetical analysis.

> Betting is the more difficult part of the game because it is largely psychology. At the same time, a player has to be gifted with the quality that we call judgement because his betting must be dictated by the manner in which the other players are betting, and how they, on their part will interpret his betting . . . A good poker player is inscrutable and unpredictable because he varies his game to make the most with his good hands and lose the least with his bad ones. (2001: 180–81)

In playing poker, then, certain elements of dialogue are in operation besides the fact that they are turn-taking interpersonal encounters. To begin with there is the cognitive engagement: the game demands, even in the simplest form, a great deal of local knowledge and analytical ability. Consider an example from Hamlyn's book. A hand has been dealt: 10 sp., 6 sp., 5 sp., 2 sp., and 9 hearts. Since a pair of 10's is of small value, the player's aim must be to discard heart 9 hoping to draw a spade to fill in the flush. There are 47 cards from which to draw, and of them only nine are spades. It follows, therefore, that the odds against drawing a spade are 38 to 9 or approximately 4 ¼ to 1 (2001: 180).

This is a beginning calculation and judgment, with further ones to be made by using the number of players still in the game and the odds the table is giving. Clearly, one cannot play this game unless one is alert, attentive, and able and willing to undertake at least a little exercise in analytical and probabilistic reasoning.

Further, this game could not be played without "betting." Betting is the act of putting something that one values, as well as something that is valued in the eyes of the other players, at *risk* and experiencing the *peripeteia* of waiting for the probability to turn in one's favor. This is true even when one is betting on a lotto game with astronomical odds: there is at least a chance, however minuscule, of wining as opposed to not betting at all, in which case the chance of winning is certainly zero.

However, what exactly is one betting in poker? It is typically a game played face to face, eyeball to eyeball—indeed, self to self. *In putting one's money on the table, then, one is not just putting some coins or notes or other items of value but one's self into the combat with other selves.* The money, in view of its complex symbolic significance, is able to determine a very complex engagement between the selves of the players. In such combats, money is a token for the self and it is the self that is in play when one bets.

Money, whatever the theories that economists have devised about it, gains its standing as a sign that is validated in dialogic interaction. It has no value unless at least two parties are willing to acknowledge it as a medium of exchange and display a certain resistance to parting with it. It is, in fact, a dialogic medium. Owning it and controlling it bring with it esteem and honor and, above all, power over others. Controlling money gives the agent, to begin with, structural powers: he or she can control social, economic, and political institutions, providing he or she has enough of it. Second, money confers symbolic power: even if one does not use it, members of society will defer to one and accede to one's wishes. Finally, it confers interactional power: in face-to-face interactions, the control over money enables the agent to receive services from another, obtain his or her goods by means of exchange, and generally dominate the other. These latter exchanges are often neutral and rational transactions—but often enough they are the situations in which deference and *abjectification* are demanded and dramatized. It is in such interactional moments that the full symbolic power of having money becomes manifested. The gifts that are unequal, the demands from the others that are domineering, the expectations that place oneself as master or mistress are derivatives of the power of money. Even in services provided in "rational institutions," the buyer and the customer are given deference and forgiven lapses in decorum, manners, and civility because the buyer and the customer have money and are paying for the services.

Money, then, is the most pervasive sign of the self in modern capitalist society, an encapsulated vehicle of the worth of a self, a collapsed unit that is also marvelously flexible: it can be exchanged more readily than any other sign, and it can be counted in very precise units and used to measure the self in whose possession it is, both by the owner and by others. It can be accumulated and hoarded more efficiently than other signs over time and transported across space with relative ease. It can be used in small doses or in large ones to express and assert the self and elicit measured responses from others. Money, in fact, forces the self to consider itself as much a political economy as a symbolic construction. It is this instrument that a person stakes in modern betting games.

In poker, these interactional meanings of money are brought fully to the fore. In it, money as a sign and manifestation of the power of the agent is brought to the table and used to assert the self, dominate the selves of others, and give the emotional and interactional significance of the self full presence and play. The wagering of money allows the self to experience various emotions, not as a static sense of being, but in undulating currents of joy and despair. In playing this game one will win, if one has the winning combination of cards, not only money but also esteem and self-fulfillment. If one loses, sorrow and despair may be the fruits. No matter; in either case, that player has given play to his or her emotions and staked his or her vital presence in the world.

Louis Zurcher, in a study of friendly poker players, using some of Erving Goffman's ideas, observes:

> If betting is low relative to the financial capacities of the players, interest may be lacking in the game and they may not take it seriously. If converse-

> ly, players feel that betting is too high then interest may be "strangled" by a concern for the money they could lose . . . The core members understood the impact of someone "who couldn't afford to lose" or "who didn't care about losing." In their view, the former makes you feel guilty if you win and the latter is no challenge because if he is not really losing anything, you are not really winning anything. (1970: 182)

These observations and analyses were made about a game in which the maximum bet was only 25 cents and the amount each player started with was $30.00. Clearly, the contest was not really about money in any absolutist sense but as a measure of one's self. If one is playing with an investment of money that is too low in terms of one's wealth, and that one doesn't particularly care about losing, then one's self is not involved in it and there is really no contest of selves. Conversely, if the other is playing and risking money that he or she can't afford—that is, it is not a *real* representation of his or her wealth—then again the players face an illegitimate token of self and the game lacks flavor and a win can induce guilt rather than euphoria.

To play the game of poker further demands not only that one has the tokens of value with which to give presence to one's self but that one has the necessary skills and wisdom and strength of character to go forward with the play. Such tests of character, nerve, and wisdom are undertaken by what are essentially dialogic moves with which one narrates his or her own self and engages the minds and selves of the others, cognitively and emotionally.

In playing poker, one is confronted with the complex and ambiguous information that is being made available by the others, information that one must interpret as well as he or she may, thereby engaging the others dialogically, and then stake one's self in it. One can see this more clearly in the aspect of poker playing called "bluffing." David Sklansky observes that "bluffing" is an extremely important aspect of poker and continues:

> An opponent who knows you never bluff is much less likely to play his hand incorrectly. Any time you bet, he will know you are betting for value. He will play only when he figures he has a better hand then yours or when he is getting a sufficient pot—odds to call with more cards to come. Bluffing, then, or the possibility that you might be bluffing is another way of keeping your opponent guessing. Your occasional bluffs disguise not just the hands with which you are, in fact, bluffing but also your legitimate hands with which your opponents know you *might* be bluffing. (1999: 163)

Bluffing then is a part of a very complex process of seeking not only to know the mind of the other but also to control what the other is allowed to think is in your mind—and hand. This mutual reading of the other's mind, the deception and the counterdeception, the attempted deception that may fail or succeed, and the move that is not a deception but is taken as one by the other—these are, in fact, indicators of not only a significant conversation but a very complex one suggesting mirrors facing each other, some of which may be distorting mirrors. Deceptions and bluffing they may be, but there is no denying a cognitive engagement between two or more minds, a locking of selves in meaningful combat.

Such combative engagement, indeed, is the very essence of poker—a continuous confrontation with the mind of the other, a conversation by means other than words. Bluffing apart, each player must read the other and respond to him or her. Sklansky notes:

> Most commonly, you analyze the meaning of an opponent's check, bet or raise, and in the open-handed games, you look at his exposed cards and try to judge from them what his entire hand might be. You then combine the plays he has made throughout the hand with his exposed hand cards and come to a determination about his most likely hand. (1999: 223)

Bellin supplies us with a concrete example:

> Morty opens the betting with $30. Dr. Liam raises the bet to $100. Amy folds, and then Joey Millman thinks for a second and calls $100 cold. Now I have to try to figure out what the hell is going on. The best thing anyone could have at the moment is three of a kind (a set). I am pretty sure that no one has a set of kings because the betting was too light before the flop for somebody to have "cowboys" as their pocket cards. But, still somebody might have a set of 6's and 7's. It could be Morty, maybe Dr. Liam; Joe's cold calls tell me he's probably got a king with a nice kicker. If he was on a bigger flush draw than mine—if he were holding A of clubs and 4 of clubs, let us say—he would have tried to end the hand right there with a huge raise. So I put him on the pair of kings and go about trying to figure out what the rest of the table is holding. (Bellin 2002: 11–12)

There is a systematic attempt to interpret the cues given by the others, taking their role as smart and competent and rational players, cues interpreted within the frame of Texas "hold-them high poker" and action taken on that basis. One of the cues that poker players are often able to use in their interpretational activity is the unmeant gestures that other players give off. These are called "tells" in the trade and are nicely illustrated by this story that Bellin recounts:

> A guy walks into a bar and notices three men and a dog playing poker. The dog is playing beautifully. "That's a very smart dog," the man says.

> "Not really" says one of the players. "Every time he gets a good hand, he wags his tail." (2002: 93)

The "tell" is then a communicative gesture that one makes without any intentionality that the other is still able to interpret and use, if not to read what is in the other's mind, then in his or her hand. Here is a telling example:

> Stover was peppered with practical tells. It's not that he wasn't smart enough to figure them out and make corrections, it's just that he didn't really care enough to change. If the flop was three cards of the same suit, and Stover didn't look at his pocket cards, I always knew he had a flush ... If, after checking his cards, he called any bets, then I knew he didn't have his flush yet, but one of his pocket cards definitely matched his suit on the board, and, therefore, he needed one of the two cards left to make the flush. (Bellin, 2002: 101-02)

The tell, as an unmeant gesture, becomes a sign that is subject to a systematic interpretational process and is used as the basis of an action. It is not a conversation in the strict sense but a dialogic interaction is going on, nevertheless. While one person is interpreting the tells of the other, in this case, Stover, there is no doubt that Stover is also interpreting the tells of his opponent and using them for his own purposes. In other words, poker has a complex dialogic process in which both meant gestures and unmeant gestures are orchestrated to conduct a significant conversation.

The presence of the "tell" in a game and the data that players use to continue to play, along with other information against other players, define one aspect of a dialogic interaction that occurs in everyday life. In everyday life, conversations are conducted to establish a dialogic relationship in which there are information, presentation, and selective concealment; typically, there is no attempt to deliberately outwit each other. Nevertheless, there are moments in an interaction, and there are types of interactions that are conducted with a great deal of wariness and circumspection. In bargaining for a sale between a seller and a buyer, for example, there is typically a move to outwit the other. In cross-examination in courtrooms, too, there is always an attempt to trap the other into revealing information the other does not want to reveal. In relationships between suspicious spouses or employees and employers, one can find a wariness and an inquisitiveness.

It is this quality of significant conversation that is idealized in poker: while the expressions that are given are read, it is the unmeant gestures in the form of a "tell" or in the way certain cards are selected or discarded that are the focus of interest, and the aim is to outwit the other—albeit through conversational means. Often a player's attempt to manage his or her emotions during play becomes a "tell" in its own right. Consider a case reported by Bellin:

> Chris also has a funny tendency to separate his winnings from his buy-in. This doesn't make much of a difference in limit games, but in no-limit, that is a huge disadvantage. A player who stacks his chips this way is obviously very concerned with his outcome. He likes to know he is up. So whenever we are playing no limit, if Chris has the $300 stacked separately from his two grand buy-out, I know that unless he's got a huge hand, any raise over that $300 will usually knock him out because he would not want to end with less money than he started with. (Bellin, 2002: 101)

Here is a player who is a very cautious player and who manages his money with full cognizance of his responsibility to conserve it—even if he happens to be gambling. He recognizes his money has other, and later, uses for it after the game is over—even if it is to play again some other time. He does not want to relinquish the power that the money represents too readily or too hastily.

Yet it is all too possible to abdicate such a commitment to emotion management that Chris displayed and become carried away—indeed, "to go on the tilt" as the gamblers say or be "on the chase." In a study of poker players, Basil Browne writes: "The term tilt is used by some frequent poker players to describe what happens to them or what happened to another poker player in sessions where they lost huge amounts of money or lost control" (1989: 3).

Two situations where such tilting can occur are "needling" and "bad beats." In needling, the other players at the table tease, insult, and challenge the player and undermine his or her self-concept. This often follows a "bad beat," where the needled player has lost a very good hand to a slightly better one. The needled player gets upset and tries to get even immediately with the needle-artists by playing aggressively. The needled player typically raises the needle-artist with a weak hand in an attempt to get even, and a third player often wins the pot.

By going on tilt and undertaking a chase, the players are, in fact, constructing a narrative of self. This narrative links earlier episodes to later ones, with each later one derived directly or indirectly from the earlier one. The soliloquy of this self can be constituted as follows: he is insulting me and I will get even with him, by beating him this time. It didn't work last time, I will try again.

In another form, this soliloquy can proceed as follows: I lost the last pot only by a small margin due to bad luck. Next time I will win and, again, next time I will win. If the bad beat and the needling occur together, one has a potent brew with which to become intoxicated with the humiliation of the self and the urge to recoup the self in an ongoing narrative process.

It is, however, not only the players who are on "tilt" and doing a "chase" who are constructing a narrative of self by playing, but all players. The plays are truncated into discrete episodes that can be assembled into a continuous series. Each episode within a particular game—or between different games and gaming—provides opportunities to either claim a victory for the self or a defeat. Each such moment is also an occasion to remember what happened in the past along the same lines and to anticipate a future. Such remembrances of the past episodes of wining or losing and anticipating futures of the same are the elements of the self's quiddity, its narrative substance. This is made evident not so much in the high-stakes games of professional players, but in local sociable games. In them, too, selves are put into play and narratives constructed, albeit with smaller tokens and currencies—the narrative of friendship.

Poker has played a major role in sustaining friendships in American society for a long time—at least in American male society. In fact, according to a study by Irving Crespi, he found that only 7% of card players reported that they play with people they have met at card games. Friends are mentioned by 83%, neighbors by 44 %, and 87% of card players said that they play in their own homes and 73% in the homes of their friends. And Crespi concludes that card playing is most often engaged in by families and friends in each others' homes. That is, card playing is preeminently a primary group activity (1956: 718–19).

Primary groups are, in fact, sustained by *dialogic activity*—with the help of cards or without them. Crespi quotes a poker player:

> Cards are a universal game. It is something to pass the time. We play for the enjoyment of the game and the spirit of companionship ... I play poker not for the game but for the social relationships, getting together with friends—relaxation. Bridge is more difficult. You have to concentrate on the game. That takes the pleasure out of playing. (1956: 720)

Evidently, some would consider too much cognitive engagement difficult to take and stick to poker rather than bridge. In any case, it is clear that card playing is a sociable activity that enables groups to hang out and undertake significant conversations with words as well as with the cards. Such conversations with cards allow selves to interact with each other and as the game develops to put into play and narrate a self—as winner, loser, adept, skillful player, weak, incompetent player, sore loser, graceful winner, cheat, honest player, and so forth.

Here is one example of such a narrative: "We play for small stakes. The idea is not to win or lose a great deal. We can't afford it and it might create animosity ... I am a mediocre player. Some of the others are excellent. We start playing immediately. The bastards are after my money" (Crespi, 1956).

Louis Zurcher's (1970) study of a continuing poker game among a group of friends reinforces these observations by Crespi. He describes a group of friends who met regularly and played poker once a week. The games were in each other's homes; no women and children were allowed and no alcoholic beverages were permitted. The game was played with small stakes and losing money was not likely to bankrupt anyone—or even make a serious dent in his finances. Frequently, new members were invited to join the group, and if they were suitable and congenial, they were invited back.

The game usually began on schedule and all the attention was focused on the playing. No external topics were allowed into the conversation—no politics, no religion, no brags or complaints about wife, children, or the job. After each play and during the game, the players were allowed to "tease" each other, even needle each other but within certain bounds of decorum and always in a play frame. Often the regular members of the group would be forced to leave the group because of their jobs, and replacements for them had to be found. At the end of the day's play, the host would provide a snack, and now conversations are conducted and plans are made for the next meeting. It is clear then that poker becomes a medium for the constitution and existence of the group and is, in fact, used, not to make money or even lose money, but to gather together and undertake significant conversations with the cards and without them.

Playing poker enables an actor to achieve a variety of states of mind and being. To begin with, it permits him or her to achieve a potent sense of being in charge of his or her own actions. As a player and participant, he or she makes his or her own decisions, without either supervision or consultation. Moreover, he or she puts his or her own worth, as a measure and token of his or her self at risk and into play. To be in charge of one's economic resources is to be an agent in his or her right, to use such agency as one may wish—even to risk loss and ruin.

Second, such powers of agency are achieved and enjoyed in dialogic encounters with one's peers—peers in skill and monetary worth at least, but often enough in terms of class, caste, and ethnicity, too. The game becomes a conversation carried on with cards and coins around a table, a continuation of one carried on elsewhere with more standard vehicles.

Third, the ongoing processes of the game as it is being played as well as the events preceding the playing and following the playing enable the player and his or her fellow players to construct a narrative of the self for each player. Before the game, the player is evaluated in terms of a number of variables and then allowed to enter the game—not just having enough money, but also the other factors mentioned earlier such as skill level, race, ethnicity, and class, and in some friendly games, conviviality and decorousness as Zurcher's (1970) study showed.

Once the actual playing begins, the actor enters the play by means of his or her tokens and displays his or her worth, care, and control regarding the money, intelligence, perspicacity—judgment, the ability to take the role and attitude of the other players by reading their moves and "tells," and so forth. Every move puts the self into play, and each move is an episode in the construction of the narrative of the self as a sagacious and competent player or a foolish and emotionally overwrought player who is "chasing" and on "tilt" and so on.

Once the playing is over, a particular identity is fixed on the players. This may be a reinforcement of an already existing one or amendments and changes to it. Further, there are often postgame conversations in which the player-self is pushed into the background and the everyday selves—involving jobs, careers, wives, children, politics, etc.—are allowed into the dialogic process. Games function as interregnums in the ongoing tribulations of life in which different rules are brought into operation, a time of carnivals and orgies. The poker game is more like an orgy, though the profligacy is not with sex, food, and drink but with money. What in ordinary life is subject to rules of thrift, prudence, and miserliness, disciplined management and control is treated more cavalierly. Money, the embodiment of power and influence in the world, the source of most of the satisfactions of life, is treated, if not with total abandonment, at least with little regard for its utility and is used to give play to the self and activate emotions at times of joy and elation, but more often at times of sorrow and loss.

The very structure of the game is subtly organized to give play to the exercise of a measure of power and control and to have it put to the test in various encounters with the consequent emotional impact on the self. *In fact, the structure of the game provides for opportunities to give presence and play to emotions and the self.* Once the cards have been dealt and the chanciness of life represented in the distribution of strengths and weaknesses, certain distributions become more powerful than others. Nevertheless, in the actual play, skill, cunning, and luck can sometimes make the initially powerful lose and the initially powerless win. The first can become the last and the last can become the first.

It is this inherent cognitive complexity and interpretational activism that makes games such as poker and bridge, and board games like chess, so very attractive. Sociologists and social psychologists have described processes in small groups and stressed the importance of the primary groups and primary relationships in the life of a person. However, it is not enough to be merely with someone; rather one must engage the other both cognitively and emotionally or else one will face the deadliest eventuality for such a relationship: boredom and ennui—which may be defined as the absence of cognitive complexity in one's communicative relationships and weak emotional involvement.

The Self in the Labyrinth: Chess

Chess is the queen of all board games. The modern game of chess belongs to a family of games derived from an ancient Indian game called *Chaturang.* In this game a contest between two players is staged on a board consisting of 64 squares. The pieces with which this contest is conducted represent a rajah (king) and the four divisions of the military—infantry, cavalry, elephants, and boatmen. A version of this game reached the kingdom of Persia in the seventh century and eventually reached Europe through the Arab trade routes or was brought back to Europe by the crusaders. The game changed in various ways as it traveled, but the basic structure remained the same.

It has been suggested that the game was devised as an instrument for the training of soldiers in the art and science of war—or at least of generalship. All these claims may well be true and might be well defended. However, it is possible to argue that, within these frameworks themselves, chess and many other board games are broader allegories. Indeed *battle* itself may be treated as an allegory.

The notion of chess as a struggle by an agent against the world or another force is found in medieval allegories of the game as a struggle between a sinner and the Devil. In the fifteenth-century morality play, *Destructorium Vitrorum,* one can read, "On this chessboard, the Devil plays against a Sinner. The Devil cries 'check,' attacking the sinner with the dart of sin. Unless the latter replies 'Nede' though penitent, the Devil cries 'mate' and hauls the sinner off to Hell" (cited in Yachnin, 1982: 324).

A medieval text claims: "The world resembles a chess board which is checkered white and black, the colors showing the two conditions of life and death or praise and blame. The chessmen are men of this world who have common birth, occupy different stations and hold different titles in this life, who contend together and finally have a common fate which levels all ranks" (in Yachnin, 1982: 321–23). In other words, people are born, achieve different ranks, and contend with each other, but all end up in the grave.

The game here is conceived as a contest between the Devil and the player as a sinner—but across the board from each player is just another player (i.e., another sinner). The Devil, however, is the unseen player and the players are playing against him as well. The devilry is in the contest itself insofar as every decision each of the players make tests his or her will and dedication, resolve and Christian virtue. The player, himself or herself, is in a contest that precedes the moves he or she will make on the board to advance his pieces, faces temptation, pride, envy, and so on, and thereby puts his or her soul in the balance. To make one move is to yield to the Devil's blandishments and to make another is to resist them.

It is not, then, that chess is an allegory of a limited sort—i.e., to a battle in warfare—but both "battles" and "chess" are allegories of the struggles of a self to the finding of dialogue and meaning in its existence in the world of everyday life. Such a world is full of complexities and contradictions; unpredictable forms and unforeseeable twists, challenges, refutations, and frustrations; and occasional successes and joys, too. Such a search can be compared to finding one's way through a maze or a labyrinth, and chess—as many other less complicated board games—*represents* this labyrinth. The labyrinth is not a place, but a metaphor. It is a labyrinth that one does not merely *read* and imaginatively reconstruct and experience vicariously, but enters, actively and practically, by moving, maneuvering, and overcoming the resistances of the adversary and traversing demanding space-ways. The imbricated patterns on the board represent a labyrinth and the complex rules of chess guide the moves of the player—Ariadne's thread. The pieces are the tokens of the self, and the contingencies these pieces face represent the various forms of resistance that an agent faces in the trajectory of his or her life.

The space in which chess and its analogues are played is comparable to the "labyrinth" that one can find in many mythologies. The most elaborate of such a labyrinth is associated with the myths of Knossos in Crete. In this story, Parsiphae, the queen of Crete, has conceived a grand passion for a snow-white bull that had emerged from the sea. With the help of the master craftsman Daedalus, who devises a contraption, she was able to copulate with the bull. A monster is born of this union, the Minotaur. It goes on the rampage and soon Daedalus is summoned again to construct a place where it can be entrapped and rendered harmless—except that it had to be fed young men and women periodically. This place was the "labyrinth" from which it was impossible to escape, and even Daedalus had difficulties finding his way out.

In the second part of this myth, Ariadne, the daughter of the king of Minos, falls in love with Theseus, one of the youths brought from Athens to feed the Minotaur, and gives him a means of escaping the labyrinth. Once again, Daedalus comes to the rescue and gives Ariadne a linen thread that the hero can tie to the entrance and unwind as he goes and then can follow back after his deed is done.

There are many interpretations of this myth. Joseph Campbell sees it as the hero in all of us, who has to seek adventure and is saved from its dangers: "By virtue of the inherited symbolic aids of society, the rites of passage, the grace-yielding sacraments given to mankind of old by the redeemers and handed down through the millenniums" (1956: 23).

Campbell argues that the thread that Ariadne gave Theseus symbolizes these traditional sacraments insofar as "centuries of husbandry, decades of diligent culling, the work of numerous hearts and hands, have gone into the backing, sorting, and spinning of this tightly twisted yarn" (1956: 24).

No doubt, there is a certain plausibility to this interpretation. Yet, before one goes to the labyrinth as a metaphor for the imagination, "the labyrinth without the heart and within" as Campbell put it (1956: 23), one must recognize it as a place that is said to have been specifically constructed to offer a challenge to any intrepid intruder. It is, to begin with, a spatial challenge that the intruder has to face: how to move in the labyrinthine ways and overcome their confusions and then master a "monster" and return home. The intricate spatial arrangement, with various twists and turns and loops, is surely also a mimesis of the life of a human and the confusing pathways that he or she has to navigate. One can do this with the aid of a good woman as Theseus did, a good man, or even all by oneself, if necessary.

Narrating the Self Through Chess

The general ideology of games like chess (and checkers) is different from those in which dice are used to introduce the element of chance. The latter games represent the fundamental uncertainty that is seen by human beings as a necessary part of the narrative structure of life: fortunes are reversed toward misfortune or better fortune often enough in such narratives. In games like chess and the watered-down chess that is checkers, chance is eliminated and the game turns on the skill, wisdom, and perspicacity of the players—not to speak of experience and boldness of character. These idealize the rational and purposeful capacities of human beings, their value as symbolic creatures who can plan, anticipate, calculate game-developing situations and the quality and moves of the opposing players, and make the moves accordingly. Physical strength, musculoskeletal coordination, physical dexterity, height, weight, and timing are eliminated as factors along with chance. It celebrates the human being as one in charge of his or her destiny, one who can master the essential qualifications to manage it and control it and face the resistance of the world confidently. The chess player does not depend on lady luck or the turn of the ball or the direction of the wind or the lay of the ground or the character of the ball or the stickiness of the wicket but on his or her own competence and mastery. This self is, however, pitted into a complex pattern of squares from which tokens are moved—not in a simple sense as in checkers—but again in a very intricate and complex pattern dictated by different rules for the different pieces.

In a succinct statement about chess, Bobby Fischer notes: "Chess is played by two players who move by turns ... The object of chess is to attack the enemy king in such a way that it cannot escape capture. Once this is done, the king is 'checkmated' and the game is terminated" (1972: 20). Though the object of the game may be to capture the king in a technical sense, the real aim of the game is to manage, transverse, and capture territory—that is, space marked out as squares on the board. In chess, each piece has its own variable power, and this is manifested in the shape of the moves each can make. To begin with, there is the *rook*—it can move only in straight lines, up the board or down the board. It can also move any number of squares horizontally or vertically. However, it is not allowed to move into a square occupied by another piece, from its own side, nor can it jump over another piece and move to the next square. Next, there is the *bishop*: it can move any number of squares along the diagonals only. If the opponent's piece stands in the way, it can capture it and have it removed from the board. The queen in chess is the most powerful and valuable piece, and it can move in any direction and can move any number of squares but cannot jump over pieces. The king is the most important piece in chess, though it is not as powerful as the queen. If the king is lost, the game is lost. The king can move one square in any direction, and the two kings from the opposing sides must remain one square apart from each other. The knight has a more complex set of powers: "it can move two squares up and one over or one square down and two over, or any such combination" says James Eade (1996: 32). Finally, there is the pawn, which can move one square forward but cannot move backward or sideways.

It can be seen that the pieces of chess are differentiated in subtle ways so that, in fact, subtle and complex combinations can be syntactically constructed. One can compare chess to checkers in this regard and see that, in the latter, such complexities are absent, making it a game with a limited capacity to elicit cognitive engagement. In making the necessary moves in chess, an agent has to consider simultaneously a variety of moves and the outcomes thereof before deciding on his or her next step. To give a simple illustration, consider the following position: The white rook is checking the black king. There are three way of escaping attack (Fisher, 1972: 20):

1. Capturing the checking piece.
2. Interposing a piece between the king and the checking piece.
3. Fleeing to a square where the king will not be in check.

Each of these moves will have to be in full consideration of the likely rejoinders from the adversary as well as the responses one can make to the rejoinder. The objects that are manipulated in chess are two in number—the pieces, tokens of variegated power and influence in the game, and the spaces they are occupying now and will occupy in the future. These objects are also tokens of the selves that are playing the game. Every move that occurs to these objects carries the self of the player who made them. These moves dealing with objects, albeit tokens, and with space, miniaturized and formalized though it may be, are acts that are "reaching into the future" (Mead, 1938: 12). The moves that are made in chess are, in fact, the manipulation of space in a social act, space that is of small compass in actual measurements but is significant nevertheless for the self. Indeed, one can appreciate the Persian emperor's exasperation at the seeming differences between managing large spaces and small ones. He is said to have remarked, "Strange that I who rule the world from Indus in the East to the Andalus in the West cannot manage thirty-two chess-men in a space of two cubits by two" (quoted in Fuller, 1977: 53).

The territory in chess may be demarcated into two cubits by two cubits, but it represents much more than that. In playing chess—and chesslike games—an agent is playing with space that has been transformed into a meaningful place, and is engaging in social acts of perception and construal and manipulation. The pieces that he or she moves upward and downward and diagonally and sideways are merely the objects and instruments with which the player takes measure of the demarcated territory and "manipulates" it so that he or she can achieve dominance and sovereignty. The variable powers of the pieces are the powers that the players are given at the beginning of the game. Their variability in the powers of the pieces enables a very complex syntax to be constructed by the selves of the two players with each other on the one hand, and between the places on the board and the players on the other.

Once the place is perceived and construed in terms of the pieces that occupy various spaces on the board, the game begins with the agents taking turns—with each turn having the potential of becoming decisive after the initial steps have been accomplished. Indeed, players often take a long time to think through to the next move. The initial moves mount an attack that the other player attempts to counter in one way or another. As the pieces move and the game advances, the selves of the players will move forward in variable sequences defined by the moves.

Once the earlier stages are accomplished, the action moves into the middle game. There is "... no arsenal of theory for use in the middle game," notes James Eade. He continues, "The absence of any vast repository of standardized middle-game theory means that you are on your own during this phase of the play—but it also means that this part of the game is where your own personal creativity can shine through the most" (1996: 179).

That is to say, this is the moment in the game when one can give full play to one's chess-self and its imagination and cunningness and chess-wisdom.

The last narrative structure of the game and the self that is narrated through the game is the end game. Eade comments:

> Just as the middle game flows logically from the opening, the *end game* develops from the middle game. In many cases, you can even anticipate the end game as early as the opening, where one side plays for an advantage in power structure that the player can truly exploit only in the end game. (1996: 191)

From the opening gambit onward, the game moves following a narrative logic—one move eliciting a response from the other side that, in turn, elicits a return move, with each move having both a contrarian and a continuing relationship to the earlier ones. And, insofar as each move is a calculated strike for victory, glory, and conquest, each implicates the self and narrates it into a presence at the table, across the board, among the places and pieces of the game.

In these board games, space that has been converted into a playing arena is defined in terms of squares and their combinations—in straight lines up or down the board ("files" in chess) and sideways ("ranks"), or diagonally. In other games, different patterns of movement are created. The fundamental theme in all these games is, however, the same: using the spatial configurations as the basis for the construction of resistance and opportunity for the self to confront and control and give play to itself. These qualities of the rule-bound spatial configuration, insofar as they can be tackled only by the cognitive and emotional engagement that an agent can bring to them, enable a self to manifest itself and experience various ebbs and eddies of its presence. The adversary is also offering resistance, in addition to the resistance given by the rules of the game, and giving usually more effective resistance as well at times: Opportunities for the self to sense its presence are many. In the playing occasion, the ebbs and flows of the self's presence are defined by minor victories and defeats, moments of elation or dejection, and ultimately a full victory or a defeat and deflation of the self.

The construction and experiencing of these moments enable an agent to narrate a self into being both to enjoy the pleasures of its existence and to obtain a "tragic sense of life."

The Self and the Pastoral: Golf

Games are played in spaces that have been transformed into places of play. In certain games, however, such transformed space acquires special qualities. In golf the space is transformed in such a way that it becomes a special place with complex features that players must seek to understand as completely as possible in order to deal with it, play against it, and experience its special qualities. In tennis the players also implicate themselves in the space that has been transformed by being subject to intricate measurements. All actions taken in the game must meet the demands of the measured place, and the agent must be made to recognize them. In both these games, the self finds itself having to deal with space and place in minute ways and to recognize it as a *narrative other* in these games.

Space is transformed into a re-creation of a presumptive natural environment in golf. Critics and commentators in literature have identified certain poems, plays, and novels as, in William Empson's phrase, "Versions of the Pastoral" (1957). One definition of the pastoral puts it this way:

> Though the definitions of pastoral are diverse, we will take it to mean: the genre of literature which idealizes country life through a sharp contrast between city and country, the implied withdrawal from a complex to a simple world, the urban awareness of rural life and the resulting tensions between value systems, the intense nostalgia for a Golden-Age past and

> the creation of a circumscribed and remote pastoral world characterized by the harmony between man and nature and by an atmosphere of idyllic contentment—a world in which country life stripped of its most coarse features, is made palatable to urban society. (Squires, 1970: 303)

The earliest pastoral forms—at least in the Western tradition—were composed by Theocritus. Shackford observes: "The first pastoral poet of whom we have historical record was Theocritus, who was living in the presence of a pastoral tradition as characteristic as the epic tradition that we call Homer, listening to songs sung by shepherds in Sicilian pastures, shaped the concrete, enduring beauty of the pastoral idyll" (1904: 584).

Virgil composed his versions of the pastoral in the *Eclogue* of which Bruno Snell observes:

> In this, and other pastoral poems, a shepherd-singer is depicted, facing the various seasons of the year and the varying landscapes through which he wanders in an idealized way. The shepherd's domain was Arcadia and in it he wandered, a land distant from the sordid realities of the present—a far-away land overlaid with the golden haze of unreality. (1953: 282)

These versions of the pastoral can be found in a variety of later forms. Empson finds them in Shakespeare's plays, Marvell's poems, Milton's elegies, and the *Beggars' Opera,* as well as in Lewis Carroll's *Alice in Wonderland.* Others consider Thomas Hardy's novels—particularly, *Far from the Madding Crowd*—as "modified pastorals" (Squires, 1970).

Shakespeare's *As You Like It* is a clear manifestation of the pastoral—albeit a very complex and ambiguous one. In this play, people who live in courts, in the midst of luxury and plenty, served by menials of many kinds, repair to the forest of Arden and affect to live a rural or at least a "forestry" life. In the forest, they live a simple life in which the rigid hierarchies of the court are diluted to some extent and everyone is forced to make changes in their styles of life. Paul Alpers observes that, faced with these circumstances, they don't get carried away into the hazes of a dream, but are forced to "accept and reconcile man to the stresses and realities of the situation" (1972: 353). But it is also the case, he notes, that "the exiled Duke is called 'happy'—the word that, first sounded by Virgil, echoes and re-echoes through pastoral literature—because he can, as Shakespeare puts it, 'translate the stubbornness of fortune into so quiet and so sweet a style'" (II.1.18–20; 1972: 353).

The confrontation between such "happiness" and the realities of the stresses of life at court/city becomes the central theme of this play. In Andrew Marvell's "The Garden" (in Williams 1952: 141–42), once again we encounter the contrast between "city and the idyllic purity of the garden," the world of "labor" and "toil," and the joy of being in the garden and contemplating it.

How vainly men themselves amaze
To win the palm, the oak, or bays;
And their incessant labors see
Crowned from single herb, or tree,
Whose short and narrow-vergèd shade
Does prudently their toils upraid;
While all flowers and all trees do close
To weave the garlands of repose!

In the next stanza, this pastoral imagery is mixed with the idea of "Quiet" "Innocence" and "Solitude":

Fair Quiet, have I found thee here,
And Innocence, thy sister dear?
Mistaken long, I sought you then
In busy companies of men;
Your sacred plants, if here below,
Only among the plants will grow;
Society is all but rude
To this delicious solitude.

The quietude of the garden and its freedom from the noise, confusion, and corruption of the "society" are neatly drawn here. Marvell goes on developing these ideas through a variety of complex images and expressing a preference for "green thoughts in a green shade." One can imagine a person taking a walk in the garden, a refugee from the "busy company of men," while "the mind, from pleasure less, withdraws into its happiness." Such a garden also recalls, according to the poet, the primal garden:

Such was that happy garden-state,
While man there walk'd without a mate:
After a place so pure and sweet,
What other help could yet be meet?

Empson, in a somewhat tortured reading of the poem, has this to say about these lines:

> "We are quiet in the country, but our dullness gives a sober and self-knowing happiness more intellectuality than that of the over-stimulated pleasures of the town. The players of the country give a repose and intellectual release which make my mind less worrying and introspective." (1957: 124–25).

In each of these works, we have an author creating a text that represents a favored way to live, extolling it and displaying its allure in contrast to urban or semiurban life. The author depicts a sylvan forest, a rural enclave, a wonderland to which one can retreat from the corruptions of the city and the royal court, from toil, mammon, and politics—but only by reading about it. The pastoral is made available to an agent in his or her imagination, and it is only by deconstructing the text that he or she can enter the forest, the "ecology" of Virgil, or the forest of Arden or the village and the wonderland. Typically, such pleasures of the text were to be had, sitting down and focusing on printed or enacted texts. The pastoral is, indeed, written by and for the urban people who long to be away from the urban but cannot yet do anything—or much—about it. These people, "the ordinary people" as Paul Alpers calls them, are in the court or city where they always are: "It is a truism that the pastoral is for sophisticated people. The question still remains—what use do sophisticated people make of pastoral poetry, what do courtiers do when they are in the country?" (1972: 353).

Marvell may have walked in his garden contemplatively, and the other authors of the various pastorals may have had direct experience of the pasture, but the written versions of them were read as texts or seen as performed ones. Yet a garden is not a sylvan arena in its own right but a simulation of one. It is organized and structured by a human designer according to his or her aesthetic and horticultural preferences. A garden is a territory wrested from the wild, but containing certain elements of the wild, now properly tamed and arranged in an orderly manner.

It is a tame place and has been used as symbolic of a variety of themes. Perhaps the most famous of such thematic gardens is the "Islamic garden" as a version of paradise. There were many imitations of this theme in the wake of the spread of Islam into southern Europe and India. These were real gardens as well as renderings of gardens in poetry and in the decorative arts on mosque walls and in carpets (Cammann, 1975).

These gardens, representing "paradise," were cultivated according to certain theological, agricultural, and aesthetic principles and people used them for a variety of purposes. For the Arab and Persian people, the garden was a version of paradise—indeed a precursor of the heaven for which this life, too, was precursor. For a desert people, these gardens had no doubt a special appeal—but there are also distinct allusions to the Eden of the creation myths. "For those who believe and do righteous works, We will cause them to enter gardens underneath which rivers flow to dwell there eternally. They shall have purified companions and We will cause them to enter abundant shade," says the Quran. James Dickie comments, "Indeed one can understand neither the Islamic garden nor the attitude of the Muslim towards his garden until one realizes that the terrestrial garden is considered a reflection or rather an anticipation, of Paradise" (1968: 238).

These "paradises" were imagined and represented in many poems in the Muslim world but they were also constructed as real places in the heartlands as well as on the periphery of Islamic civilization. One can find them in Granada, the Islamic outpost in Spain, and in Kashmir, on the other side of the Islamic empires of old. Even when the Arabs moved out of the desert, their imagination wanted the antithesis of the desert. Julie Scott Meisami observes:

> The mediaeval Islamic garden was a *horos condusus,* walled off and protected from the outside world; within, its design was rigidly formal, and in its inner space was filled with those elements that man finds most pleasing in nature. Its essential features included running water . . . and a pool to reflect the beauties of sky and garden; trees of various sorts . . . flowers, colorful and sweet-smelling; grass. (1985: 231)

Gardens may be representations of condensed nature or of paradise imagined by a desert people, but they are also places in which people walked, sat, cavorted, and experienced the order, color, structure, smell of the vegetation, and the sound of the water. *The gardens, as the pastures, were then not merely literary conceits, but were actual places, meaningfully rendered out of mere space, humanized, symbolically transformed, and used in a physical and manual way.* The people walked in them, lived in them, smelt their various odors, felt their various resonances, heard their various sounds, and often ate their products. They also dug into the land with their hands, and hands extended by implements, and converted it into human uses for work, leisure, and worship.

While the poets and dramatists could only write about them or see them performed, many others experienced the garden and the pastorality by actually being in them and feeling them underfoot and around them—by playing games in them. Football, before its systematization and commercialization, was a folk, and even a ritualist practice undertaken on the rural fields and landscapes. Summarizing a number of studies on the origin of football, Eric Dunning observes, "Such games were traditionally associated with religious festivals such as Shrovetide, Easter and Christmas. However, they could also be played on an *ad hoc* basis at any time in the autumn, winter or spring. They were played across the country and through the streets of towns and often by females as well as by males" (1999: 88). It was, nevertheless, a rough game with indeterminate rules, but a game played by the people of the pasture over the land in which they lived and which they cultivated to make a living. The playing of ball may even have been a ritual in which the ball represented the sun, as is believed by some scholars (Marples, 1954: 12–13). It may have adopted Christian overtones later, but it was for all that a ritual interaction and celebration of the ground on which they lived, an apprehension of its features—it hardness and softness, its bends and curves, its undulations and flatness, its resistances and allowances—by agents moving across them in pursuit of a ball and fellow agents. Cricket, before it became urbanized and commercialized, when it was still "village cricket," and even baseball, its derivative, were rural games with strong elements of the pastoral. Such a game of summer cricket, A. J. Forrest says, was played "among echoing sounds and leafy splendor in an arena cordoned off by prodigal foliage" (1957: 17).

This pastorality and even the "prodigal foliage" are evident most clearly in the game of golf as it is played today, highly commercialized though it may be. Golf has made a deliberate attempt to simulate a pastoral scene and a garden environment. In the golf that is played today, one sees a representation of the pastoral scene, with some variations—indeed, a complex pastorality that includes not only the countryside but also at times mountains and the seashore. In playing games on the village green, one actually entered the pasture and the garden, as it were, *corporeally,* and felt and smelled it and, above all, touched it.

Golf, as it is played today, represents a deliberate creation of the pastoral from origins that were not quite so pastoral. While hitting a ball-like object with a stick may have been done everywhere in the world, an identifiable early version of golf, it appears, was played in Scotland and Holland. Nevertheless, the origins of modern golf are hard to pin down, though Scotland is often credited with it. Holland is said to have a stronger claim insofar as there was a great deal of trade between Scotland and Holland. It is thought probable that these traders brought the game to Scotland. Steven van Hagel has done extensive archival research in Holland, and he traces the game to a Dutch game, *spell metten kolve,* and concludes that the game was being played in Holland from the thirteenth century onward (Concannon, 1995: 13).

The first allusion of golf in Scotland occurred in 1457, when King James banned the playing of football and golf because it was interfering with archery practice. These games, as well as the practice of archery, so necessary to the defense of the realm, were played on the sandy patch of land that separated agricultural and pasture land from the sea—the patch that "linked" the two, hence "links." However, both golf and football continued to be played, and eventually the kings of Scotland took up the game and it gained in popularity. Many of the Stuart kings became devoted to the game, with James IV of Scotland leading the way. When James VI of Scotland became king of England, he introduced the game to English court circles and built a course at Blackheath, near his palace. Still, the game was considered an index of frivolity and irresponsibility. The Earl of Moray, one of the witnesses against Mary, Queen of Scots, before she was found guilty and executed, testified that a few days after her husband was murdered, she played "golf and pall-mall in the fields beside Seton" after which "she did abuse her body with Bothwell" (Concannon, 1995: 24).

David Stirk observes that the modern game, with its rules and ceremonies, was first given shape by the Masons and eventually became systematized at Leith and later at St. Andrews in Scotland.

> Though St. Andrews is known as the home of golf, Leith was, in fact, the birth place of organized golf and the concept of the Golf Club ... The first formal rules were established at Leith in 1744. When St. Andrews Club was formed, the members laid down their own rules of play, but it differed scarcely from those at Leith." (1987: 72)

From these beginnings the modern game evolved, going through various vicissitudes and triumphs. It became a court game and a game favored by many social clubs who often cherished conviviality and dipsomania more than sport, but nevertheless played the game, too. The Freemasons used it in their pursuit of conviviality and power and gave it a strong push in popularity. It was the Freemasons who introduced the game to the United States (Stirk, 1987).

Golf expanded in popularity and, by the late eighteenth century, it was being played all over—in western Europe and the United States. This game was played on systematically designed courses that took account of the local topography in their structure. These courses had to be built away from the city, and the emergence of the railway enabled players to travel to these refuges from the city.

The railways, both the short-distance commuter systems as well as the longer-distance systems, became the link between the cities and factories, as part of the industrial revolution. The railways also were the links between the city and the country, between the commerce and the money of the city, and between the estates and farms and hunting and playing grounds of the landed gentry as well. Stirk notes:

> The effects of railways on the habits and movements of golfers may be seen in the records of a nineteenth century annual pilgrimage. In the late 1860s, Blackheath members formed a regular habit of attending the spring and autumn meetings at Westward Ho, at the time, the only true links outside Scotland. From there, Blackheath and Westward Ho members entrained for Liverpool to play in the spring and autumn meetings at Holylake, the even newer links of the Royal Liverpool Golf Club. Also, playing at Holylake were golfers who had come south from Pestwick, St. Andrews, Muirfield and other clubs.
>
> At the end of the Holylake meeting, the whole company of golfers went north by rail to play at St. Andrews. The annual migration was made possible by rail travel and the careful arrangement of club dates. (Stirk, 1987: 77, 84)

While this may be an extreme example of itinerant golfers using the railways, there is no doubt that to many others the availability of the rail system made it possible to travel to a golf link and engage their passion as well as enjoy the country. In fact, Stirk notes the rapid rise of golf after rail travel became common (1987: 77).

The railways, then, linked the two separate entities, the city and the country, emphasizing the pastoral theme once again. Eventually, golfers were to use automobiles and planes to reach their choice retreats from the city. And in cities, golf courses were set up in the city's precincts itself—or close enough—as an oasis in the desert, for the urbanites to relax and breathe freely. Whether one plays in the city itself or in a different place to which one travels, the theme of separation is established tightly and one leaves the cares of the city and adopts another set of cares with different challenges and opportunities.

The Golf Course: The Playful Paradise

The place to which golfers thus repaired was constructed by using the principle of miniaturization. "The cleverer I am at miniaturizing the world, the better I possess it," observes Gaston Bachelard. He continues, "But in doing this, it must be understood that the values become condensed and enriched in miniature" (1964: 150). He goes on to describe the process by which writers can construct miniaturized universes. The golf course is one example of a spatial world, a world full of natural phenomena—flora, lakes, mountains—at least hills—depressions and ravines, sandy stretches and verdant stretches, and even fauna that may sometimes wander in unexpectedly—that are miniaturized and presented for action by the player for an experience of total immersion and contemplation.

The course, then, is a miniaturization of the ecology of the Earth—without, however, the snow and ice. The vegetation, the greenery, the softly undulating fairways and greens, the sand suggesting the sea and the ponds of water—and in some golf courses the distant mountains—recreate the natural environment in miniature. Some golf courses are situated in mountainous ravines or coastal ambiences, and the designer takes these features in constructing the course. The playing of the game involves not only maneuvering the ball across fairways and greens into holes while avoiding the hazards or dealing with them, but also participating in the logic and the sensibility of the environment of trees, rivers, seas, and mountains. For example, the course at Old Works Golf Club, Anaconda, Montana, takes account of the surroundings. The mountainous terrain becomes a backdrop to the golf course that is situated in a valley between the hills. Pebble Beach Golf Links in California is situated right on the beach, with the sea and even a jetty in the background. "A course," says Alister MacKenzie, "should have beautiful surroundings and all the artificial features should have so natural an appearance that a stranger is unable to distinguish them from nature itself" (in Nicklaus and Millard, 2002: 84).

Playing golf in these courses enables one not only to escape the "city" but also to go to the beach, the mountains, and the forests—sometimes all at the same time. The form of the course follows the functions for which it was designed. Nicklaus continues:

> A large part of the designer's work is deciding where and how (and where not) to insert his hazards. For example, I don't necessarily care to force the golfer to hit the ball 240 yards. What I like to make him decide is between the glory of the long ball and the practicability of another alternative. One part of forcing the golfer to make a decision is working with the land; the other part is creating man-made hazards such as bunkers, water plantings or mounds. It all goes back to the routing. If there's a beautiful, natural fairway site that just cries out for a bunker in a certain position, then I'll work harder on that fairway strategy and that strategy will dictate the green shape and the bunkering. Or there may be a great green site that just calls out for a bunker or certain type of pitch or roll and I do that green first and let the green dictate the form of the fairway. (2002: 190)

Sometimes, the course is "etched into canyons" as Kathleen McCleary puts it, describing the course in Rustic Canyon, California. About these courses, Mike Keiser, a designer, says, "My definition of a great golf course is one that a non-golfer will have as much fun walking in it as a golfer" (McCleary, 2003).

A golf course is a re-creation of nature in which a miniaturized form of various features of the natural world are collapsed into a unified whole. The re-creation can take many forms—but the basic premise remains unchanged: it is a representation of natural forms in such a way that a human agent can enter it, walk in it, and incorporate the various features of the ground and the things that grow on the ground into his or her acts and performances. Some golf courses fit seamlessly into the surrounding landscape, often incorporating the land and sea into one coherent text. It is a garden, a pastoral landscape, and an environment in which a player can breathe freely, and walk easily—at least a little more freely and easily than in places of work in the city.

Into this complex game an agent casts himself or herself. The game's possibilities allow for various responses that give presence to the self in an ecoform. Henri Lefebvre contends that today "holiday" marks a "moment of departure." Such a moment was "formerly contingent but now a necessary moment and when this moment arrives people seek qualitative space. The qualities they seek have names: 'sun, snow, sea'" (1994: 353). The contemporary golf scene manages to pack at least two of these spaces into one coherent system and offers it to people so that they can situate a narrative of their selves in it for a while.

The Self in the Physical World: The Contact Experience

The golfer is able to undertake a dialogue with the environs as well as narrate a self by coming into contact with the physical world. It is a very subtle and complex contact. In this it is different from football, for example, where the contact is more direct and, indeed, gross. Consider here the comments of a player:

> To be able to make a golf ball go high or low, curve under trees or around trees or over trees and then be able to roll it over the ground into a hole or out of the sand. It's just fascinating, really. There are so many facets and you have to be proficient in so many different areas that it is just hard. (Fran, quoted in Crosset 1995: 97–98)

She does not talk of meeting another player in combat but of imagining a contact with the trees and the ground, a hole in the ground—and to consummate this contact in all its fullness and richness, a player has to become "proficient in so many different areas." Such proficiency, however complete it may be, is a means of handling the world of physical objects and incorporating one's self into them. The club is really an extension of one's hand.

As Harry Cotton, a writer on golf, put it: "A golfer is only as good as his hands" (quoted in Plimpton, 1968: 51). The hands and their extension allow a player to experience the world in his or her immediate vicinity as real and tangible phenomena. In Mead's words, "Things are not real as seen or heard or smelled; they are real as actually or potentially experienced through contact" (1938: 364).

Even in the earlier version of the game, the club and the ball were instruments with which the players took the measure of the environment in which they lived—the ice and the snow, the country roads and lanes, and the landscape itself. In other words, the game was a way of coming to terms and interacting with the spaces in which they were forced to live and converting them into social and communal places. To take a club in hand, put a ball on the ground—icy or dry—and to address the ball and drive across the space forward, at one target or another, is to seek an intimacy with the space and understand it. Neither the cold and the ice nor the rough country and its equally unwelcome lanes were going to detract these seekers after integration into the environment and communion with the landscape. The primary encounter, in golf, unlike most other games, is not with a human adversary but with the ground itself. The narrative other, then, is the course and its special features, not the other players, and the combat is with these features. The other players are secondary in the narrative of golf. It is not that there is no competitiveness in golf. Far from this being the case, golf is as full of competitors, hustlers, gamblers, and entrepreneurs as any other modern game. Such competitiveness is, however, indirect and occurs only in the tallying of the scores at the end of the game and not in direct encounters between the players. It is a solitary quest, this game of golf, though other players and caddies may hover around as one plays. This is nicely put by the great master of golf himself:

> I think youngsters tend to get caught up in the competition, that is beating other players or hitting a ball longer than their friends can. When you really start looking at golf holes and particular golf shots from a strategic standpoint, the true beauty of the game presents itself. That's when you learn that golf is really about playing the course, about beating the golf course rather than the other players. (Nicklaus and Millard, 2002: 17)

I would add that it is not only about beating the course but, above all, perceiving and construing it, living in it, participating with it, walking across it, and examining its pliancy, responsiveness, cooperation, and friendliness and about taking its measure along these lines. Nicklaus claims that golf is a "giant jigsaw puzzle" in which the tees, fairways, and greens and the bunkers and hazards are the individual pieces. It is, however, a puzzle that a player walks his or her way through and, indeed, is comparable to a labyrinth.

The self that is playing golf gains its actuality and presence by means of this contact with the physical world achieved through the club and the ball. There is the *actual* contact as one drives or putts the ball and there is the *potential* contact as the player takes account of the physical surrounding—the trees and bushes, the sand and the water, the rough and the smooth—as he or she drives or putts the ball. The ball becomes the messenger between the player and the environment and between the environment and the player. And the messages may not always be happy ones. They may come twisted and deformed, maliciously turned and shaped.

Et in Arcadia Ego

The golf course is, however, not merely a place of retreat from urban confusions and anxieties, not merely a simulation with tees, fairways, hazards, roughs, and greens with holes in them but an arena in which there is indeed "ego"—even in Arcadia, there is play of the self. The phrase, *Et in Arcadia Ego*—perhaps one of the most famous Latin lines—has many manifestations and many translations and emendations. To begin with, it was used in Virgil's eclogues to indicate that even in Arcadia, "human suffering in superhumanly perfect surroundings creates a dissonance. The dissonance, once felt, had to be resolved and it was resolved in that vespertinal mixture of sadness and tranquility which is Virgil's most personal contribution to poetry," observes Erwin Panofsky in a disquisition on the meaning of the Latin phrase (1982: 300). This mixture of happiness and sorrow is contained in these words and in one rendering that, in Panofsky's words, "they conjure up the retrospective vision of an unsurpassable happiness, enjoyed in the past, unattainable ever after, yet enduringly alive in the memory: a bygone happiness ended by death" (1982: 296). It has also been translated to mean that all present happiness is menaced by the possibility of death. Memory and anticipation play their part in one's relation to his or her presence in Arcadia. Even in Arcadia, in the midst of present or recollected happiness, there is sorrow and suffering, and the vicissitudes and tribulations that a self must experience, the vagaries of success and failure, of victory and defeat, of death, sudden or anticipated. The self has to face the plays of the moment as well as recollect those of the past and anticipate those yet to come.

The golf course is a version of Arcadia that is apprehended by participating in the game on the ground physically and mentally. The golfer walks into the ecoform; feels its presence under foot and in the surround; feels it in the body; sees its features with the eyes; smells the trees, the flowers, and the waters; and engages them with his or her hands—albeit one extended with a club. Not only does the player engage the environs but apprehends the Arcadia in the course of playing the game and adjusts his or her presence in it according to its demands. These demands—which constitute the structure of the game itself—can be met only just so, thereby providing both victory and defeat, joy and sorrow, birth, rebirth, and death, sudden or slow—symbolically, of course—all on his or her own insofar as the player does not address the ball to another player and he or she does not answer him or her. Each player plays with his or her own ball and the dialogue is with the course, the ground, the trees, the bushes, the sand, the water, the wind, and at times the rain.

In the ongoing narrative of the self in golf, a player has to face many vicissitudes. At times one can experience failure after failure. George Plimpton (1968) describes one of his golfing experiences this way from a diary he kept of his intrepid adventures into the professional tour of golf:

> I found that one bad shot was almost invariably followed by another, and then another, until there was a whole stretch of them to assault one's poise.
>
> 5th—Fair drive. Long iron to right of green, ball lodging under tire of Cushman's pick-up truck. Truck carefully moved. Poked ball on green with six iron. Three-putted, missing two-footer.
>
> 6th—Feeling low about two-footer. Apologized to Bruno. Hit drive out of bounds. Hit another drive out of bounds. Apologized again. Picked up and left Bruno responsible for the hole.
>
> 7th—Hit drive 15 feet into gully in appalling mental condition.

This is rather a rare experience and, with the exception of the rank beginner, the golfer will have a series of qualified successes and failures with the attendant emotions given play.

The game begins with a drive from the "tee," and it begins a series of moves that can bring varying degrees of joy and sorrow. The drive also begins a quest for a perfection that is never reached. Even the best golfer in the world can find the goal of the drive coming up at least a little short. At the next stage of the game, one gets a chance to remedy the defects of the previous move, and once again it is open to the possibility of both a little joy and a little sorrow. It is not as good as one wanted it to be and not as bad as one could have feared. And once again, the player has a chance to remedy the ill effects of the earlier move and improve the next move. And so it goes until the *coup de grace* of the putt, and even here the player has to face the experience of not getting it quite perfect.

Every move that a golfer makes in this contemplative walk across the course is fraught with uncertainty, with the realization that the quest for perfection and completeness will come up short. One cannot bank on a perfect drive or a perfect putt or any other strokes in between.The moves in the game will nearly always fail to reach the goal; there will always be further and costly steps to take before consummation.The climax is always marked by the sorrows of not having quite made a perfect game, tempered only by the realization that one has played a little better than another distant fellow. Golf, as a game, in its very structure enables its players to understand the nature of an imperfect world and that, even in Arcadia, there is sorrow and failure.

These experiences are felt as a result of moves that the player himself or herself puts together, alone and unaided and uninterrupted by the others. He or she did this by exercising his or her own ability to judge, calculate, and contemplate. The joys and sorrows that result from these moves, too, are the player's own achievement, the result of his or her enterprise and industry, and his or her own to savor or to mourn. The emotions of these golf moments are delicately nuanced ones and totally personal. It is quite unlike the joy of hitting an ace or serving a ball in tennis or scoring a touchdown in football. The latter are decisive and final achievements and one can jump for joy or dance around the end zone. But even when one putts the ball into the hole, there is the qualification that goes with it: Why didn't I get an eagle or even a hole in one? If one goes over par, there is the sorrow of it, of course, but there is also the expectation, unless it is the last hole, that the next will be better. Joy and sorrow occur in various mixes and combinations in this game, and in varying shades and colors, and there is always the next hole to look forward to, the game to play. Such experiencing of emotions, including the rage and frustration that come when one has played a bad shot, however, are kept under strict control. "Golf cannot be played in anger or in any mood of emotional excess," observes Plimpton (1968: 92), not a great golfer but a keen and articulate student of the game.

Nevertheless, even in golf, in which emotional discipline and control are central to the successful execution of its moves as well as part of its ethos and etiquette, there are cases where golfers lose control and vent their anger and frustration.This venting is always against oneself and never against another player or official. In this game one does not glare at a linesman or address curses at him or her or at the umpire. He or she does not throw sand toward the umpire or try to bump him or her as an irate player runs down the field. Instead, when golf players miss a putt, they hit their bodies with the club. Plimpton tells of a player who "missed a putt and hit himself with the putter much harder in the reflex of his disappointment than he intended to and his knees buckled and he fell to the green" (1968: 93). Another player went a little further:

> If Shackleford hit a bad hook, he would take his right hand, which had come too powerfully into the shot and caused the fault, and he would look at it as if it were disembodied and then carry it over to a tree and hit it against the trunk. He'd shout things at it such as "Take it ... that'll teach you." (Plimpton, 1968: 94)

Plimpton also reports of players who, in their occasional excess of joy, throw their clubs in the air or let out shouts and exclamations. Yet these are rare occasions, emotional balance being maintained most of the time.

Still, there is a difference in the sorrows and joys in the Arcadia of the golf course: just as one does not play against another player in a confrontational style and plays by himself or herself, the joys and sorrows are also not dependent on the actions of others—except at the end of the game when the final scores are tallied. *Every instance of joy and sorrow is created by one's own actions and not by another person's moves.* No superordinate's calumny, no insolence of office, no subordinate's rebellion or inefficiency, no vagaries of the economic system or tribulations of the domestic interactions can be held responsible for the emotions of the game: it is just the "solitary ego" in search for self in Arcadia.

George Simmel described the as the "psychological conditions which the metropolis creates. With each crossing of the street, with the tempo and multiplicity of economic, occupational and social life, the city sets up a deep contrast with small town and rural life with reference to the sensory foundations of psychic life" (1950: 410). Sociologists and social philosophers before Simmel as well as after him have worked this theme extensively—in one way or another (Karp, Stone, and Yoels, 1977).

The golfing Arcadia is built to accommodate both the fantasies and nerves of the city dweller, one who is tired or constrained by the city's streets, squares, lights and shadows, and its boutiques and coffee houses. The city dweller is one who works and lives in relations of domination where alienation and negativity of self are abundant. However high in the hierarchy of relations he or she may be placed, there is no escaping the experience of being answerable to someone else and having one's acts and attitudes challenged and sometimes repudiated. Such challenges and repudiations may come from superordinates and consociates as well as sometimes from subordinates, too. And, at other times such repudiations come from the world of objects and events. A product one designed or supervised may not "sell" as predicted; a market forecast made may not have turned up correctly and a person one hired may cut up, and so on. Even if one is a successful and widely respected official, the constraints of attempts to control others, direct them, manage them, and sometimes reprimand them can be wearing and guilt- and shame-inducing experiences.

To sum up, the self is put into play in golf by the player's speaking to the objects of attention, addressing not only the ball but the environment, by means of hands extended by the club. And these objects do make a response, thereby establishing a dialogic relationship. The self is, no doubt, a process and not a structure, but it is a process that in its ongoingness meets with resistance that it confronts, the outcomes of such confrontation becoming a meaning for the self. And this resistance, of course, is of variable strength and challenge and such variabilities come to qualify the meaning for the self. In the playing of all games, these variabilities are programmed into the very structure of the game. In golf, these variabilities of strength are organized with greater subtleties and graces than in most other games—if not, all other games with the exception of billiards and its variations. The drive demands skills that are different from the "up-and-down" strategy necessary to get out of the sand trap, and the moves on the green call for more delicate touches and moves. The self that emerges out of the playing of golf—and that is put into play through both simultaneous and sequential moves—carries these subtleties and delicacies, control and discipline. The golfer's self is a soft-spoken one as it maneuvers the ball through the fairways and greens as well as perhaps outside the course. These pulsations of the self—those of the emotions of joy and sorrow as well as the cognition of the efficient and inefficient execution of moves, and the related judgments of victory and defeat—as they occur in golf are the result of one's own private enterprise and endeavor. One drives and the ball goes the distance. One gets a perfect up and down from the sand trap and then takes more shots than par to reach the hole, and none of these results are the results of the resistance offered by another player. The golfer is the captain of his or her swings, drives, chips, and putts and master of his or her self—emotions and cognitions and all.

The poets wrote about the gardens, architects and horticulturalists constructed them, and even ordinary human agents converted the wilderness, small and large, into gardens. The physical gardens allowed people to walk in them and participate in their essential features, while the poetic gardens allowed vicarious participation as well. The golf course allowed participation in the pastoral, too, but with a difference—a player could become more actively involved with the garden by means of the club and the balls, as objective extensions of his or her self, and engage with it emotionally and cognitively by means of the game and its properties. Not a cold pastoral, but a warm one in which a player can immerse himself or herself in practical ways.

Golf is, then, that unique pursuit: a sociable game that allows a solitary quest in which one can put a self into play against the environment; a test of character and a walk in the country—a pastoral *flanerie,* as it were, as opposed to the urban one described by Gleber (1999). Golf also provides ample opportunities to experience the exhilaration of seeking perfection and the challenge of solving various problems and failing in them, more often than not, and an opportunity to experience the angst of imperfection, since the ball nearly always falls shorter than one wants it to. Social engagement, emotional experience, and cognitive involvement, ecological contact, and the constant presence of failure and suffering are simultaneously served in the game.

The Measured Self: Tennis

There are a few games that are played in narrowly circumscribed spaces and may be called "court games." While tennis is the most famous of these games, one can include badminton, squash, and table tennis in this category. The fundamental element of these games is the management of an object—a ball or a shuttlecock—within very precisely defined boundaries in space. In these games, the player uses an instrument to serve and drive an object in order to land it in a particular place.

Among these games, tennis is the oldest one. One of the earliest allusions to tennis occurs in John Gower's poem to Henry IV written about 1400, and by that time tennis, an early version of the modern game, had been well established. This relationship between Henry IV and tennis was evident also in a ballad produced apparently at about the same time. In response to a request from the King of France by Henry's messengers, he is told:

> Your master young and of a tender age,
> Not fitting to come under my decree.
> Therefore I will send him three tennis balls
> And along with them he may learn to play.
> (Noel and Clark, 1924)

Shakespeare, in his play *Henry V,* also takes this association between the young king and his playfulness into account. Here the Dauphin sends him a "treasure" through his own ambassador. Henry bids his uncle, the Duke of Exeter, to open the treasure:

King Henry: What treasure uncle?
Duke of Exeter: Tennis balls, my liege.
King Henry: We are glad the Dauphin is so pleasant with us.
His present and your pains, we thank you for.

Act 1 (11)

This was not a very tactful or diplomatic comment on Henry's youth given his inexperience in statecraft and on his reputation as a frivolous youth when he was Prince Hal: "You savor too much of your youth," the Dauphin tells him through his messengers.

The game for which these balls were to be used was called "court tennis" and was played in European courts by royal young men and presumably women, too, on indoor courts of play. In the Shakespearean play, the dialogue uses tennis to define Henry, the king of England, as a frivolous and inexperienced young man better able to play tennis than wage war against France. Henry treats this as an insult and promises great suffering for the people of France in recompense. This early form of tennis was no doubt a very genteel game and was no more than paddling the ball across a barrier to the other side. Its origins are as obscure as they were unremarkable. However, by the late nineteenth century, this game, having been played in royal households, in schools, and in the colleges at Cambridge and Oxford under many guises, evolved into the modern game of "lawn tennis." The game was systematized and marketed by Major Walton Clapton Wingfield. He created equipment that could be bought and sold—a portable court and a net—and that could be put to use wherever two posts could be erected, to string a net. The box also included a set of written rules, and the game was set on its course as a national and international pastime with a certain uniformity. The rules were changed in some ways as the game progressed, but the basic structure of the game remains unchanged. It became a game in which measuring one's moves and placing them within very precise boundaries was the main theme.

Placing the Self

Human beings live in space that they convert into places for their selves. They do this by a variety of means—by using principles of design, putting up personal markers, decorating, and above all by drawing boundaries. The self is defined and understood in terms of these boundaries: "My house," "my room," "my office," "my corner of the street," are not merely names of places but an assertion of the self's presence in these places, and they give a sense of boundaries to the self and the spatial limits of its power and influence.

In relating to other selves, too, the self claims a certain space for itself and acts toward others in terms of this space—a culturally defined sense of place (Hall, 1958). There is, then, a sense of relational space between actors who are in each other's presence, an area that one does not typically transcend. Invading another's space is often viewed as an attack on the other's self, a challenge and a claim of power and control over the other. Such rights to one's own space, to control and dominate it and to protect it are defined in the laws and practices of many cultures.

In acting in the world, in giving presence to one's self in the social world, one situates it in a scene that is defined by boundaries of some sort or another. Further, in such acting, an agent also takes into account the nature of terrain on which one is situated: rough mountainous ones, roads and lanes, beaches, water or snow and ice, and so forth. In situating one's self and body on these various terrains—*the boundaries underfoot*—he or she has to negotiate its physical features and relate them to the self. Can I climb this mountain? Can I walk on this ice? Can I swim in this ocean? How should I walk on this road—can I run on it? Such queries to the self are assessed by the agent himself or herself on the basis of his or her own capacities to undertake these tasks as well as his or her sense of rights, obligations, duties, and responsibilities. Two issues are involved in such assessments: Can I do this and should I do this?

In undertaking these moves, the agent has to take a measure of his or her self and act accordingly. Furthermore, in the actual manifestations of these moves, in their qualities of addressivity and answerability, the agent has to constantly measure the self and the other—indeed, measure his or her gestures with varying degrees of accuracy and set them forth. Once this issue is faced, a third question is raised: How should I perform these tasks? They surely must be undertaken with maximum efficiency as well as propriety and "rationality."

In the game of tennis, every move is a measured one and any error in the presumptive measurements will elicit a demerit. Every move, in fact, is a measured address to the other and elicits disciplined answers. Deference to the other and the demeanor that is presented to him or her must conform to a sense of optimum measures, just as anger, affection, and other emotions must do so. In gift giving and expression and praising someone, once again the appropriate "ratio," to use Kenneth Burke's concept, must be maintained between "act" and "scene." For Burke, the concept of "ratio" contains a variety of meanings, all of which were relevant to his larger purpose in investigating the grammar of motives, but for us here the relevant meaning is this: "reckoning, calculating and computing of things" (1969a: 151), that is, the reckoning and calculating of the relationship between phenomena—including the ratio of act, self, and interaction. It is safe to say that the *ratio-centric* management of the expressiveness of one's acts in terms of the identity of self and other is pervasive in social interaction as well as in one's use of places in the world. In the game of tennis—which is played within multiple boundaries—this theme is represented in mythic form. *Indeed, tennis can be considered a structure for the management of the ratios of act and scene and of the self's relation to them—a structure that enables agents to actively practice such ratios.* To play tennis, more than any other game, or to be emotionally involved in watching it, is to engage the self in the significance of ratios, economies, and measurements in the social and the interactional life, to recognize boundaries, limits, and perimeters. The boundaries within which a single agent has to drive and place the token of the self, which is the ball, with the help of the extension of his or her body, which is the racquet, is the exemplification of the measured processes by which the self is to be presented.

The arena of play in tennis is a rectangle with another rectangle inside—a container and the contained—clearly marked on a well-prepared ground. Space is also marked vertically: the ball must be dispatched from one side to the other above a certain height achieved by placing a net of three feet in the middle of the court. This net also separates the playing arena horizontally into two halves, each "owned" or occupied by one player (or a set of two in doubles games). Once again, we can see that wide-open spaces have been delimited and humanized by inscribing boundaries on them and enabling agents to act within them. The acts that are to be performed in these places, and through them, will now have an economy and an intelligibility and a sense of place. Every significant act by the players who stand on one side of the rectangle must be executed in terms of these rectangular divisions. The beginning act of the game—the serve—is contained in the inner container, and once it is successfully executed by the server, the opponent returns it, and the game is in progress. All subsequent moves of the game are conducted within the outer boundaries of the court until a point is scored by a player who managed to keep his or her moves within the boundaries, without hitting the net that bifurcates the rectangle. Each move in the game is a move that measures the space of the court, confronts the precisely demarcated boundaries, and articulates the self of the player with the various moves. The move can be a drive along the sidelines, a cross court drive, a drop shot, a cunning passing shot, or an overhead smash, and each such move carries the self forward. If the move is successful, the self is vindicated and if it is not—well, there is another chance to do so in the next series of moves.

The self that is given play in these dialogic processes has very fixed boundaries, established by the formal rules of the game, constraining the acts that the self can undertake and giving such constraints a spatial structure.The spatial boundaries convert the playing arena into places in which selves must learn to operate.These spatial boundaries of tennis are truly the metaphorical versions of the social, economic, and moral boundaries within which all selves must operate in everyday life.The game of tennis is a myth that not only represents the combative and cooperative processes that are the imperative of social life but also indicates, visually and operationally, the boundaries under which such cooperative and combative processes have to be undertaken.

The moves that tennis players make—like those made in court games of all kinds—are truly entries of the self into demarcated spaces. Such moves are not like the magic incantations of those who seek to enter the *mandala,* certainly. Nevertheless, there are interesting analogies: the court is, in fact, a mandala and the players deal with it both meditatively and practically. It is space that is objectified by the actor, rendered into an object, and related to the self by means of the instrumentalities of the racquet and the ball. The ball and the racquet become the analogues of words and allow a communicative intimacy to emerge between players and the ground, between self and place, between self and the adversary each functioning as a narrative other. Indeed, it could be said that these objects—court, ball and racquet, and adversary—enable an agent to narrate a self into being, however, temporarily. Every move in the game is an attempt to keep within very strict boundaries, and every loss in the game is a measure of the degree to which a player has transgressed those boundaries.

In tennis then, as in all court games, every time a player serves or returns service, makes a drive or a drop, or an overhead smash, he or she is touching the world of objects around him or her, contacting them and connecting his or her self to them in delicately measured moves. An inch, a part of an inch, out of the lines of the various boundaries—horizontal or vertical—and the player knows that he or she has stepped out of bounds, has let his or her self be a little looser than he or she should have, has allowed it to wander a bit more than what was good for him or her.

The Dialogic of Tennis

In this game between two players on each side of the net, one "serves" the ball so that the other player can attempt to return it. The opening serve must be made from the right side of the court, and the serve must land in the left side of the opponent's court. The tennis court has, unlike all other games, ten boundaries—four outer boundaries indicating the playing area and four inner boundaries—counting the net—indicating the boundaries for the service. The serve must fall within these boundaries, but once the service has been returned, the entire court becomes the playing area. A server, then, begins his act with certain constraints. He or she is bound by these rules of service—in addition to the rule about the placement of his or her feet before the service. The act that he or she produces is a disciplined act, a move within certain preestablished parameters. Nevertheless, it has the potential to become a creative act: the server can send the ball down the center line or he or she can angle it to the corner of the service arena or put it short and in the middle of the arena. These moves are selected after gauging where the opponent is standing in order to receive the service. In addition, he or she can send a strong, forceful serve full of pace and speed or a gentle, spinning one—again making a choice on the basis of the opponent's stance, known strengths and weaknesses and so on.

In any case, the serve is a dialogic act addressed to the other and imbued with answerability—but with certain complications that are unique to gaming encounters. It is addressed to the other: the server takes, understands, and interprets the other's stance and role and sends the ball accordingly. It is an answerable act: The server not only takes the position of the receiver but also takes his or her own role, as defined by the rules of service in tennis, and puts them into practice. He or she serves the ball within the boundaries of the service court so that the other has a chance of answering it. However, there is a difference between everyday dialogic encounters and the ones in tennis: one addresses the act and imbues it with addressivity and answerability but also takes steps to ensure that the answer that, in fact, comes is a missed or erroneous return. One serves then—for that matter, makes all moves in the game—to address the other but hopes for an error and takes steps to ensure that this is the answer that he or she will get.

The opponent who answers the service, if he or she is able to return it, is now in a position to address the server, and he or she, too, will seek to imbue the return not only with answerability—that is, by sticking to the rules of the game like putting the return within the boundaries, for instance—but also with unreturnability. And so the game proceeds from service to return and return to another return until one player misses a shot or the ball lands outside the relevant boundaries or in the net.

Further, as the game proceeds, "points" are won or lost and accumulated into a pattern, eventually determining a winner or loser, additively. In each moment of this progression, various emotions are given play—joy and sorrow, rage and resentment, apprehension and fear. Each such experience of emotionality, too, defines the presence of a self and a certification of one's participation in a dialogic process where tangible objects like racquets and balls, court and boundaries, as well as opponents, supporters, and revilers from the audience, umpires and linesmen are actively operational.

In playing the game of tennis—or table tennis, badminton, or squash—then, one undertakes acts that have a certain degree of creativity and autonomy and are directed toward others from whom one anticipates an answer. These acts situate a player in a defined *place* where he or she feels at home, which he or she understands, where he or she knows how to act, as well as where people understand clearly his or her moves, objectives, and self. Further, he or she will also be able in these situations to use various material objects—balls, racquets, and so on—in a familiar way and exercise mastery over them. Here is a first-person description of a match by Helen Jacobs against the legendary Helen Willis Moody:

> It appeared from the opening of the first set that Helen was going to play me as she had in every one of our meetings—playing chiefly to my forehand and, at the first evidence of my being off balance, using the short cross court drive to the opposite side. It was at its best a devastating placement which I was determined to prevent. To do this, I put everything I could into the force and placement of my service with the intention of drawing Helen out of the court for the drive to the opposite side, then going to the net. (Phillips, 1999: 76)

Helen Jacobs describes in this short passage the acts and responses of a game of tennis as well as all the anticipation and imaginings that each player has to go through in order to make an effective interaction. It is not a simple case of taking the role of the other, but of taking it several steps ahead of the other and taking steps to thwart the effects on one's own game—and life. Each act is a creative and assertive move calculated and determined in terms of its probable effects and executed in a moment of play.

In tennis, the process of taking the role of the other and developing acts that are addressive and answerable are more complex than those in most interactions of everyday life: One expects an answer from the other accordingly, but the player will also seek to ensure that the answer will be deceptive in one way or another. To play the game at all, one must take the role and attitude of the other. In doing so, one serves the ball within the specified inner boundaries of the court and sends the ball to the player on the other side of the net. The other player anticipates this move and positions himself or herself accordingly, and when the ball is received, the player attempts to return it to the server. This may be termed the first order of the process of taking the role of the other. In the second order of this process, the server sends the ball across the net in the hope that it will have such a pace and/or position that the other will not be able to return it and the server can win a point. Similarly, if the receiver does manage to retrieve the serve, he or she would use pace, positioning, and spin to ensure that the other will not be able to return it. The dialogic of tennis is really an argument or debate in which, on the one hand, an agent does want to engage the other and, on the other hand, seeks to undermine the efficacy, sufficiency, and rhetorical vigor of the response from the other.

The game is, in fact, a very systematic dialogue conducted by means of sending the ball across the net to the other side. In this dialogue, space converted into meaningful place delimits the nature of the dialogue. The defined space limits the moves that each player can make enabling each of them to take the role of the other with a certain degree of measured precision. Furthermore, in this dialogue, there are what may be termed *warranted interruptions* occasioned by the failure of one player to make the correct responsive move.

In the dialogic game that is tennis, the meaning is created by the players' observing the formal rules of the game about the management of space by means of ball and racquet, by converting it into places of significance interpreted and applied by the players themselves or an umpire, as well as by operating various secondary rules of performance. Meaning is constituted in its fullness, not only in terms of the logic of the game but by dramas of performance. The narrative of self that is thus created and the plays of the self as they are conducted are bound by a variety of rules, and it is in their observance as well as in their occasional violation that selves are presented and asserted. Such a presentation of self and its assertion lead to the construction of a narrative self by the episodic accumulation of such presentations and assertions made according to these various rules.

The assertion and play of the self are also manifested in the struggle that a game—insofar as it is a *match*—elicits. Indeed, tennis games are confrontations between players of more or less equal strength and skill. In such confrontations, games are well contested. The players struggle against each other with their services, drives, placements, and drop shots and this is recorded in the score. A player may win the first set easily, find himself or herself challenged in the second set, and then lose it. This situation may be reversed in the third set and he or she may prevail in the fourth set, leading to a fifth and final set: 6/2, 4/6, 6/2, 5/7. And the final set may go to a tiebreaker with one person finally winning by two points.

Here is a fine description of the processes of asserting oneself by serving and the use by the other of "placement" to answer the serve while keeping one's faith to the last. The game was a Davis Cup match between the United States and Germany in 1937. Hitler had come to power and was eager to have Germans prove their manly prowess at all sporting engagements. He was listening to the description of the game between the American Don Budge and the German Baron von Cramm on the radio. Queen Mary of England was there also to watch the game played on the center court at Wimbledon on July 30, 1937. In any case, here is Budge's superb description of the game that conveys very nicely the drama of tennis that is inherent to the game itself as well as the special action in this one:

> There was no reason why I shouldn't hold serve. I was moving well; I was getting it in deep, and Cramm had not been able to take more than two points off it in any game so far. Besides, I had fresh new balls. And the fact was that my reasoning was absolutely correct, I did serve well in the whole game. I held up the new balls and showed them to Cramm across the net. Right away, I smashed a beauty at him. I clicked right in. I never touched his return. I moved over and hit another beautiful first serve. I never touched his return. I hit another beautiful first serve and never touched his return. I hit my fourth straight beautiful first serve. As a matter of fact, the only thing I hit in the game was beautiful first

> serves. And that was all he hit back. I never touched the fourth return either. Cramm had broken my back at love with four fantastic placements. (in Baltzell, 1995: 292)

A self can be asserted but the answer from the other, in this case with adroit placement of the ball, can place one's self, too. Budge couldn't respond in his turn to the answers from Cramm because they were out of his reach, despite his own best efforts at delivering superb serves. The return squelched him and he had to accept defeat in this game. Budge, however, was able to stretch the game to five sets and win the final one—defeating Cramm and the Third Reich in one fell swoop.

Narrating the Self in Tennis

The systematic performance of the dialogic of tennis leads to the emergence of a narrative of the self. The self that is narrated in the moves made by the player in tennis is that of an agent who is able to execute disciplined and precisely controlled moves and who can manage his or her emotions and attitudes with decorum. Such a narrative is achieved by observing the rules of the game, both constitutive and regulative ones, as scrupulously as possible. By putting the rules of the game into play, one narrates a self as the game proceeds—the narrative of a disciplined and ethical self capable of controlling his or her emotions and managing defeat and victory with grace and dignity.

In typical amateur games, there are no umpires and the game's progress depends on the mutual trust between opposing players regarding the judgment of the placement of the ball within the prescribed boundaries. The following of these rules, their application, depends, then, on the "character" of the players, their commitment to a conception of "honor" or "decorum." If these commitments were not kept habitually and systematically, the game could not be played and the player who was habitually and systematically given to violating them would be excluded from the game.

Once umpiring by a nonplaying third party became standard practice, another set of problems of conduct emerged. The umpiring was sometimes done by a lone figure, but eventually he was given assistants in the form of line judges and net judges. The new problem was this: how should players treat the umpire and the line judges if they disagreed with the "call"? One approach to this problem, followed by most, if not all players, is contained in the following words from Perry Jones, tennis player and promoter and spy for the United States during the war years:

> All close balls are good, if you remember that you will never cheat an opponent. In tournament tennis, you don't question a call by an umpire or a linesman. You continue to play. And don't think too much when you

> play a big match. Just try to hit the ball well. Oh yes, keep your sneakers clean. (quoted in Baltzell, 1995: 219)

Not only, then, are there the rules of the game, codified in some form or another, but there are also the rules about how the rules are to be interpreted and used for acting. Jones's views on this matter could be supplemented here from the magnificent memoirs of his cricketing days by C. L. R. James. The memoirs and the game itself are not just about cricket. As James put it, "What do they know of cricket, who only cricket know?" (1983: 9). James writes: "We were a motley crew ... Yet rapidly we learned to obey the umpire's decision without question, however irrational it was. We learned to play with the team which meant subordinating your personal inclinations and even interests to the good of the whole" (1983: 34).

In addition to these rules, there was the final rule about how to win and how to lose. In every game, there is going to be a winner and a loser and the disportment of self after the decision has been reached must be conducted according to the rules. There is a good description of this in the aftermath of the match between the aristocratic Baron Gottfried von Cramm and the American commoner described earlier.

> Gottfried, the noble loser, had to wait patiently at the net, waiting patiently for me, the winner, to get up off the ground. I rose finally, bewildered and rushed towards him. I tried to hug him but before I could, he stopped me and took my hand. "Don," he said, evenly and with remarkable composure, "this was the absolutely, the finest match I ever played in my life. I am very happy that I could have played it against you, whom I like so much." And then he pumped my hand: "Congratulations." (in Baltzell, 1995: 298)

Baltzell considers these regulative rules of the game a legacy of the upper-class "gentlemanly" code by which even everyday social life was conducted. This may well be true in a very limited sense. It is difficult to believe, however, that the robber barons and the rapacious capitalists and slave traders whose children became the American "gentlemen" observed these rules in their everyday life outside their homes and clubs. They must have evolved later. These regulative rules, whatever their origin in English "public" schools and their American imitations, as Baltzell claims, were absolutely necessary *functionally* for the games to exist and to allow them to be played continually. I have seen servant girls play the game called *Sokattan* in Sri Lanka with the same sense of decorum and observance of these rules as Baltzell's gentlemen. *Indeed, no game could be played at all if the rules of conduct, deportment, and manners that surround the game—the regulative rules—are not observed just as interactions of conversations could not be easefully conducted without them.* While some interactions can proceed even when these rules are violated and a relationship maintained for a while—a quarrel, for example, or a quarrelsome relationship—no game can proceed without them. If every call—or many calls—in tennis were going to be disputed or repudiated, if every decision by an umpire in cricket—or too many—were going to be challenged, the games could not be played at all. Once the decision is challenged, then there has to be an appeal procedure, and this will delay the game and leave another official whose decision can also be challenged. The practice of accepting calls and decisions on the court and field and taking them as final is necessary for the game to proceed again. If there is to be an appeal to a higher authority, it should be swift and short, allowing the game to proceed. These appeal procedures entered many games only when they ceased to be really games and became jobs and careers for the players. Similarly, the practice of winning with grace and decorum and losing with dignity and composure means that the two players can play again and again without making it into a permanently acrimonious exchange. Insofar as these games were first played by friends and acquaintances, people belonging to the same social circles, who perforce have to meet again, the secondary rules had to be observed so that the meeting and sociability could continue to occur. In Goffman's words, they were the rules of "deference" and "demeanor" with which the "interaction order" of the game was maintained (1967).

In the evolution of tennis into a commercial enterprise and media event, it also attracted a large number of players who came from what Baltzell would call the nongentlemanly set. Many of them came from poor white social circles and eventually some black players were able to gain entry too. In addition, a large number of players from eastern Europe, who were definitely not Anglo-Saxon Protestant gentlemen also came into the game. In spite of the entry of the hoi polloi and the money changers into the game, the regulative rules continued to be observed—with some exceptions. These exceptions reveal in a very particular way, the function of these regulative rules in tennis. They reveal, too, the different narratives of self that emerged when they were violated—narratives that were eventually rejected.

It was, in fact, left to two white, upper-middle-class men, suburban though not perhaps either Anglo-Saxon or Protestant, who were to violate the regulative rules, with the help of a couple of eastern Europeans, and bring them into question and the game into disrepute. Here is the outraged comment from Baltzell: "I should think that tennis lovers of all social classes would *desperately* want to *discourage* the wider appeal that characters like Nastasie brought to Flushing Meadows" (1995: 365).

These words were written about a game between Eli Nastasie from Czechoslovakia and John McEnroe of the United States in which the decisions made by the umpire led to a near riot by the crowd. Nastasie's refusal to accept the umpire's ruling was the immediate provocation, though it followed constant bickering by the two players.

In another incident in his career of great tennis and even greater controversy, McEnroe again threw "tantrums," notes Baltzell, often containing all the elements of taboo conduct. "All through the Wimbledon tournament that year, McEnroe displayed an adolescent sense of injustice untempered by any sense of adult civility," Baltzell observes. He quotes two Wimbledon historians as having written: "Never in the history of sports was there so public a display of bad court manners when temperament caused him to go beyond acceptability in his opening match on court one against Tom Gullikson. His offensiveness to officials was established as an example of what sportsmanship should not be" (1995: 369).

He threw thirteen "tantrums," used obscenities repeatedly, and insulted linesmen by alluding to their ethnic origins. "After one crude outburst, Lady Diana Spencer, betrothed to Prince Charles at that time, left the royal box," notes Baltzell and quotes an observer's joke: "The wedding is off. Her ears are no longer virgin" (1995: 309)—it being the case that the mother of the future king of England should be a guaranteed virgin.

Here, then, we have an instance of the systematic violation of the regulative rules of the game. Another consistent offender in this regard was Jimmy Connors—again upper-middle class and wealthy enough, and white, though neither Anglo-Saxon nor Protestant—to use Baltzell's characterization.

Did the game remain a game, remain "tennis" in spite of all this? Indubitably so—because all the other players did observe the regulative rules of performance. McEnroe, Connors, Nastasie, and a couple of others—like the one who insulted an umpire to his face and had his wife slap him later—were able to get away with it because officials were too timid and greedy to enforce the rules. There is no point in having rules, if they are not enforced and if officials are afraid to alienate the millions of television viewers, the sponsors of the game, and the advertisers, and choose to accept the infractions. To censure a player was, of course, to alienate the fans, but more significantly, if such censure leads to the award of the game, set, and match to the opponent, the game will end prematurely. If a leading player is thus eliminated, and if he is otherwise such an interesting player as McEnroe, there is loss of audience as well as an empty time slot on the television schedule to fill. No official, with one eye on cash flow would want that.

Nevertheless, it finally happened and brought home the importance of the regulative rules into the game. McEnroe, in the fourth-round match of the Australian Open championship, was playing against Michael Pernfors. Here is Baltzell on this:

> Then at 5:30 on Sunday afternoon, January 21st, 1980, the axe fell. In the fourth set, McEnroe was first given a warning for glaring menacingly at a lines-woman and then a point penalty for abusing his racket—McEnroe put up what he knew was a hopeless argument. The supervising official

> of grand slam tournaments was called in to settle the dispute. Just as he was walking away from the court, McEnroe yelled at him in a loud voice "Go fuck your mother." The official and the umpire conferred for a moment and then made an unprecedented announcement: Verbal abuse and audible obscenity, Mr. McEnroe. Default; game set and match, Pernfors. (1995: 375)

McEnroe, Nastasie, and Connors then did not fully understand that measured shots they played on the marked ground were paralleled by the measured presentations of self they had to undertake on the court. *McEnroe's offense in this case and on many other occasions, too, was that while his strokes with his racquet, more often than not, remained within bounds, his attitudes and gestures were out of bounds.* They could be said to have overestimated their measurements, violated the ratios, and repudiated the economy of the game and its relationship to a self.

To the extent that both the constitutive rules and regulative rules are observed, the gaming procedures develop a narrative of the self in an orderly manner. In addition to the orderly and measured dialogue and narrative that the procedures of tennis allow for the self, the game also demands a certain commitment and determination in order to be successful. It was an excessive commitment to the game and fighting to win that no doubt prompted McEnroe, Connors, and Nastasie to go so far in their indecorous behavior.

In these interactional series, the agent asserts his or her self and puts it into play, no doubt, but processes like grit, determination, dedication, and discipline are also in evidence. Further, in these moves in the game the player has to battle not only the skills, grit, and determination of the opponent but also his or her own fatigue and the wind and rain, and at times, the hostility or indifference of the crowd, if it is a public event, as well as the waning of one's own confidence and determination. Each player can have these qualities in a necessary sufficiency and one will lose and another will win. Each player will be able to congratulate himself or herself—and will be congratulated by others—for having displayed these qualities in the course of the game. Nevertheless, there is a difference between winner and loser that cannot be obscured under certain circumstances: Player A wins the first two sets and seems to be coasting to an easy win in the third set, when Player B seems to revive himself or herself as if from a slumber, "pulls out all the stops," and wins that set and the next two sets and the match. These matches come to a point in the last set and the destiny of the player is on the line in the few remaining moves of the game. Boris Becker put this issue nicely, "The fifth set is not about tennis." Yes, indeed—it is about character and self.

The game then enables one to put not only one self into play but, at times, to narrate a particular character into existence, convert a game into a "test of character" in Goffman's usage of these terms. He puts it this way:

> These capacities (or lack of them) for standing correct and steady in the face of sudden pressures are crucial; they do not specify the activity of the individual, but how he will manage himself in the activity. I will refer to these maintenance properties as an individual's *character.* (1967: 217)

While Goffman gives boxing as an example of "fighting heart" and "never admitting defeat"—it is in tennis, with the relatively slower and systematic accumulation of points, that one finds a good example of this. Consider a player in a championship match who is losing 6/2 and 6/4 in the first two sets and then finds himself or herself down 4/1 in the third set. Two more sets to the opponent and he or she will be out of the game. Many a player has fought out of this predicament, winning that set and the next two. In this situation, with both players facing each other for the decisive fifth set, a combat myth is set in place. The player who won the first two sets and then lost the next two faces a test of character of his or her own just as the other player does: does the former give up in despair and abandon the fight? Does the second player claim, "I have put up enough of a fight" and wind down? Typically, neither of these developments is known to occur. There are many instances of "epic" fifth sets where both players put their "character" to the test and win this test—let alone the game itself.

These features of the performance of the self in tight situations can be related to many ethical and religious prescriptions. From the Judeo-Christian tradition alone, there is the example of Job, to begin with, and the doctrine that Martin Luther and John Calvin enunciated—the doctrine of the "calling" (Weber, 1958a). In such ethical prescriptions, the recommendation is to keep the struggle going, try to move ahead irrespective of the odds stacked against one—or as we might say, play the game and show "game."

The Self at Bay: Baseball, Cricket, and Stickball

In various myths, one can find as an axial event the combat between the protagonists. In such combats the hero confronts one adversary—or a series of adversaries in succession—and emerges triumphant. The classic encounter is in the form of a duel between equally or nearly matched opponents and was incorporated into the chivalric and aristocratic traditions of medieval Europe (Kiernan, 1989).

This form of the myth represents a common human experience: an agent's having to confront another for social or economic advantage, political progress, and individual esteem. A variation on this theme is the confrontation between two groups of agents: tribes, clans, gangs, platoons, armies. In such combat one fights as a member of a team, expects and receives support from other members of the group.

There are, however, other forms of combat in everyday life. In such combats, an individual agent faces a group of people arrayed against him or her. Such confrontations can occur within normal groups themselves: in a family an individual can be singled out for special consideration. He or she can be made a "scapegoat" and forced to constantly defend himself or herself against the others. The same process can occur in all groups formed at work and play, in neighborhoods and gangs, and so on. In such confrontations, an agent has to prove himself or herself as strong, competent, and able to take what is thrown at him or her. One narrative form of this is found very clearly in Henrik Ibsen's Dr. Stockman in *Enemy of the People.* Faced with betrayal and abandonment by both kith and kin, alone and isolated, he exclaims, "The strongest man in the work is he who stands most alone." One can become an "enemy of the people" and decide to fight the people as well as one may. Such a conception assumes that an individual has a certain degree of autonomy and that his or her self is not a mere substrate of the social or ideological process. The human agent, constituted as he or she is by the interactional and discursive processes to which he or she has been subjected, is nevertheless able to act on his or her own volition and reap the consequences.

With such an autonomous sense of being, he or she can feel himself or herself in competition and contests with others, many others, against whom he or she must win, must outwit, disarm, best, and so on. Again and again an agent can feel his or her self questioned, challenged, put to the test, subjected to demands that he or she should put up or shut up. This is a call for effective performance, an attempt to seek perfection, work hard, and prove oneself as a worthy member of the group. Such is the experience of the self encircled by others who demand certain performances from it. Such demands are met in a number of ways: hunting, where one can provide leadership and bring forth the best kill; being the best general; providing leadership in an organization as well as succeeding individually.

In these pursuits, an agent stands, if not alone, at least above the others and often has to confront them and deal with their questions, criticisms, and objections. The obverse of this "singleness" is the case where an individual is forced to defend a decision or action against an array of others—those who "gang up" against an agent, or merely disagree or want to undermine or lynch one at any cost. An individual has to handle the situation as best as he or she can and the manner of handling it will confer esteem or dis-esteem on one and will be used to estimate his or her character. One can "cut and run." He or she can display cowardice and incompetence or he or she can "face up" to the challenge, display courage and confidence in the handling of the adversaries.

This is a common enough experience in the lives of most people—it happens at least a few times. One is forced to defend a position, an opinion, a stand, a claim, an assertion and do it competently and courageously all on one's own. *This role is analogous to that of the sacrificial object in myth and ritual.* It stands alone—a scapegoat—and faces the challenges of many sorts. The extreme example of this is the scapegoat well-expressed in the gospel according to John. In the meeting of the Pharisees, as reported by John: "And one of them Caiphas being the high priest that year said unto them, Ye know nothing at all. Nor consider that it is expedient for us, that one man should die for the people, and that the whole nation perish not'" (John 11:49–50). Kenneth Burke comments on this:

> With a culture formed about the idea of redemption by the sacrifice of a Crucified Christ just what does happen in an era of post-Christian science, when the ways of the socialization have been secularized? Does the need for the vicarage of the Sacrificial King merely dwindle away? Or must some other person or persons, individual or corporate, real or fictive, take over the redemptive role? (Burke, 1969b: 31)

Having invoked the Judeo-Christian scriptures as his exemplary text, Burke goes further with it and argues that such expiation is achieved by the creation of a "victim" and the offering of a sacrifice. Burke argues, "The principle of personal victimage was introduced incipiently, so far as theology goes, in connection with the covenant involving Abraham's willingness to sacrifice his beloved son Isaac on the altar of God's governance ..." (1961: 216–17).

This sacrificial principle is "reaffirmed anew" by the fact that the covenants in the Bible are broken again and again, thus making it necessary to seek redemption again and again. Victimage then becomes the favored mode by which such redemption is achieved—victimage really being "redemption by vicarious atonement" (Burke, 1961: 217).

In displaying his willingness to sacrifice Isaac and making the necessary preparations for it, Abraham was essentially acknowledging his submissiveness to God's authority and defining his own place in a hierarchy: This sacrifice also defines a father's authority: The father as a patriarch has the right to offer his son's life to anyone. That is, he can kill him, give him away and sell him into slavery, abandon him in order to save the family or the tribe. Switching to a different religious tradition, a perusal of Agamemnon's sacrifice of his daughter Iphigenia also reveals the play of the principle sacrificing the one for the god of the many. Agamemnon had offended the goddess Artemis by boasting that he was a better hunter than she was, or alternatively, by killing a deer that was sacred to her. She punished him by becalming the seas when Agamemnon was ready to go to Troy for the war, which prevented him from sailing. Kalshis, the seer, announced that she could be appeased by sacrificing Iphigenia. She was summoned and was about to be sacrificed when Artemis intervened and saved her, substituting a goat in her place. In other versions of the myth, she was, in fact, sacrificed, earning her mother Clytemnestra's wrath against Agamemnon.

What exactly then is a sacrifice? In all sacrificial rites, one can discover certain common elements:

I. An individual surrenders something of significance to him or her, or something to which he or she is committed, intellectually and emotionally—a son, a daughter.

II. One surrenders something that is identified with him or her. In many societies, hair is sacrificed, for example, in fulfillment of vows. In an elaborate study of the rituals of the Semites, Julian Morgenstern observes, "Among many primitive peoples, hair is regarded as the particular seat of life, vitality, and strength, and in consequence, as possessing a positive character of sanctity." (1966: 84)

III. In other societies, one offers as sacrifice objects that are *valuable* to the devotee—food, wine, oil, animals, money, gold and silver, for example. In these cases, and in one version of the story of Iphigenia, an animal is substituted for a human being. The lamb has a certain economic value and it can be communally consumed after the sacrifice. In many parts of the world, animals are still sacrificed and then eaten together with other members of the community. In the Vedic rituals of Brahminical Hinduism, "ghee" (clarified butter) is offered to the fire god Agni, and in one form of the sacrifice a horse is killed and its remains subjected to various treatments (de Bary et al., 1958: 26-27). In what may be termed the supreme sacrifice, one offers his or her body as a sacrifice. When a devotee becomes a monk or a nun, or a *sannyasin,* he or she is, in fact, surrendering his or her body to God's governance. Further, in some religions, self-immolation is practiced as a sacrificial ritual. Besides actual physical punishment visited on the body, such sacrifices include fasts, penances, and selective consumption of items of food. The pain and deprivation that the body is made to experience—with its consequent impact on the self—is interpreted as one of surrender to God's will and sovereignty. The various elements that are sacrificed, then, can be summarily described as either the self itself, or surrogates for the self, or in semiotic terms, signs of the self. They stand for the self, represent the self as symbols or icons or indices. An abandonment of these signs, a surrender of them, elicits almost the same conditions and emotions as the surrendering of the self itself.

It is clear then in performing sacrificial rites, an agent is, in fact, surrendering himself or herself—*its worth and presence and its esteem and regard*—in the form of a token to an external entity. A sacrifice that does not cost something to the sacrificer is no sacrifice at all. The self is put at risk by submitting it to pain and loss in anticipation of rewards in this world or in the afterlife. *The money, the lamb, the goat, the hair, and the boy are not the real offerings of the sacrifice but, insofar as these are mere*

tokens of the self, it is the self that is the offering, albeit an indirect and a voluntary one. In other words, a sacrifice has both a sacrificer and a victim on the surface, but in reality, the agent is both a sacrificer and a symbolic victim.

Victimage in Games

These themes are represented in various games. Indeed, games were used throughout the ancient world as structures and occasions in which either human beings or animals were offered as sacrifices. In the Minoan civilization of ancient Crete, there is evidence that bulls were sacrificed in the central courts of the palaces of Knossos, Phaistos, and Malia at the conclusion of acrobatic games. In Mesoamerica, one can find evidence of the central place of ball games in the ritual life of the people as well as ball courts as public places of great importance. In such places, a variety of rituals were performed as essential elements of the ball games. After surveying a great deal of the archeological evidence, John Gerard Fox observes, "These combined sets of data point to the use of ball courts for a variety of related ritual practices including the playing of ball games, ritual feasting and other rites involving the burning of incense, the use of figurines, and in some areas, human sacrifice" (1996: 491-92).

The games were then not set apart from other activities as frivolous or leisurely pursuits but were integrated with political and religious systems. The essence of the ball game, observes Esther Pasztory, "seems to be a contest between opposing forces, which may be represented by male twins or a couple of contests that often involve a cyclically recurring pattern of death, rebirth, and revenge. In each case, one contestant is devoured or beheaded (an act ritually recalled by the practice of human sacrifice) as a result of which great benefits inure to society especially in the form of agricultural fertility" (1972: 209-10). Other scholars have stressed the relationship between ball games and the cosmic order of Mesoamerican speculations. Linda Schaete and David Freidel have suggested, for instance, that ball courts were viewed as "portals" to the Mayan other world and human sacrifices as means of sending people there (1991). It is true though that the victims of these sacrifices were those who lost in the game.

It is clear that ball games in Mesoamerica were anything but ludic events. These themes of play as ritual and sacrifice are transformed and represented in certain contemporary games, too. An individual is put out to face an array of adversaries who do everything possible—within the rules of the game—to undermine him or her. He or she becomes a *virtual scapegoat,* for a while as he or she elicits the ire of the opposing team as well as that of their supporters and, if he or she fails to deliver, that of his or her own team and its supporters, too. He may go out as a hero to face the adversaries and come back as a goat—or conversely, he may go out as a goat and come back as a hero or even go and return as a hero. Unlike sacrifices in many religious and mythological forums, in games there is always the possibility that an agent can escape the fate of being a victim. Nevertheless, every time a player goes out to face his or her adversaries, he or she is taking his or her reputation as a sacrificial offering. This reputation is either a verbally rendered one or one that is enumerated in the form of a "record" or "average" or "won-lost" listing, sometimes accompanied by details about stunningly heroic deeds or deeply humiliating ones. As the player goes in to perform, he or she has a record, an average, and a reputation that confers on him or her a certain status, a place in a hierarchy. And when he or she leaves the arena of play, these variables have been put to the test, and if he or she is a batter in baseball—where getting a "hit" is more difficult than in any other game—more often than not, he or she leaves the arena humbled.

These games are usually played in broad fields that are different from football and hockey fields. Hit-and-run games are played by teams, but there is no continuous interaction with each other all the time. In baseball, there is the batter and a pitcher, a catcher and a fielder who are sporadically united, but usually the confrontation is between the batter and the pitcher.The same structure of activities obtains in cricket and other allied games.The axial event in these games is, in fact, a single player standing alone in an appointed place and facing an array of opponents, seeking to keep him or her at bay.

These games are, in fact, mimetic structures of an encircled self, by, if not necessarily hostile forces, at least critical ones. In these games, the self is not only put to the test, but continuously challenged and repudiated, asked to come forth with his or her best performance, to face its others in a contest of will and character. Unlike chess or tennis or even football, the self is alone against a *host* of others, none of whom is sympathetic or supportive. It is the hero against the world; Hercules against the Hydra. It is also Tom, Dick, Harry, Tanya, Deborah, and Henrietta against the family, the neighbors, the colleagues, the staff, and so on.

Many games can be examined as exemplars of the theme of self against the world, of victim facing hostile forces, in order to bring redemption to himself or herself or to those who identify with him or her—the few as in local games, or to the multitudes as in regional, national, or international games.This claim applies to all games that are played and supported by various fans and followers where the team becomes the sacrificial victim—the valuable item put at risk—but is more starkly and subtly realized in games where a single individual is allowed to face an array of adversaries. In such games, the individual agents, representing "us," face the enemy, the many others, and put themselves at risk on our behalf, giving the occasion for emotional play and catharsis. Furthermore, in the playing of these games the themes of birth and death are enacted symbolically: one begins the game, and the "outing" of the player by the actions of the others is a death *represented,* a goat or lamb sacrificed.

I will take four games—a folk game played in South Asia, cricket, baseball, and an urban game played in New York City—to exemplify these claims.

The Stick Game

These kinds of games are found in many societies. In southern Asia, a game called *Gulli-Danda* in Hindi, *Kitti-Pull* in Tamil, and *Chuck-Gudu* in Sinhalese is played. These games have the structure of one against all, of a victim facing his or her challengers, an agent putting his or her self forward, and putting it at risk.

In this game two sticks are used, one shorter than the other. The long stick is called *danda* and the short one *gulli.* In playing this game, the danda holder would lay the gulli across an elongated hole in the ground and with the danda held under the gulli, scoop it up and throw it as far as he or she could, and the fielders try to catch the awkwardly shaped gulli hurtling toward them. If the stick is caught, which seldom happens, it means you are out and someone else takes the danda to repeat the action. If it is not caught, you lay the danda across the hole and the fielders have another chance to "out" you by trying to hit the danda with the gulli from the point where the gulli has landed. The gulli is usually missed and now one has to hit the gulli on the ground in such a way as to make it rise up so you can hit it again, as far as you can, while the field tries to catch it. One of the fielders then tries to throw the gulli, once again from where it has dropped and tries hitting the danda that was laid across the hole. If the fielder hits the danda, the player is out, and if he or she doesn't hit the danda, the player wins a point or a "run." Needless to say, being a folk-game, it has many local variations.

In an alternative version, the player will drop the small stick with one hand and hit it toward the others. As the small stick travels toward the adversaries, they try to catch it. If it is caught, the hitter is out, but if it falls on the ground, he or she scores a point. If the small stick falls on the ground, the distance from the hitter's hole to the stick is measured by the big stick and this becomes his or her score. When he or she gets out, other members of the team will take his or her place and continue until everyone is rendered out.

Clearly, this is a game in which an agent is alone in the field and has to face the many adversaries and allow himself or herself to be challenged and put to the test and either be vindicated as a winner or humiliated as a loser. The player does have teammates, but they follow him or her only in the performance of the axial act and are not there to help him or her. It is just him or her and his or her adversaries.

Cricket

In the game of cricket, a batsman, along with a partner, goes to the pitch on either side of which is a wicket—three stumps and a pair of bails on top of them. Each batsman stands in front of these wickets, with a crease marked on the pitch indicating a safe area. Facing the batsman on the opposing side is the bowler whose task is to send the ball toward the batsman and the wicket. At any moment in the game, a batsman is facing the bowler and arrayed against him or her are the adversaries who, in alliance with the bowler, will seek to get the better of the batsman. In cricket, these fielders occupy positions that have strange names, the origins of which are lost in antiquity. To begin with, behind the wicket is the wicket-keeper. He or she catches the balls that are not hit by the batsman and tries to get him or her out by stumping the wickets, should the batsman be outside the crease. In addition, there are the following fielding positions: first slip, second slip, and third slip on one side of the wicket; gully, silly point, silly mid-off, and silly mid-on; leg slip, short legs—forward and backward. These positions are called "close-catching positions," which are used when the ball is being bowled slowly. In the mid-field there are the cover-point, extra-cover, mid-off and mid-on, mid-wicket, square leg, short third-man. In addition, there are positions in the outfield. All these positions are not occupied all the time; rather, the captain, depending on the type of bowling being practiced, will set the field accordingly. In any case, it will be seen that the batsman is a lone figure encircled by a number of people whose only mission is to outwit him or her. He or she has to face the ball being sent to him by the bowler, study and deal with it as well as he or she can, and dispatch it in such a way that it is not caught on the fly by an adversary and is long enough so that he or she can run to the other side of the pitch. If, however, he or she manages to send it out of bounds along the ground, he or she gets four runs, and if on the fly, he or she gets six. If the ball is short of the boundary, the batsman and his or her partner run toward the other side of the pitch, often frantically, before the ball is collected by a fielder and thrown toward the wicket. At the wicket, another player, the bowler or the wicket-keeper, will catch it and try to stump the wicket before the batsman reaches the crease. If he or she makes it to the crease, he or she is not out, but if he or she doesn't, he or she is out. There is also another way of being out—the leg-before-wicket. This is a judgment made by the umpire, on an appeal by the bowler that the batsman blocked the ball hitting the wicket with the padded legs.

In this game, the batsman is standing alone at the wicket surrounded by eleven adversaries, all of them intent on doing him or her symbolic harm. The bowler is the main instrument of attack, with the others playing supporting roles. He or she has at his or her disposal various techniques to discombobulate the batsman: a) length: the distance the ball bounces on the pitch from the batsman's usual position; b) speed: fast, medium, slow swing; c) spin: the off-cutter; the leg-cutter; off-spin; leg-spin, googly. Bowlers specialize in one set of these ways of delivering a ball and the fielding positions are set according to these strategies of bowling.

Against these various modes of attack, the batsman plays what are called "strokes." A stroke is a way of hitting the ball with a particular stance and movement of hands, arms, and body that are both safe and visually elegant. Indeed, one of the best epithets in cricket is to be called a "stylish" batsman. Each stroke is selected on the basis of the ball that is delivered—its length, bounce, spin, cut, and placement. On certain deliveries, the batsman plays "back" and on others, he or she plays "forward" or "cuts" and "hooks" and "drives" and at times, swings at a "loose" ball to hit it high over the boundaries for six runs. The rule of good batsmanship is always, or nearly always to watch the bowler carefully, interpret the nature of the delivery quickly, and play the stroke that is appropriate to the nature of the delivery—the pace, the length, the bounce, the spin, the swing. For a good and successful player, there is then the goodness of fit between the nature of the delivery that he or she is facing and the selection of the stroke.

In playing all these strokes to the balls that are delivered to him or her by a cunning and calculating bowler, filled with malicious forethought, the batsman has twin objectives: to guard his or her wicket from being hit by the ball and to hit the ball so that he or she can score runs by adroit placement of the ball. The bat has a flat surface enabling a batsman to have good control over the direction of the ball. Armed with the bat then, he or she will defend his or her wicket and aim to score at the same time: the twin tensions of the art of batsmanship. These are also the twin tensions of the interactional confrontations of everyday life: Defend, guard, protect the self, and simultaneously seek to win credit for it by acting with dignity and decorum, with style and poise and panache, if one can manage it. Every move of the batsman is a move that is both defensive in this sense and aggressive at the same time.

Here is a description by C. L .R. James, on a stylish batsman, Wilton St. Hill, facing a fast bowler, George John:

> I do not remember any more frightening a sight at cricket than John running, jumping and let loose at his terrific pace and St. Hill playing back as if he had known that he would have to do so long before the ball was bowled and was somewhat bored by the whole business ... In all his strokes, even the most defensive, the ball always traveled. I have taken people who knew nothing about cricket to see him and as soon as they saw his easy, erect rhythmic back-stroke to the fast bowler, they burst into murmurs of admiration. His right torso was always towards point, left elbow high and left wrist a fulcrum. (James, 1983: 89)

Here, then, we have a batsman, poised and ready to take the particular delivery that is coming toward him and handle it in such a way that while avoiding a demerit, he simultaneously gains credit by hitting the ball for a score. James continues his description of St. Hill:

> No one I have ever seen, neither Bradman, nor Sobers, saw the ball more quickly, nor made up his mind earlier. Time; he always had plenty of time. From firm feet, he watched the ball until it was within easy reach and only then brought his bat to it with his wrists. He never appeared to be flurried, never caught in two minds. (1983: 88)

The bowlers are sometimes ferocious "speed-merchants" and, at other times, are cunning and manipulative in their attacks. In spite of the fact that so many players are arrayed against him or her, a good batsman always finds a way to score runs against a bowler, often amassing large totals. Good bowling, it is said, wins matches in cricket and a good one is the one who smothers the batsman's skills and keeps him or her from scoring. Still, many batsmen become legendary run-getters and drive the bowlers and their side to distraction.

Such a one was Don Bradman, the Australian—a legend in cricket in the thirties, forties, and early fifties. He was unbeatable by any bowler of the time, and new strategies were brought into play when England faced Australia in 1932–33. This confrontation was a controversial one with politics and diplomacy becoming involved. For us here, it illustrates the thesis that the batsman is a lone figure when he or she is at the crease, facing the bowler and the bowler's teammates as he or she has to deal with the situation as well as he or she can. Bradman was too good a player, too successful a run-getter, arrogant and self-centered and avaricious to boot. The English side, under the leadership of its captain Douglas Jardine, an equally arrogant and domineering character, devised a strategy to beat him. It was called "bodyline bowling"—which meant bowling at the body of the player instead of the wicket. Here is a description: "The mechanics of bodyline are simple. The requirement is for short-pitched fast bowling aimed at the batsman's body at shoulder length with seven or eight men on the legside (Blofeld, 2002: 110).

The batsman was, in fact, in a trap. With a strong, heavy, and hard ball hurtling toward his or her body and seven of the ten fielders hovering over him or her, the player had little chance of playing straight and correct strokes. He or she had to defend not the symbol of his or her dignity and honor in the shape of his or her wicket but his or her life this time. Not quite cricket, some would say, but in defending the imperial honor of England and cutting Bradman down to size proved stronger than the ethics of the sport. When it was put into practice, several Australian players were hit and one Woodruff suffered a head injury. Woodruff made a comment to Plum Warner, the English manager, when the latter went to the dressing room to commiserate with Woodruff, that is both memorable and significant: "I don't want to see you Mr. Warner. There are two teams out there. One is trying to play cricket and the other is not" (in Blofeld, 2002: 110–12).

The English team won the five match series 4 to 1, and Bradman had, in fact, been smothered. This issue became a matter of serious confrontation between England and Australia, and eventually, the rules were changed in order to minimize the risk of injury. Bodyline bowling as such vanished from the scene, after a brief display of imperial arrogance and ruthlessness, but aggressive bowling of bouncers remained a tactic that a fast bowler would often use to intimidate a good stroke-playing batsman. Douglas Jardine and his killer-bowlers Harold Larwood and Brian Voce may not have violated the rules of the game, but they did challenge its ethos and its conventions, and eventually, these conventions were made into rules that an umpire could enforce.

While all the players on a team were not expected to bat well, the few who were skilled batsmen going in early to bat were expected to make the runs. In their work at the crease, certain fundamental features of rational, calculated action, action that carries the stamp of what Max Weber called "inner-worldly asceticism" are manifested (1958a). Every ball that is delivered to the player must be judged as it comes toward him or her and the appropriate stroke selected to deal with it. If it is a delivery that has a length and a placement that is difficult to hit, the batsman is expected to play a defensive block and protect his or her wicket from being hit. There is no rule that demands that he or she should take a swing at every ball and he or she cannot be ordered out if he or she misses. Indeed, he or she can keep on blocking and stay at the wicket without any penalty. The rhythm of batting is to block certain balls, with no score being made, hit the balls that are easy to hit, and all the time wait patiently for such a ball to come along. Patience and judgment as well as deferred gratification and calculated moves to defend his or her interests by protecting his or her wicket are the hallmarks of a good batsman.

Even though cricket emerged before the full development of Protestant culture, it incorporated the theses about investing prudently, deferring present gratification, and waiting patiently for the returns into its batting philosophy. Hanif Muhamad, a Pakistani batsman who held many records, would often bat for two days in a five-day match and was known for his "legendary patience." One of the greatest batsmen of all time, Donald Bradman, was known for his "ability to pick up the line and flight of the ball swiftly, to *assess* in a moment what shot to use and dispatch the ball to the desired part of the ground" (Hutchinson, 2002). Brian Lara, another record-making batsman from Jamaica, was adept in his timing and his ability to make a ball-by-ball assessment of what to hit, what to merely block, and what to leave alone.

With a repertory of strokes, intelligence, and character, the batsman generally dominates the game, driving the bowlers and fielders to distraction and amassing a large number of runs. The batsman may be at bay, encircled by determined adversaries, but most of them come out winners.

It is in the art and craft of batsmanship, too, that one finds what may be termed the *drama of cricket,* and the dramatic tension is between two protagonists. One of them is delivering balls to the other to get him or her out of the game. To meet the onslaught of the fielding team, the batsman has to treat every move with studied circumspection. The stroke to be played, the stance to be taken, the direction and placement of the ball after it is hit are all under the batsman's control. It is in this contact between batsman and bowler on the one hand and between him or her and the fielder on the other that the drama of the game resides. *Every delivery and the responses to it by the batsman and then the fielders are fraught with this drama of confrontation between a solitary agent and an array of adversaries.* Even if the batsman parries the ball with a defensive block, the quality of the ball that made him or her do this becomes an interesting detail. The length, the bounce, the spin, the direction of the break, on the one hand, and the manner in which it was dealt with by the batsman and fielders, on the other, are the stuff to which the player and the well-informed spectator pay attention. *The drama is in the details.* Not being fully informed of the subtleties of the game playing and not paying attention to the details may make the game boring.

In the theater, audiences are expected to pay attention to every word, gesture, and movement that characters make on the stage and use them to come to a conclusion about the meaning of the proceedings on stage. Every such move is drenched with significance. In cricket and baseball, the same is true. This is given fine expression by C. L. R. James:

> The total spectacle consists of and must consist of a series of individual isolated episodes, each in itself completely self-contained. Each has its beginning, the ball bowled; its middle, the stroke played; its end, runs, no runs, dismissal. Within the fluctuating interest of the rise or fall of the game as a whole, there is this unending series of events, each single one fraught with immense possibilities of expectation and realization. (1983: 193)

In every move in the game there is, then, the tension of anticipation and attention, and also soon, remembering, the realization of expectations fulfilled or thwarted, the self vindicated or thwarted. James concludes that such a "structurally perfect relation between event and design, episode and continuity, the battle and the campaign, the part and the whole is not found in lawn tennis or soccer but only in baseball and cricket. In baseball alone does the encounter between the two representative protagonists approach the definiteness of the individual series of episodes in cricket which constitutes the whole" (1983: 193).

Cricket as Carnival

Yet this drama proved a little too delicate for most people and the number of spectators began to dwindle in the fifties and the sixties. Five-day "test matches" proved too demanding of time and attention. These were also rather serious and even rather stodgy affairs, all the players clad in immaculate white flannels and white shirts and the regulation cricket sweaters and players' often trying to behave with a controlled politesse and emotional restraint.

It was under these circumstances that cricket, already a mimesis and miniaturization of social themes, attempted a further miniaturization—a temporal one. The playing time was reduced to one day and each team was allowed to bat for only 60 overs ("over"—a series of six bowls per bowler). At the end of sixty overs—even if the whole team had not been rendered out, the inning was finished and the other team took over and attempted to beat the score made by the first team. This changed a crucial aspect of the game: instead of guarding his or her wicket and seeking runs only when it was safe to do so, the batsmen were profligate and enthusiastic run-getters. No more cultivation of patience, deferred gratification, and rational calculation. Rather, there was a reckless adventurism, instant gratification, and emotional thrusts and parries. Spectator participation in the earlier forms of cricket were measured and disciplined with partisanship tempered by appreciation for the skills and style displayed by the adversaries. In the new cricket, active, emotionally driven, crudely partisan, and at times insulting involvement was encouraged. These radical changes in cricket were compounded by the costumes that the players wore. Instead of the staid and neutral cricketing whites, now each player wore colorful clothes with the logos of sponsoring commercial firms displayed prominently. Each team wore uniforms made in primary colors and with the logos they became in effect multicolored outfits: the players were dressed in motley garments, becoming, in fact, jesters and clowns. Instead of the scapegoat, in carnival cricket, we have the analogue: jesters, clowns, and pranksters as the focus of various emotional attitudes. The advertising logos on their clothes, in fact, make them "grotesque" in Mikhail Bakhtin's sense of term. He gives a nice summary of this: "The essential principle of grotesque realism is degradation, that is, the lowering of all that is high, spiritual, ideal, abstract" (1984: 19). The conduct of the players, too, was more activist and undisciplined, with frequent and unmerited appeals to umpires and at times even engaging in arguments with them. Next, there is the time limit to a day and a limited number of overs changing the strategies and tactics of the game re bowling, batting, follow-ons, and intermissions. Finally, the players often encouraged and participated in the expression of sectarian loyalties by the crowd—wild singing, drum beating, and flag waving, with occasional "pitch invasions" by fans to show appreciation of a player.

Emotional expressiveness, jesters and clowns, dancing and singing, ritual abuse and overt hostility and crude partisanship—the list was complete in the move to make cricket a carnival. Now the drama of the game was not in the subtleties with which the batsman and the bowler handled each other, not in the finer points and style of batsmanship but in the mere hitting and the running, allowing not only the quick piling up of runs but also the roaring approbation of an untutored crowd. It is not that such behavior by the crowd was not known in earlier years. Dominic Malcolm, in fact, has examined the historical record and describes many instances of crowd violence in the early years of cricket. He conceded, however, that such behavior began to decline when the game came into its own in the nineteenth century and politeness, decorum, and restraint became the rule rather than the exception (1999). That is to say, before the nineteenth century and the march of the "civilizing process," as Norbert Elias and Eric Dunning (1986) would call it, cricket had certain unruly elements. Nevertheless, with the one-day time limit and limited number of overs, cricket was more than the occasional rowdiness: it was a carnival. In the new game, the move was to hit the ball as frequently as possible with a certain sense of abandonment.

The new cricket was, in fact, gaming in a Rabelaisian manner. It was an ironic parody and a display of derision, muted and unconscious, toward the trappings of traditional cricket, its aristocratic provenance, its elitist ambience, and its sober and orderly habits and repressive emotionality. It marked the decline of the Protestant ethic and of the cultivation of deferred gratification and was, in fact, a manifestation of the new age of permissiveness and emotional free play and commercial excess. Still, the basic structure of the game remained stable: the one against many; in this case the many included an unruly mass of partisan spectators.

Baseball

There are many theories of the origins of baseball, many of them merely romantic legends created by one interested party or another. It is generally agreed, however, that its origins are in the English games of cricket and "rounders." In the latter game, the player stands in place and a soft rubber ball is thrown at him or her and once the ball is hit, he or she runs to various bases. If he or she misses and does not hit the ball after swinging at it three times, he or she is out. He or she can also fly out or he or she can be tagged out. This game was played in England and the English immigrants played it on the eastern seaboard of America. They, no doubt, played a version of cricket, too. Various features of both games were incorporated into the emerging baseball (Seymour, 1960). Once baseball began to take root, it gained a life of its own and devised new rules and conventions. Distances between bases were changed, and it has become the tight, geometrically coordinated, and challenging game it is today. As in other games mentioned here, it, too, is a game in which the axial point is a single player standing by himself or herself and facing a number of adversaries who want to undermine him or her in one way or another. A pitcher will throw trickily designed balls at the batter and if he or she manages to hit one, it must land in fair territory—and even then it may be caught or fielded and the player driven out of the game.

The theme of an individual struggling against difficult, if not impossible, odds is depicted with an unmatched poetic intensity in baseball. In this game, unlike cricket, the batter gets only a few chances to show his or her mettle: three strikes and the batter is out. The bat is round, making it difficult to direct the ball to a precise location, with the batter being caught out often. The distances between bases are short, with each base being guarded by a quick-moving fielder. There are other hazards: double and triple plays to be avoided, "spikes" to be evaded, and so on. In organized games today, from Little League games to major league ones, the manager of the team as well as various coaches watching each base give signals to the base runners to help them negotiate the bases better. These moves do make the role of the batter less of a lonely quest than it would be otherwise. Nevertheless, these helpers of the runners are aberrations in the purity of the entrepreneurial game, introduced after the game became commercialized.

Baseball is, in fact, a game in which the fielding team and its pitchers have the upper hand and the batter is the one at bay. The scores in baseball are very low compared with those of all other games. The umpire has a bigger role in this game than in all other games, too, because whether a ball crosses "home plate" and at the right height is not determined by any tactile signs but purely by the interpretation of the umpire. "It is a strike only when I call it a strike," an umpire is said to have observed, allowing both his role in the game and his hermeneutic powers to be collapsed into a single sentence. He or she, too, participates in hemming the batter in and keeping him or her at bay. The batter goes to the mound and faces the various adversaries who have their own guiles and skills with which to outwit him or her. Baseball, unlike cricket, is a pitcher's game: he or she controls the game and usually gets most players out of the game. The balls fly from the player's bat in unexpected directions, and he or she has no choice but to run to first base where the baseman there is waiting to tag him or her out, if he gets the ball in time. Time and space are nicely coordinated in baseball and to get to a base is to have mastered this simultaneity—to have measured space and time simultaneously.

The batter in baseball has to make quick moves and indeed has a series of restricted choices. Whether he or she swings at the ball or not, if the umpire decides that it has crossed the plate, he or she gets a strike and three such strikes and he or she is out. If he or she swings and misses the ball, even if it does not cross the plate, he or she gets a strike; if he or she hits the ball even if it is not long enough, he or she will have to run and will be rendered out by the first baseman and sometimes contribute to the outing of a teammate by a double play; and finally, if he or she hits the ball and it is a fly ball, he or she will be caught out. The only way for him or her to stay long at base is to swing and hit a foul ball, and after the first two hits, they will not be counted as strikes. For the baseball batter, there is no room for deferred gratification: it is hit now and run, if he or she can.

While this is true of all batters, a couple of cases illustrate the theme that baseball as a game represents the self at bay in a rather exaggerated way. Jackie Robinson was the first black player to play in major league baseball. Until the owner of the Brooklyn Dodgers invited him to play for the team, baseball had followed a segregated course. There was a white league and a black league and the twain never met. Branch Ricky, prompted by a combination of greed (the hope of attracting black spectators to the stadium) and Christian piety, signed Robinson to his team. Once this happened, there were the usual threats from racists outside the leagues and even from newspaper and radio commentators. The significant phenomenon for the argument here is that on the field itself, the adversarial team put into play the thesis that a batter is a self at bay and should be treated as such. To begin with, there was the taunting. It begins in the dugout and continues onto the field. Jules Tygiel quotes a sports writer, Roy Stockton: "Probably the greatest cruelty in the American sports picture is the abuse that is showered on the players from the rival dugout." He continues, "These exchanges held no topic sacred. Frequent targets included personal problems, appearance, ethnicity and race ... In the 1935 world series, according to umpire George Moriarty, the Chicago Cubs crucified Hank Greenberg because he was a Jew and taunted umpire Dolly Stark as a 'Christ Killer'" (1983: 182).

Robinson was to be submitted to a kind of treatment that "exceeded," writes Tygiel, "even baseball's broadly defined sense of propriety" (1983: 182). It was begun by the manager of the Phillies, Ben Chapman, an Alabama native—and his instructions to his players reveal not only his racism but also a particular definition of male character and its place in baseball. Here is Tygiel's description:

> Chapman ordered his players to challenge Robinson with a stream of racial taunts "to see if he can take it." From the moment the two clubs took the field for their first contest, the Phillies, led by Chapman unleashed a torrent of insults at the black athlete. "At no time in my life have I heard racial venom and dugout abuse to match the abuse that Ben sprayed on Robinson that night," Tygiel quotes Harold Parrot. (1983: 182)

The racial aspect of the attack on Greenberg and Robinson, however, was another dimension—no doubt a crueler one—of the ethos of the game. This ethos is to put an individual in a difficult situation and "see if he can take it." Indeed, Chapman defended his action along these lines: "We will treat Robinson the same way as we treat Hank Greenberg of the Pirates,

Clint Hartung of the Giants ... or any other man who is likely to step up to the plate to beat us ... There is not a man who has come to the big leagues since baseball has been played who has not been ridden" (in Tygiel, 1983: 183).

In Chapman's judgment, every player is challenged in this way, and clearly, it is a continuation of the basic theme of the game: the self at bay taunted and tormented by an array of adversaries. In addition to these taunts, Robinson was to face balls thrown to his head and body while fielding and guarding bases: runners would crash into him and use the spikes on their shoes to injure him. In one game, writes Tygiel, "the Cardinal's outfielder Joe Medwick spiked Robinson on the left foot leaving a bloody gash. Two days later, Robinson barely moved his leg in time to avoid Enos Slaughter's spikes, but on another occasion, Slaughter slashed Robinson on the left leg dropping the injured athlete to the ground" (1983: 202–03).

The availability of Greenberg, the "Jew," and Robinson, the "Negro," to the players and spectators of the period brought an added dimension to the need for a victim to be taunted and put at bay, on the one hand, and for Greenberg and Robinson and their respective supporters, on the other hand, to enact the theme of a hero encircled. Indeed, Greenberg was not merely ethnically a Jew in these dramas but a representative of the arch-enemy of Christian civilization: the "Christ killer" in person, standing there, alone, with bat in hand. Similarly, Robinson was the archetypical African American, threatening in his skills, speed, strength, and baseball acumen to the white American male; for his supporters, both when he was at bat and when he was in the field, he was the hero facing the ignorant armies of the night.

Eventually, Robinson was accepted fully in the major leagues and many other black players followed suit. He faced the racism of the society, as well as the ruthless competitiveness enshrined in the game itself, with both skill and aplomb to become one of the great players of the game—black or white. Tygiel, after describing many of Robinson's trials by ordeal, nevertheless, concludes that Robinson's story is a drama of "the rugged and righteous individual confronting the angry mob. It is a tale of courage and heroics and triumph. Epic in its proportions, the Robinson legend has persevered ... because the myth, which rarely deviates from reality, fits our national perceptions of fair play and social progress" (1983: 208).

It is a drama, a tale, a legend, and a myth all rolled into one for Tygiel. It is, however, ambiguous in its meaning as a myth: heroism and fair play and social progress combined with ruthlessness and possessive individualism that is the ethos of the game. Patriotic writers—Michael Novak, for instance, and Bartlett Giametti—have tended to stress the individualistic aspect of the game, its commitment to equality of opportunity, and its demand that it is performance that counts. The game, however, represents more than these sterling and stirring virtues. Baseball, it turns out, is also the quintessential game of American capitalism, the Protestant ethic in its ruthless aspect—the Protestant ethic and the spirit of ruthlessness. Never give a sucker an even break; make him or her pay his or her dues; make him or her work as hard as you can drive him or her; exploit all the chinks in his or her armor and see whether he or she can take it. And, if he or she cannot—well, you know, the fit survive.

Baseball, then, is an American myth, though not quite in the sense imagined by certain other scholars. It is a myth that is enacted, again and again, in every move made in the game. It is an enacted myth, a performance that demands close attention if one is to appreciate the geometrical precision of its moves and the drama that is allowed to unfold. To the unwary and untutored, it is a game full of lethargic moments interrupted with sudden bursts of energy. Far from this being true, each initial move of the game—the pitch to the batter—is a dramatic gesture with a precise narrative intention. If it is a pitch with "no outs" and no strikes or balls called yet, it has a different dramatic significance than the opposite of this—three balls and a two-strike pitch. Even that changes if there is a player on first base, or players on first base and second base, or if the bases are loaded. Again, the score, the innings of the game, the early innings or the ninth inning, become elements in defining the significance of just one pitch. Further, the rational and aesthetic qualities of the pitch itself—is it a fast ball, curve ball, an inside ball, outside ball, or a change-up—are subject to judgment and analysis by the true connoisseur. Every moment of the nine-inning game has great dramatic significance if the teams are evenly matched and adroitly managed.

Yet, it can be seen that the drama in baseball is achieved by baiting the batter and putting him or her in a corner. Once again, the pitcher has all the advantages and with the aid of the other fielders, he has the batter cornered. Nevertheless, the batter hits and moves to the base and, despite attempted interruptions, reaches it and is declared "safe." Once again, the myth of alien forces against which one has to contend and arrive at a safe place is enacted and this adds to the dramatic tension. The player does this again and again and, barring successful interruptions, reaches "home." Here again, he or she has at times to fight the guardian of the gates to the home with some force before he or she is declared safely "home." This systematic *contentiousness* defines the game, and in the confrontations with the nature of the pitch that is thrown to the player, the tactical moves that have to be made, and the struggle against the pitcher, sufficient drama is created. As in cricket, the drama is in the details.

Stickball

This is an exquisitely miniaturized version of baseball that used to be played on the streets of New York City. It illustrates the theme of an agent facing a hostile world in more complex ways even than baseball. The children of various neighborhoods, poor and without too many resources for summertime recreation, played this game. Reporting a study of a New York neighborhood in the thirties of the last century, Frederick Thrasher describes the scene so well that it deserves to be quoted at some length:

> The lack of attractive home life and of other effective wholesome leisure-time interests makes it inevitable that a very large proportion of the boy population from the earliest ages up, spends its time on the streets. The younger boys play on the side-walks and in the streets in their own blocks. This play takes place after school in the afternoon and, in many cases, until late at night; during vacation time, of course, it goes on all day long . . . Summer street play in this area is varied and active. The most popular street game, in spite of the difficulties and hazards of city traffic and interference by the police, is the universally played stickball.
>
> In Intervale, the large number of boys who by choice or necessity play in the streets creates a situation in which social interaction is intense, constant, and ubiquitous . . . It is, however, the real world of the boy and the young man and, as informal education, it probably represents the most powerful set of social and moral forces which function in the development of youthful behavior patterns and personalities in this district. It is the social complex within which delinquent activities flourish and within which the delinquent personality is largely developed. An analysis of this social world and the various factors which enter into it, therefore, is essential. (1934: 472-73)

Stickball is played with a stick, usually a broom handle and a hard rubber ball. It is played on a stretch of street between two and three city blocks or on empty paved school yards. The area is demarcated by the manhole covers of the underground sewage disposal system. The game has many of the rules of baseball and others are improvised as the situation demands. There are many versions of the game, two of which are *fungo*, where the hitter drops the ball on the ground and hits it on the first bounce to be fielded by the others; and the "purest" form of stickball, in which a pitcher throws the ball toward the hitter on one bounce and the hitter is expected to swing at it. And significantly, if the hitter doesn't swing, especially at a good pitch, he is ridiculed by both his adversaries and his teammates.

These games, played by more or less randomly selected teams, are indeed "pickup" games. They bring a sense of adventure—the players having to deal not only with the gaming adversaries, but also streetcars, pedestrians, police officers, and automobiles. Essentially, however, the game is that of a child with a difficult life, struggling against adverse circumstances and seeking to hold his or her own, risking his or her self in a circle of friends and acquaintances who have temporarily become adversaries.

In a remarkable study of play in the city, Amanda Dargan and Steven Zeitline say, "Play is one of the ways we develop a sense of neighborhood in a large city. Play is one of the ways a city street becomes 'our block'" (1990: 10). Stickball allows the children of the street to domesticate the place where they play. The street, an alien and usually a foreboding space filled with various hazards, is taken on, challenged, and converted into an arena where their selves are put into play. The dangers and challenges of the streets are not evaded or ignored: rather, they are incorporated into the very structure of the game. The manhole covers become not only markers of the territory of the game but the territory of the self, an extension of home, a familiar and manageable place.

The players make the space of their play their own, but for all that, such a place also marks the deprivation and oppression to which they were subject. They had to play on the street, in "sewers," and face hazards of various kinds only because they were not provided with the facilities for play in schools, parks, and recreation centers. The games of the street were simultaneously a measure of their alienation and their attempts to overcome it. The selves of the players of stickball are at bay, encircled and engulfed not only by the game itself but also by the society in which they lived. The social game is represented in the street game with great fidelity.

Martin Gold (1976) claims that delinquent activities by young boys in urban scenes are continuations of the pickup games of basketball and stickball. The children, driven to the streets for their play, become members of teams with which they play stickball. A hitter goes out to hit the ball and in certain circumstances he or she is derided by his or her adversaries as well as by his teammates. In addition, he or she as well as the other players are playing against the street hazards and the police. The delinquent activities that occur also become a manifestation of the main theme: me against the others, us against the hazards that have become routinized. A pickup game of stickball with a hitter standing against the world of adversaries, a pickup game of petty thievery and violent attacks on another gang—all are woven together by a self at bay and meeting its demands in one way or another.

In the stick games, cricket, baseball, and stickball, it will be seen that an individual agent is made to face a variety of others and answer their moves and seek to overcome their maneuvers and strategies. These moves are designed to construct and sustain the integrity of the self, on the one hand, and give it a feeling of autonomy: I aim to do this and I can resist the antagonistic moves of others. Conversely, as the players go onto the field to face their adversaries, they are also putting their selves on an altar and facing the risk of humiliation. Autonomy of the self and its integrity and the possibility of victimage are nicely blended in these hit-and-run games.

Soccer and American Football: The Structures of Cooperation and Conflict

In a brilliant analysis of soccer, Norbert Elias and Eric Dunning argue that the essential features of the playing of soccer demonstrate the shortcomings of various approaches to the study of groups. These studies, they aver, do not take into account the dynamic configurations that groups display. If one observes soccer as it is being played, one can see the constantly changing configurations, the same as those that occur in actual groups of all kinds. They write:

> The initial configuration from which the players start changes into other configurations of players in a continuous movement. It is to this continuous movement of players to which we refer when we use the term "game-pattern" ... One observes small groups of living human beings changing their relations in constant interdependence with each other ... This moving and regrouping of interdependent players in response to each is the game. (1966: 389; 390)

Later in the same article, they extend this analysis of soccer to develop certain themes of a "configurational sociology." They assert, discussing the tensions that these configured relationships create, that "one can neither understand nor explain its character from the 'interaction' of the individual players" (1966: 397). Yet it seems to me that these configurations are started by acts and interactions and continue as a series of interactions.

In American sociology, an approach that calls itself "network analysis" has argued a case that is similar to the one advanced by Elias and Dunning here and elsewhere. One of its recent theorists, Stephen Fuchs, has observed, very succinctly, and in a prophetic mode: "In the beginning, there were networks. Networks are fields of forces. They do not consist of nodes. Nodes are outcome of networks. Nodes without relationships are nodes without qualities" (2001: 337).

Describing the basic principles of network analysis, Barry Wellman observes that as a result of the network theorists' dislike for "psychology," they dismiss as nonstructural any explanation that treats "social processes as the sum of individual actors' personal attributes and internalized norms ... Since they are concerned with individual motives for action, they are ultimately psychological and not sociological" (1983: 162).

Compare these views of the configurationists and networkers with Maurice Merleau-Ponty's description of an individual in action in the phenomenal world—and, fortunately for me, he uses soccer as his exemplar:

> For the player in action, the football field is not an "object" that is, the ideal term which can give rise to an indefinite multiplicity of perceptual

> views and remain equivalent under its apparent transformations. It is pervaded with lines of force (the "yard lines"; those which demarcate "penalty areas") and articulated within sectors (for example, the opening between adversaries) which calls for certain modes of action as if the players were unaware of it.
>
> The field itself is not given to him or her, but present as the immanent term of his practical intention; the player becomes one with it and feels the direction of the "goal," for example, just as immediately as the vertical and horizontal plane of his body ... Each maneuver undertaken by the player modifies the character of the field and establishes in it new lines of force where the action in turn unfolds and is accomplished, again altering the phenomenal field. (1959: 168-69)

These observations are no doubt true. Nevertheless, it is also the case that a player passes the ball to another player and he or she in turn passes it to another "in the opening between the adversaries" in order to establish an interaction and a network of relations that leads to the scoring of a goal—the objective of the game. Merleau-Ponty does not seem to think that this is of any importance. He is interested only in the "consciousness" of the player, which is "nothing other than the dialectic of milieu and action" (1959: 169).

This kind of analysis of action sequences, exemplified by Merleau-Ponty's observations, is frightened of the individual agent's being contaminated by the intrusion of an other into his or her consciousness or even admitting that the dialectic of action can be influenced by the force of the other. It is fundamentally a Calvinist theory of the relationship between self and other. The configurationists and networkers, in turn, are terrified of being haunted by the ghost of Emile Durkheim. What Fuchs calls "nodes" and what Wellman calls "individual motives for action" are no doubt dependent on structures of social relations. *Nevertheless, these nodes in a network are imbued with qualities of self-consciousness and identity, and their actions are based on both their social motives and their awareness of their respective places in a network of interactive relations.* Networks are emergent structures, consequences of knowledgeable and thought-centric human agency, while human acts are interdependent with social structures. Only theories that cannot handle *simultaneity* will insist on giving priority to networks over nodes or nodes over networks. They are simultaneous occurrences except that, as a *practical* matter, only agents can act, while "network" is a *theoretical* conceptualization for the agent. He or she has to *conceive* it and indeed conceives it in variable valences: some conceive their relevant networks with a small compass and others in much larger systems.

Long before sociology emerged, this theme had been beautifully embodied in football in all its variants. They are able to both incorporate the phenomenology of action and the embeddedness of such action in networks of relationships very nicely. Further, field games condense into their form the imperatives of human social organization—cooperation and conflict—without giving priority to either. In such games, with two teams of agents arrayed against each other, the game begins with an agent from the attacking team passing the ball to another member of the team as the other team seeks to take the ball away from the initial player. The entire game is then a series of passes, attempted interceptions, and successful ones, with fouls of various kinds and out-of-bounds moves, constituting interruptions that stop the game, which is resumed only after suitable penalties. Different from two-person games like chess or tennis or two-member team games like bridge or doubles tennis, in football, in all its variants, a player addresses the ball to a teammate and he or she may then address it to another teammate while the adversarial players try to interrupt this address and start a dialogue of their own. The structure that emerges out of these moves in field games of this sort can be described as a dynamic network of cooperation and conflict. As these relationships develop, they create the emergent reality of a coordinated series of moves that are organically related to each other so long as they are not interrupted by fouls, leading the team toward a single goal. This emergent reality of coordinated moves is further enhanced by the emergent emotionality of the network of actors. Working together they generate a shared and assertive excitement and energetics that become stronger as the prospect of reaching the goal increases.

Positions and Agents

In football—American and association—as in all field games, a structure of positions is established as the game begins. At this stage, the network of positions is a static and lifeless mathematical model indicating how players are tied to each other. In field games, every player has a position in a pattern of relationships to the other players—positions that have exactly reciprocal ones on the other side of the field, too. Once this static network is assembled, an agent *addresses* an object to another and the network becomes a set of dynamic actors interacting complexly with each other. In fact, every move in the game is a pass to another player except the final one in the end zone. Every move is, in other words, an answerable address made to another, moves that actively construct a moving network that is constantly changing its configurations. The players, in fact, engage in a chain of interactional relationships in which they address the ball to another who in turn addresses it to another while an antagonist tries to interrupt the address and initiate his or her own dialogic series. In these braids of dyadic relationships, often accompanied by interruptions, it is the individual's initial interactional moves that create the dialogue and the emergence of the network of relationships. *In the beginning is the dialogue,* constituted out of addresses and answers and networks emerge only after the dialogue has been initiated.

This moving network always creates its dialogue within itself in constant awareness of the active presence of another network of relationships that is only waiting to enter into an *adversarial dialogue.* Every move that the agent in the soccer field makes, then, is in terms of a dual awareness: a friendly partner and an adversary who will try to interrupt the dialogue. While the passes are between two players, the rest of the players on both sides move and act in terms of these passes with their collective eye on the ball. These games incorporate the processes of cooperation and conflict achieved by and through the dialogic agency of individual actors emerging into coordinated teams of actors. The player passes the ball (the first move in the game is the pass), which initiates a dialogue and constructs a network of relationships and challenges in one seamless system. Every player creates a new configuration, a newly emergent form of life, with his or her moves as he or she activates the network of relationships. In the beginning is the acting agent, and until he or she acts, neither a dialogue nor a network is real. It is, of course, the case that the actor as such has a history, and is endowed with a memory, in which is inscribed a version of his or her identity that will include a conceptualization of his or her position in a network of relations. This is a far cry from reifying networks as concrete and autochthonous entities with a life of their own. *Networks, with varying ranges, are strategies that a player uses, with varying degrees of power and volition, to get on with his or her game.* These networks and the identities that are embedded in them are, after all, transient ones that can be deconstructed, with new networks and alternate identities constructed readily.

This form of life is the true exemplar of the phenomenon that G. H. Mead and George Simmel among others discussed in terms of the emergence of new forms out of the combination of more primitive ones. In Mead's words, "When things get together, there then arises something that was not there before, and that character is something that cannot be stated in terms of the elements which go to make up the combination" (1938: 641). This view of the emergence of new forms of life rejects the mechanical view of groups as static positions with units within them and accepts a teleological view of the kaleidoscopic nature of groups as members interact with each other and systematically negotiate an interactional order between them.

The Plays and Narratives of the Self in Soccer

Soccer has eleven players, but only one of them is allowed to touch the ball with his or her hands, and that, too, only in a demarcated territory near his or her goal. The other players are expected to move the ball with their feet, abdomen, shoulders, and heads toward the enemy's side and put the ball between two goalposts. Clearly, actions here not only "imply" goals but are oriented toward them. These actions have to occur within a clearly and precisely marked territory. There is, to begin with, the outer periphery, a rectangle. Any time the ball moves outside this territory, play is halted and a new beginning made with a "throw-in" within this rectangle. There are two other units, one before each goal post marked as the "penalty" area. This piece of territory is a place of particular danger to the side that owns it because any infractions of the rules within it will be punished by the enemy being given a "penalty kick" (that is, one without challenge by the enemy player, except for the goalkeeper). This usually results in a score.

The interactions between agents are controlled by rather precise rules. An agent can challenge the other if he or she is in possession of the ball and can try to dispossess him or her of it, but this can be done with only minimum physical contact, no rough or violent moves, no "tackling," no moves from behind the player, no use of elbows against the other, no tugging of the other's clothes, and no "head butting." In fact, it is an interaction order. If any one of these rules is violated, a "foul" is called by the referee and a "free kick" is given to the aggrieved party. If the fouling has been repetitive or dangerous or willfully violent, the player is given a warning (yellow card) or exiled from the game (red card). The fundamental tension necessary for the game, its essential antagonisms, is to be found in the interaction between an agent and his or her adversary in a face-to-face encounter: each player should indeed confront the other and seek to outwit the other, but such a move must be undertaken within the precise set of rules that have been prescribed. To violate unwittingly or willfully will elicit a penalty that will cause the player to lose face, and the team to lose face and the game.

Soccer, then, is defined by very precise rules that are put into operation within a demarcated territory by well-defined agents. The actions that each play sets in motion have, however, a design to them. To begin with, they are individuated actions: each player moves the ball according to his own will, judgment, emotionality, aim, skill and dexterity, specialization, sense of honor and decorum and commitment. He or she can dribble, dodge, cut, fake, tap, and kick the ball to the best of his or her ability while he or she controls the ball. He or she does this in order to evade and thwart the enemy player and the enemy team, to generally outwit them by any and all means that are sanctioned by the rules. Secondly, he or she has to be cognizant of the fact that as a member of a team he or she and the team can save face only if he or she develops his or her own plays and then passes the ball to a teammate. In other words, his or her moves are an *integral* part of a larger structure of moves: *He or she received the ball from someone else, after the other had put his or her own individual skills into the play, and passed the ball to him or her, and it is his or her duty to do the same.* In this way, a chain of interdependence is constituted and the team—or the offensive line of the team—moves forward jointly to fulfill a common purpose. "For this moving and re-grouping of interdependent plays in response to each other *is* the game," observe Norbert Elias and Eric Dunning (1966: 390). These moves, articulated within such an interdependent structure, manifest both the narrative intention of the self as well as that of the team.

The ball is an instrument for the communication of this narrative intention. It is wonderfully flexible: it moves readily and unambiguously from player to player and changes its value in relation to the space in which it finds itself. It is an instrument that is more or less continuously in motion and its value changes as its placement changes. Nearer the center of the field, it can be handled in a rough and ready way, but near the goalmouth, in the penalty area, it has to be handled differently: too much roughness against another player in this area will result in a costly penalty, just as too indelicate a handling of the ball—should I say, footing?—would make scoring a goal more difficult. Further, the instrumental value of the ball changes if the ball goes out of the playing arena: depending on who touched the ball last, it becomes the unchallenged instrument of the side that has the right to use it. Similarly, after a "foul" has been declared, the befouled side gets a "free kick" and the instrumental value of the ball changes.

In contrast to tennis or chess, soccer and similar field games stress the interdependence of selves and the significance of coordinated labor, divided in terms of specializations of functions. Before the selves are in conflict with the others, they are engaged in cooperative construction of each other, passing supportive moves and seeking successful integration. It is into this narrative of the self that an agent casts himself or herself, where every move is intended to be a gift for the team as it is for the receiving agent. Every move he or she makes is at once an agentic one as well as a contribution to the organization's orientations. *It is a move that is simultaneously centered on the self, on a cooperative other and on an antagonistic one.* The ball becomes the token with which these processes are recreated. Yet the cooperation with the fellow member of the team is not of the pure kind. In undertaking the passing of the ball to the team member, the player has to consider whether he or she should use the chance to play for his or her own glory or to play for the welfare of the team. In other words, there is not only conflict with the adversarial team but also competition within the group. The Meadian problematic of the relationship between the "I" and the "Me" is beautifully rendered in these field games: I should assert myself and the me would be constituted by eliciting the attitude of the other. This theme—how to use one's individual talent to advance one's own interest while considering the impact of the gesture toward the others or the general welfare—is a perennial one in the narrative of the self.

With the ball as the instrument, various actions are undertaken by an agent, actions that are directed at a "friend" or an "enemy." Each of these agents has a "character" to them: goalkeeper, defensive back (right), defensive back (left), striker, forward, and so on. Here, too, there are enemies and friends, our side and their side, and there are interactions among friends and between friends and enemies.

In this way a dynamic organization is created by the interdependent acts of the various players, with each player putting his or her self into play while simultaneously cooperating with the other. One can see an element of cooperation even in the relationship with the opposing team, since one cannot have a game without the disciplined participation of both teams. *Indeed, it is not so much an instinct of competition or an imperative to excel or win that seems to animate the playing of these games, but a desire to cooperate and interact with each other and to compete with adversaries on the basis of strict rules—rules of contact and rules of territoriality.* All the moves that an agent can make in soccer are not only constrained by the rules of contact—how he or she should relate to other players and the ball—and by rules of territory. Also, the territory on which the game is played has been converted into a place for the self, for the time being, and its every action must be undertaken in full cognizance of the marked and defined spaces. The self in these games must be managed by the rules of contact and kept within certain boundaries.

The agent operates within these constraints and constructs simultaneously a narrative for his or her own self and for the team. The center of the advance line passes the ball and it is received by a player on his or her left who passes it to another on the far left, who has run forward. He or she successfully evades a challenge from an adversary and passes the ball to a player all the way on the right who has also moved forward. He or she then evades yet another adversary and passes to the player on his or her left who advances toward the goal, evades further adversaries, and puts the ball between the goalposts. Each move in this series is a narrative moment: the self of the player who started the series, even though he or she is not involved in the later moves, as well as the respective selves of all the players become involved with the progress of the ball, with the eventual outcome giving them a boost of esteem. Conversely, the ball could have been successfully wrested from the players in question and the opposite result could have emerged: a goal may be scored against the protagonist's side with consequent loss of esteem for the agents. No matter; there is still time to struggle to remedy the situation.

Such eventualities for the self are possible not only because a structure of intricate activity has been made available for each player, but because there is a narrative other against which the players, as agents and as a team of agents, can struggle. In order for this struggle to have any significance for the narratives of the self of the player, the narrative other must have certain qualities. It must, to begin with, be a team that is strong enough to be a match for the other by providing the necessary degree of resistance. It must be a contender. Secondly, it must also be able to evoke emotional resonances: a rival club; traditional rivals; a nation's, city's, or region's adversaries.

The Plays and Narratives of the Self in Football (American)

Michael Oriard, in a comprehensive analysis of the emergence of American football, stresses its role as a narrative created by various officials and arbiters and cognoscenti on the one hand and, more crucially, newspapers and magazines on the other. "That the popular press was primary, the game itself secondary, in football's extraordinary rapid emergence as a popular spectacle and cultural force is one of the inescapable conclusions of my inquiry" (1993: XXI), he observes. For Oriard, football as such is a narrative constructed by writers of various kinds and the administrators and executives who controlled various institutions and made and changed the rules. One can, however, examine football as an effective structure in which active agents cast their selves to achieve narrative presence and imaginative efficacy. The narratives that football is able to sustain with its structures and processes, enabling various agents to use them for their purposes, are rich and varied.

Among all the games reviewed so far, American football is the one with the greatest restrictions to free agency. From its beginnings in rugby football into its modern metamorphosis, it has systematically restricted the opportunities for an agent to act on his own initiative and brought players under a tight discipline of plays and moves formulated ahead of the actual execution by coaches, tacticians, and motivators. The players on the field are like performers reading a musical score and following its specifications as minutely as possible. Nevertheless, in amateur games where this control by outsiders to the play is not that rigid, and in professional games, too, it is not possible to deny sufficient agency to a player.

The game is played by two opposing teams of eleven players given various positions on the field. Unlike other field games, the teams are given an offensive role and a defensive one alternately with different players taking on these roles. The game begins with a kickoff of the ball by one team, and after it is caught by the opposing team, the kickoff team and receiving team change personnel. New members of the team—the attacking specialists and the defending specialists—come in, and the play proceeds. The quarterback is in charge of the attack and his team goes into a "huddle" before each move and gets directions about what each player should do in the ensuing attack. It returns to the point of scrimmage, and the quarterback executes the determined moves just as the defending side tries to stop him and his associates. If the ball is successfully passed and caught, the receiver runs with it to the goal line of his adversaries until he is intercepted by one or more of the adversaries. The object of each such move is to go at least ten yards in four moves. If the team succeeds in doing this, it does it again and again until it reaches the goal line of the adversaries and scores a touchdown. If it doesn't move the ball the requisite ten yards, the team surrenders the ball to the other side by punting it, and the whole process is repeated by the other side. If one side scores a touchdown, the ball is then kicked from a specified distance between two upright goalposts above the crossbar and the team ends up with seven points. The winning team then kicks the ball back to the other team and it begins the ten-yard pilgrimage—unless one receiver is able to catch the ball and run all the way to the touchline.

The frequent interruptions of the onward flow of the game, the huddles, the time-outs, the consultation with coaches on the sidelines and the systematization and written and diagrammed structures of the moves in the play effectively retard the spontaneity and easy fluency of a game like soccer. Football is a more rationalized and calculated narrative and the consequence of a more rationally constituted self. Indeed, American football has been *as rationalized* as the other institutions and practices of Western civilization. Max Weber, while applying this thesis to society, economy, and politics also claimed that even the harmonic musical system that came into prominence after the Reformation was also based on "rational foundations." Football, too, has been subject to the same process: it has been rationalized in precisely the same way. Martindale gives an admirable summary of Weber's thesis re music:

> Musical sensitivity has been highly developed by other people. Polyphonic music is widely diffused over the earth. But the rational tone intervals, while calculated and known elsewhere, do not appear outside the West in systems of rational harmonious music in the form of the counterpoint and harmony with the formation of tone material on the basis of these triads with the harmonic third. Also, peculiar to the West are chromatics and harmonics interpreted in terms of harmony, the orchestra built around the string quartet, the systems of notation and a music possible only with print. (1964: 383-84)

Football in America followed a similar development. To follow the above listing backward—football came to depend more and more on systems of notations and diagrams that the players read and executed in the field. The rules of the games are printed and widely distributed, each rule is explained by the referee on the public address system as soon as it is violated and the play is brought to a stop. Thus, the spectators are invited to participate in the rational basis of each move in the game. These moves are executed by an orchestrated team with a few selected—"the quartet"—as the pivot around which the rest moves. The elements of the game are subject to precise mathematical calculations: the field is divided into regular intervals, the yardage of each move in the game is measured to inches, and various moves in a game are subject to precise time constraints. The division into offensive activity and defensive activity as alternate functions—rather than leaving them mixed up as in other field games—again speaks to calculated rationalization of function: each player is a *specialist* with a commitment to a *career* as a quarterback or a defensive end or a punter, and so on. If the particular specialization is not required at the moment of play, the players sit it out until they are called upon to do this duty.

While many of these features can be seen in most modern sporting forms, in American football they have reached a very special fruition. In spite of the rationalized constraints under which football is played by its practitioners, it still yields opportunities for agency and effective investment of self. Each player may have been programmed to stand in a particular place and move in a specified trajectory, but once the ball is in motion, he has to make quick judgments and instantaneous interpretations and execute strategic moves—agentic actions that enable him to participate emotionally and cognitively in a nicely orchestrated performance and give play to his self. Here is a description by Andrew Malcolm in his role as a quarterback:

> I surveyed (the scene) again. They were crowded up again, even more certain of the line plunge this time. The ball slammed up into my hands. I whirled and obviously handed off to the fullback, who was so convinced that I was handing it to him that he went to hold on. I pulled back, hid it against my hip, while I faced away from the action and the entire defense swarmed onto the fullback. One count, two counts. Casually, I looked back. And then more seriously, beyond. There was one target loping across the field, unhindered, looking at me—I lobbed the ball towards our end. He caught it. The surprised safety arrived a second later. The end carried for another six yards. First down. (1992: 145)

In a fine-grained prose, Malcolm is describing a fake move that distracted the defense and enabled Malcolm to execute a successful action that gave his team enough yardage to move the ball forward and keep "possession"—that is, the right to make the next move toward the touchline. Quarterbacks have greater freedom for agentic moves than the other players. There is no doubt that, rationalized constraints notwithstanding, they, too, can experience measures of control and creativity in their performances. A receiver has to face the oncoming defenders, duck, slide, run, feint, twist, turn as he seeks to elude them and move forward. Bureaucracy, yes; but performative agency, too.

American football gives a varied and intricately structured opportunity for narrating a self. It is played by agents who are embedded in a network of complex relationships in which they are enabled to negotiate an international order. The game proceeds in starts, spurts and stops, and restarts and, indeed, is rather a leisurely game. What football loses in narrative fluency and momentum, it gains in narrative complexity. At any moment in the game, every player is attentive to the ball as well as to other protagonists on the field, and each move that he will make is in terms of these factors. One is even allowed to tackle a player, anticipating that he may interfere later with the passage of the player with the ball. Each player on the team has a very particularized character to play and the success of the team depends on his executing it well. Such a variability of characterization gives the game its narrative complexity. The receiver has to be an "eligible" one; the quarterback can be sacked by defensive players, the ball is kicked by a specialist, and so forth. Further, once moves have been made in the first instance and "yardage" obtained, there is a pause for reflection and analysis and the devising of new moves in the huddle—at least more of the latter than the former.

Malcolm gives a description of moves from another game that can be taken as an exemplar of this process. It is a description of a return of a kickoff that led to a touchdown as well as the narration of the self while this was happening:

> The kick-off sailed high and deep into our territory. Oh my God! We would have a chance to run it back. Fast and far ... Oh my God, the ball was coming towards me, drifting end over end down and down. Oh my God, redemption was at hand ...
>
> I locked the ball into my arms ... My blockers up front were already moving to our right. So, reading our players were the defenders.
> I went to the left. (1992)

Malcolm here rejects the play that was dictated by the coach and accepted in the huddle and makes a move on his own, choosing what he thought was the better strategy. This confused his blockers, but more importantly, the adversaries, too, because they were watching the blockers. He continues:

> My blockers, unable to see me, continued to set up a return lane down the right sideline. At about the thirty-yard line, I veered right again behind the protective wing of the blockers, who thought I had been there all along. The earnest eagerness of the defenders had caused many of them to run themselves out of the play ... From despair I had shot up to determination, all in seconds. It felt good to have the initiative. I don't remember ever running faster in my life. I was not thinking of scoring a touch-down. I was thinking of my next step and the next one and the one after that.

> I was near the sideline now. I ran in silence, looking left ... There was but one defender to destroy. I veered slightly toward him, then ducked away without touching ... The last forty yards was wide open. But I poured it on anyway as fast as my short legs would go. In the end zone, I gently set the ball down; act like you've been there before, boys. (1992: 150–51)

This is, of course, a recollection of an event, but there is no need to discount the essential accuracy of the narrative intent. The player has fumbled an earlier move and was rather despondent about it and finds and takes on an opportunity to redeem himself. He makes various choices and creates a number of maneuvers, made on the spot by decisions made instantaneously, but in all these doings, he is narrating a self into being and giving it a thrust and a force. Once this narrative is complete, he is "surrounded by ecstatic teammates and fans. With defeat in sight, we had tied the game" (1992: 151).

This approval by the teammates is the denouement of this phase of the narrative of Malcolm's self. It is now not only redeemed and given a new identity—the one who by grit and determination and sound judgment and athleticism saved the side—but has also created the narrative of a player who has struggled against the odds and produced a heroic gesture. One can also see the narrative of loyalty and commitment to the team, of dedication and commitment in the face of failure.

But, sadly for Malcolm, his heroic play was deemed invalid because a linesman, unbeknown to Malcolm, had committed a foul and the ball had to be brought back to the line of scrimmage. In the end, Malcolm's team lost, providing opportunities to cast the self into the narrative of how to take a loss and how to treat the errant linesman (1992: 152).

One can get a clear picture of the multiple narratives that a self can undertake and experience in football by examining the discourse that was produced by a coach and players in a high school in New Jersey. A team of cinematographers followed the coach and recorded his interactions with members of the team and a brief one with his wife. In addition, there was one interview with two players. The coach, by using a variety of rhetorical strategies, attempts to create a structure of cooperating agents while at the same time constructing a narrative other with whom the players could struggle for supremacy.

The coach begins his discourse by creating a narrative other and eliciting commitment from his players: *Can you accept a loss to Bosco? To Passaic?*

Bosco High School is the traditional rival for the Bergen County Catholic High School whose football team was called "The Crusaders," and the coach brings it up. He mentions the other rivals, too, because the goal is to win the state championship. But Bosco High School remains a special adversary: "Nothing matters unless we beat Bosco," says the coach.

Coach: Are you doing your best? How come the team is not practicing at its best?

Player: We are just losing focus and intensity in practice ... the heat ...

Coach: Why do we lose focus? Either you want to be champions or not ... It is not a sometime thing. It is an everyday thing. It doesn't matter what the temperature is. You got to practice to the best of your ability everyday. I realize the difficulties of the challenge. No Bergen County Catholic team has ever started number one or finished number one. It has never been done before. (*The Crusaders,* 2002)

The game as conceived by the coach and his associates is a narrative of hard and committed work in which one prepares to face a difficult, if not impossible, challenge and overcome it. The commitment and dedication are defined and elicited in terms of a combat with an other: us against them, heroes against the villains, the crusaders against...

On the day of the match against Bosco High School, the coach reiterates some of the same themes: "To function in this environment, you need discipline and determination ... We have worked hard for three years for this opportunity." He then asks them to join in a "chant": "I will give my word that I will give everything I have for forty-eight minutes, so help me God." This followed by a collective prayer, invoking God's "Kingdom" and his "Power."

It is the team that is systematically featured in the conversations, and the pledge and the prayers are repeated in unison by the players. It is in this collective enterprise that each agent is expected to cast his self and move both individually and in tune with others, individually taking his role and that of his own team and that of his adversaries, and participate in a narrative that is both collective and individual.

The team comes out ahead in the first half, but gets clobbered in the end to an ignominious defeat—47 to 16.

This sets the scene for another narrative self to be enacted: How does one face defeat and handle the sorrow and the dejection? The coach talks to his staff: do they have what it takes to bounce back from such a devastating defeat and disappointment? Do they have the will to overcome adversity and take on a bigger challenge of fighting their way back at the next opportunity?

The coach then addresses the team: "I am not going to say too much. You just watch the film ... At one point in the game, we just quit. I haven't seen Bergen County Catholic give 34 points in one quarter."

A hint of humiliation and a serious charge: the players "quit" trying, gave up the struggle, withdrew their commitment and dedication to the goal. This is a serious charge in American society, given its commitment to the work ethic and all that. Quitters, retreatists, ritualists get no respect here. Advancing ambitiously toward a goal, even against bad odds and adverse conditions, is the recommended agentic process.

The coach speaks again to the assembled team:

Coach: We have to reestablish our desire to fulfill the mission. What is the mission?

Team: The state championship.

Coach: What is the mission?

Team: The state championship.

Coach: That's correct. Has anything happened to prevent us from winning a state championship?

Team: None.

Coach: What is the only thing that will prevent us from winning the state championship?

Team: Us.

Coach: You have met the enemy. It is you. It is us. (*The Crusaders,* 2002)

The coach very adroitly gets the collective participation of the team by establishing a chantlike interaction with a question and an answer that is repeated. He also has a way with pronouns—using them to both separate the role of the team in overcoming adversity—"It is you" and then acknowledging his own role in it. "It is us." The entire conversation enables the players toward an interpretation and an analysis of self and invitation to take individual and collective responsibility and not blame anyone else by giving excuses.

Once he or she has cast himself or herself into the narrative of the game, the player is able to enact the dynamics of action: he or she is able to perform both a singular agency as well as an interdependent one and thrust forward to a *telos*. The player is able to narrate commitment and loyalty to the team as well as to the self by working hard and struggling against both the resistance of the others and the environment as well as the other team's, at times, better performance; through hard work, self-commitment, facing tribulations and setbacks and betrayals and calumnies of adversaries, one fights on, keeps struggling until the end has been reached. Finally, the participation in these extremely physical and violent confrontations with each other, the wallowing in the mud or the snow, the willing exposure to pain and injury, the management of emotions with control and a stoic acceptance are all elements of what Max Weber called the "Protestant ethic." Players had to be "sober, conscientious and unusually industrious workmen who clung to their work as to a life purpose willed by God" (Weber, 1958a: 117). If one was "called" to be a football player, to be a quarterback or a linebacker, then one fulfills its demands with purpose and dedication. The combination of the Protestant ethic—adopted by Protestants as well as by others in time—and the narrative of a form of manliness and a philosophy of action and engagement of self in moves that enabled expressive agency was potent brew and captivated the country.

Football became a structure of ideas and activity—an enacted myth—that parsimoniously encapsulated several themes in neat formulations that enabled both players and spectators to engross themselves in them. Cooperation and conflict, agency and networks, autonomy and interdependence were simultaneously put into play with great structural precision and dialectical clarity.

In American football, the narrative of the self that is constructed is a self and an agent engaged in rational calculation and systematic orientation to a goal. Every move is planned—indeed diagrammed—and a geometric precision for the configurations in the field is sought. The rules demand a precision of conduct in every move and, indeed, a "golden mean" is the recommended place to be in every move: a delicate balance between "necessary roughness" and "unnecessary roughness" in tackling an adversary has to be maintained just as between proper attempts to retrieve the ball from an adversary and "pass interference." This idealization of exactitude is by the manner in which labor is allocated to different members of the team: in addition to the division between attacking segments and defending segments, there are distinctions between "eligible receivers" and "ineligible receivers" in a game in which giving the ball to another is the central move. The self that is narrated by the respective players is a self that is trapped in an iron cage.

4

The Morality of Games

Human agents live their lives and construct their selves and manage their relationships on the basis of one system of morality or another, expressed as rules and regulations derived from sources outside the acting individual and validated by others. Many of these are derived from religion, while others may be derived from secular sources. There is, however, no gainsaying the claim that human actions are based on ethical/moral principles that human agents learn from other members of a group—however misguided some of them may appear to be—and not on uncontrollable biological imperatives, the claims of certain academic propagandists notwithstanding.

These moral and ethical principles are enshrined very systematically in the individual's consciousness in one way or another, so deeply that he or she can be said to have a moral self and conduct himself or herself as a moral agent—though the morality and ethics may vary. And, one can ask, to begin with, how does an agent become a moral agent? And why does an agent follow ethical rules and regulations without *active and systematic enforcement* by others? Every major sociologist has grappled with these questions, not to speak of philosophers, and has given varied answers. For my purposes here, I will use the answers given by G. H. Mead and Pierre Bourdieu.

Self and *Habitus*

The answers given by G. H. Mead and Pierre Bourdieu—several decades apart in timing and founded on different assumptions—can be taken as fairly convincing. The observance of such rules is obviously the basis of social as well as interaction order and the order of the self. Social order and interaction order are achieved by managing the relationships between and among people by means of rules and regulations. The order of the self, too, is maintained when the self conducts its relationship with itself according to certain proscriptions and prescriptions. This forestalls not only feelings of guilt and shame but also anxiety, uncertainty, and anomie. It is when the self perceives itself as having violated one of these prescriptions as proscriptions that it experiences shame or guilt or anxiety (Sullivan, 1953).

Mead argued that each individual in a society develops a self according to the attitudes the others direct toward him or her, and social control "will depend upon the degree to which the individual does assume the attitude of those in the group who are involved with him in the same attitude" (1932: 192). *Social control is achieved by making an agent practice self-control and occurs in a self/other dynamic in which the other can be an interactional other or a generalized other.* The attitudes that these others project toward an agent become features of the self of the agent and exercise control over his or her attitudes and acts.

In Bourdieu's work, the concept of *habitus* is used to indicate that an agent may be *covertly* adapting and orienting his or her conduct to the demands of society. For Bourdieu, such adaptations and orientations are not matters of choice, but are determined by factors prior to the situation. Nevertheless, he does not rule out the operation of a reflexive consciousness completely:

> It is, of course, never ruled out that the responses of the *habitus* may be accompanied by a strategic calculation tending to carry on, quasi-consciously, the operation the *habitus* carries on in quite a different way, namely the estimation of chances which assumes the transformation of past effect into the expected objective. (1979: 76)

Habitus then is embodied, so to speak, in the agent but can be subject to a calculating rationality in order to act in specific situations. In such a conception of *habitus,* it becomes compatible to Mead's concept of a self—a self not only as a persistent way of being and doing over a period of time (insofar as being and doing receive continuing validation from one's social circles) but also as a response-structure situated in a particular time and place.

A self, cultivated and habituated over a period of time and continuing to receive validation from others, achieves a certain stability that becomes functional in the conduct of the individual. The self is able to achieve a "unity" as Mead calls it—what could also be a "coherence." Mead wrote, "The unity and structure of the complete self reflects the unity and structure of the social process as a whole ... The structure of the complete self is thus a reflection of the complete social process" (1934: 144). The unity of the complete self is achieved by systematic and stable discursive relations within a unified social process, and, to the extent that the social process remains stable and continuous, the self, too, becomes stable and continuous—indeed, becomes a *habitus.* Mead observed that "we normally organize our memories on the string of the self" (1934: 135). This memory hoisted on the string of the self is one that is achieved by the systematic incorporation of attitudes that were originally rendered to the agent by the organized social group. Postone, LiPuma, and Calhoun seem to acknowledge these positions when they observe "the *habitus* is at once intersubjective and the site of the constitution of the person-in-action; it is a system of dispositions that is both objective and subjective" (1993: 4)—though the concept of self does not figure in their argument. Nevertheless, one can recognize an affinity between the self and *habitus* as they function respectively in conduct and see certain advantages in using both self and *habitus* to handle the performances of given agents and their situational specificity.

This leads to a further question: how does an agent become a self that is implicated in the moral and ethical values of a culture, or how does an agent cultivate the practices that eventually became the *habitus*? For Mead, the self is constituted by the practices of symbolic interaction with various others from childhood and, eventually, becomes articulated as both a subjective phenomenon with a capacity for creativity and innovativeness and an objective phenomenon that responds to the attitudes of one's significant social circles. Bourdieu contends that *habitus* "is a socially constituted system of cognitive and motivating structures" (1979: 76). He further argues that these cognitive structures operate on a probabilistic basis—but using a probability theory that is different from the ones accepted by scientific statisticians:

> Unlike the estimation of probabilities which science constructs methodically . . . the practical evaluation of the likelihood of the success of a given action in a given situation brings into play a whole body of wisdom, sayings, common-places, ethical precepts ("that's not for the like of us"), and at a deeper level, the unconscious principles of the *ethos* which, being the product of a learning process dominated by a determinate type of objective regularities determines "reasonable" and "unreasonable" conduct for every agent subjected to those regularities." (1979: 77)

In addition to such prescriptions for determining "reasonable" and "unreasonable" conduct in Bourdieu's sense, a culture also seeks to provide answers to questions that human agents ask themselves and each other: about the causality of suffering, inequality of experience, the reasons for oppressions and exploitations and all forms of existentialist anguish. In addition, there are questions about why one became what one has become, and what one was before one became what one is now, and what one is going to become in the future.

While there are secular texts that answer these questions, the overwhelming majority of the people in the world rely on religious ones for the answer. Collectively, these religious texts enable believing agents to cognize an ordered and causally sensible natural and social world as well as a similarly ordered identity for the self. A chaos—or a potential chaos—is converted into a cosmos.

These "attitudes of the others" as well as the "wisdom," "sayings," and "commonplaces" can be richly endowed with themes drawn from religious narratives as well as secular ones. *Religious or secular, they must be made available to the subjects, in one way or another, before they become their subjectivities.* To think with and through these attitudes, these wise sayings, and commonplaces and to become wise with them and act on their basis, one must come to know them. They must become part of a person's self-conception or be featured in his or her own systems of practices. Agents must, in other words, be enabled to think with them and through them and act with them and through them. To be able to use these "attitudes" and "sayings" and "wisdom" for the conduct of thought and action, one must have them available as sign-systems because "we have no power of thinking without signs" (Peirce, 1955: 230). This is certainly not a debatable proposition, but if one examines these signs, it becomes clear that they are organized into systems. Ferdinand de Saussure used one vocabulary—that of "paradigms" and "syntagms"—to describe these systems or "structures," while Roman Jakobson referred to "metaphorical" and "metonymic" structures. Whichever terminology one adopts, there is no denying that human beings think not just with signs but with structures of signs.

In view of the overwhelming importance of making people think with certain defined sign-systems for the maintenance of the order of the society and the order of the self, human societies construct various structures that its members can use. That is, we construct the "inner world by hypothetical reasoning from our knowledge of external facts" and allow "our every cognition to be determined by previous cognitions" and understand that there can be no "conception of the incognizable" to use Peirce's statement again on the importance of signs in human thinking (1955: 230).

These sign-systems or structures are made available to the members of a culture at a certain stage in their lives by a variety of means. One such means may be termed the discursive mode. In such a mode, the ethical and moral perceptions of a culture are articulated in various narratives and conveyed to the prospective members of the society as well as current members in order to reinforce them. These narratives often take the form of stories in which various characters are made to act and interact with each other, creating plot lines that lead to one denouement or other. The various books of the religions of the Jews, Christians, and Muslims are such narratives. For the Hindus, there are, in addition to the *Vedas* and the *Upanishads,* the two epics, the *Mahabharata* and the *Ramayana.* In the latter, gods take human form and participate in the activities of this world and illustrate various principles of the Hindu religion. For the Buddhists, both the biographical details of the Buddha and his "discourses" to his immediate followers, collated at a later time, become the texts of morality and ethics. The preceptors of the religion as well as some of their followers read these narratives—which may be termed the metanarratives of a religious system—and make them part of their universe of discourse. They are subject to study, reflection, debate, and endless disputations.

The implicit and explicit content of these narratives is also transformed into more material forms: architectural forms (temples, churches, cathedrals), paintings, and sculptures. They are all made to reflect the thesis of the relevant religion and become instrumentations with both the cognitive and emotional basis of self and *habitus.*

There are other media, too, through which the prescriptions and proscriptions of a society are conveyed to the people and their children, which may be termed lesser vehicles. These are verbal and performative instrumentations: rituals, music, chants, magical formulas, benedictions, maledictions, and so forth. Finally, one may mention theatrical forms. In medieval Europe, religious, ethical, and moral principles were conveyed to the audience through theatrical performances. Here one may mention the "passion play"—in which various incidents from the life of Christ were depicted, with actors playing various roles—and the "morality play"—in which various "virtues" and "sins" were personified on the stage. In the plotting and the denouement, the sins were overcome by the virtues. The most famous such play was *Everyman.* It is a dramatization of the orthodox Christian's position on human salvation. It can be, no doubt, somewhat simply put as the claim that good deeds and practices can lead to the salvation of the soul. It is also a paean to the nature and significance of friendship. It has characters called "Good Deeds," "Knowledge," and "Death" as well as "Fellowship," "Kindred," "Cousin," "Goods," and so on. Everyman interacts with these characters and finds that good deeds and a tested friend rather than cousins and kin are the instruments of salvation. Everyman goes through various vicissitudes before he (or she) learns the lesson: "Even the redeemed Christian in the state of grace is capable of forgetting that his natural properties and accidents are in themselves not the instrument of salvation" and that he "demonstrates by his good deeds, he is in a state of grace" as Lawrence Ryan puts it (1957: 781).

There were other plays besides *Everyman* that directly portrayed "the Seven Deadly Sins" in combat with the "Seven Christian Virtues." These were more properly called "miracle plays," including one that came to be called the "Pater Noster" play (Craig, 1950). Both morality plays—which portrayed "everyman's" need for salvation and in which *homo humanum genus* was the protagonist in allegorical form—and miracle plays—in which various religious themes were put into conflict and the good side was made to win—reduce the themes of the metanarratives of Christianity into smaller units and parade them in easily comprehensible ways to an audience. It was believed the audience members would watch the plays and be either terrorized or cajoled into behaving in a particular way once they left the theater.

In Hindu India, the metanarratives—both the religious treatises and the epics—were reduced into manageable proportions in standard theatrical forms as well as in dances and a kind of performance that could be best described as mono theater—*harihatha* and *kathapirasangam*—in which a single performer depicts various characters from one of the epics. The Indian dance forms—*Bharata Natyam, Kathakali, Kathak,* and *Kuchipuddi* did the same. Various forms of folk theater—like the *terukkuttu* in the Tamil country of India—also represented religious themes in their performances (Frasca, 1990; 1998).

The "tea ceremony" of the Japanese is said to be a representation of Zen principles. "The Tea Way is a way designed to help the living man to the annihilation of the ego, to pave the way for the ultimate experience of enlightenment ... The essence of the Tea Way lies ... in entering the state of contemplation in which one spontaneously handles the utensils correctly and in attaining the religious attitude through which we may grasp the Buddha-nature within us," observes Horst Hammitszch in his study of the tea ceremony (1988: 63-64).

Rituals and Games

These latter structures—which may be termed the *lesser vehicles* in contrast to the metanarratives of a religion—are essentially rituals. Rituals of all kinds, in fact, are relevant for conduct and contemplation insofar as they exist as *performed* activities. Stanley Tambiah, in a subtle analysis of a performative approach to rituals, develops a semiotic and structural analysis of rituals and observes "that cosmological constructs are embedded ... in rites and rites in turn *enact* and *incarnate* cosmological conceptions" (1985: 130, emphasis added).

These rites, in a magnificently parsimonious manner, manage to share the property of both being artistic productions and instruments of knowledge: insofar as rituals have to be performed with attention to a certain perfection in form, they become *dramatic productions*; insofar as rituals are containers of ideas and are performed repetitively, they impart knowledge of a moral and ethical nature to those who witness them, in addition to reinforcing this knowledge in those who perform them.

To the list of performative structures in which cosmological principles as well as moral and ethical ones are "incarnate," one must add games. They are, in fact, ritual dramas. Lévi-Strauss has argued that rituals and games are different, despite their apparent similarity in that they are both performances based on rules:

> Games . . . appear to have a *disjunctive* effect: they end in the establishment of a difference between individual players or teams where originally there was no indication of negativity. At the end of a game, they are distinguished into winners and losers. Ritual, on the other hand, is the exact reverse: it *conjoins*, for it brings about a union between two initially separate groups. (1966: 32)

Levi-Strauss's claims are true—but only up to a point. Games do bring disjunction between opposing players and teams and social groups that the teams represent, but they also bring about union and communion among the members of the team and with the groups they represent as well as the spectators.

No matter whether there is union or dis-union, there is no doubt that rituals and games are both vehicles with which and through which the larger themes of a culture are represented and communicated on a systematic basis so that the selves and *habitus* become informed with them. Further, unlike theatrical performances, games enable a large number of people to participate in them with mind and the self and society and allow these cultural themes to be practiced and incorporated into the participants' habitual selves. *One's "unconscious" must be present in someone else's consciousness before it becomes an agent's "unconscious."* Even the "structuring of structures" must be *communicated* to a budding agent at one time or another—insofar as he or she does not acquire them by osmosis—before they come to "quasi-consciously" guide thought and action.

The Morality of Dialogue

Insofar as games are dialogic processes conducted according to very strictly observed and enforced rules, it is possible to see them as manifestations of perfect dialogues. To begin with, in games each participant is enjoined to maintain strict codes of deference and demeanor. Each player must show the respect to which the other is entitled and maintain the manners and etiquette appropriate to the situation during the actual playing. It is not that these rules—or ethos—of a game are not violated frequently but that such violations must be considered departures from the norm.

Games, in fact, approach, if not actually represent, the "ideal speech situation" that Jurgen Habermas identified as a feature of emancipated social relations. In ideal speech situations, there is "inter-subjective symmetry in the distribution of assertion and dispute, revelation and concealment, prescription and conformity among the partners of communication" (1970a: 371). These symmetries lead to the emergence of "truth" (consensus), freedom (free self-representation), and "justice" (shared norms). In such an ideal speech situation, agents are equally competent and acknowledge each other's rights and fundamental equality and undertake "undistorted" communication, as he referred to it in another paper (1970b).

The doctrine of the essential equality of human agents is enshrined in the very structure of the game. Once a game has begun, no player is allowed to play "foul" or is given greater room to maneuver or accorded special privileges because he or she is son or daughter of a powerful person or a famous player. He or she has to make his or her best contribution to the game and expect to be penalized if he or she violates the rules. Furthermore, no player is considered unimportant or of secondary significance in team games: every position, created on the principle of the division of labor, is of equal significance. In the perfect dialogue that is a game, every player is entitled to make his or her contributions to the game and is not denied such opportunities on any a priori grounds. In other words, every player is entitled to enter the dialogue and take his or her turn without unwarranted interruptions.

In the games in which one player confronts another, as in court games and some board games, and in others where a duo faces another, certain steps are taken by players to ensure that a semblance of equality is achieved in the playing. Two such steps can be summarized under the rubrics of "seeding and ranking" in many court games, handicapping in certain others like golf. Players who have a "record" are ranked according to their past performances and when knock-out tournaments are arranged, these ranks are used to ensure that only those who have reached certain standards are allowed to play in them. Further, these ranks are also used to achieve an opposite effect: they are used to "seed" the various segments of a tournament's "draw" so that all the best players do not face each other and get eliminated in the early rounds, enabling inferior players to win by default in the end. The point of these exercises is to have it both ways: to enable only skilled performers to play in a tournament and to ensure that there is continuous and accelerating competitiveness in the games.

These procedures too enable a perfect dialogue to emerge: people of equal skill compete against each other. If one had a contest between a very strong opponent and a weak one, the contest would consist of all addresses and no answers. No doubt, in the early rounds, court games are often one-sided, but that occurs despite attempts to prevent it.

In golf, the practice of handicapping is used to ensure the competitiveness of the game. Often a weaker player is pitted against a stronger player and in order for a match—that is, a perfect dialogue—to emerge, the weaker player is given an *a priori* score that the stronger player has to overcome. These steps may be taken when one is playing with friends and familiars, too, who may be less competent, to begin with, in the game. In order to make a match of it, a parent may give his or her small child a handicap just as one may do this with a friend who is just learning the game. Once the game has begun, further steps are taken to ensure that the morality of dialogue is maintained.

Insofar as games are address-and-answer processes, every step is taken to ensure that the addresses are made in such a way that it is possible for the respondent to provide an answer. This is true of all games—but can be illustrated by considering tennis. In this game, the "serve" is the opening gambit in the dialogue. The other side of the court is so large that if the serve is permitted to land on any part of the court, it would be almost impossible for the respondent to return the ball. In such an eventuality, the dialogue will stop and the game will only be a series of serves. Even now, if one player has a very powerful serve, the game does degenerate into such a state. Nevertheless, steps are taken to ensure a more perfect dialogue. The court for each player, when he or she is receiving, is given an inner boundary for purposes of the service alone. Every serve must fall within these inner boundaries and a player facing a server need watch only those boundaries, and he or she has a good chance of answering the addresses of the server. Furthermore, the server has other restrictions: his or her feet must be in a certain place and position when the serve is delivered, and it must be delivered only when the other is ready and paying attention. Insofar as the ball's placement will be distorted if it even touches the net, thereby putting the receiver at a disadvantage, the service is delivered again when that happens.

Conversely, insofar as the serve is so important in maintaining the dialogic structures of the game, and considering the difficulties it faces in keeping to the vertical boundaries of the net and the horizontal ones of the service court, the server is given two chances at the opening gambit. If the first one is fouled, a second service is permitted without penalty.

Once the service is made and the game has begun, the players make addresses and returns. The playing of the game is structured into "points," "games," and "sets": one player accumulates 60 points in units of 15 and wins a "game" so long as the other player is at least two points behind him or her. These games are accumulated into sets of six, and once again, a player wins a match if he or she is ahead of the adversary by at least two games. If either one, in the point-score or in the game-score, is not ahead of the other by at least two units, the match is played until such time as a margin of two is achieved by one player. Once a point is made, it is cumulated in units of 15 and he or she who makes the 60 with a 30-point margin is given the game. Once a game is won, the service is surrendered to the other player or players. *The strict observance of the rules of turn taking, then, allow also for the emergence of a perfect dialogue.* Unlike ordinary conversations, the turns in games do not depend on the willfulness of the participants and no one can be interrupted in the taking of these turns: everyone waits his or her turn, thereby ensuring that the most fundamental machinery of the dialogue is functioning. This is most visible in paired tennis games. It is usually the case that one member of a team in a game of doubles in tennis is a better server, and if allowed, he or she could dominate the game. Nevertheless, he or she is not given the chance to serve all the time. Every player is made to serve in rotation, allowing the other side sometimes to evade a powerful serve and thus increase its chances of rendering answers and winning games.

While turn taking and turn giving and the emergence of a more perfect dialogue are most readily visible in tennis and other court games, they are, in fact, a sine qua non of all games. Every step is taken to ensure that it occurs, even in team games where there are many players who must be accommodated into the structure of addresses and answers. Indeed, the morality of dialogue is maintained in a complete and intricate form in such games. In a game in which a group of players bands together and faces another such group, there are two forms of dialogue: one within the group and the other with the adversaries. The dialogue in the first case is maintained by passing the ball or puck to a member of one's own side and seeking to advance it to the other side of the arena and into the goal. Each side tries to do this, and it is not obliged to give the other side a turn: these turns must be taken forcibly. Nevertheless, the dialogue is made perfect by very strict rules of how the turn is to be taken. *The essential quality of these rules is that they forbid certain moves that put the other player at a gross disadvantage.* If these rules are violated, a penalty is declared and the offending party pays a forfeit and equilibrium is restored. These rules include the practice of "unnecessary roughness," "ineligible receiver," and "pass interference" in American football and tackling the other player in a "foul" manner or using the hands in soccer.

In cricket, there are various rules—not to speak of the unwritten "ethos" of the game—that prevent practices deemed to be "not quite cricket"—that is, creating an imperfect or defective dialogue. An example is bowling "wide"—that is, so wide of the standard batting area that the ball is unreachable by a batsman. When a bowler delivers the ball to a batsman in this way, he or she is making it impossible for him or her, a priori, to be able to provide an answer. Scratching and scuffing the shiny new ball used at the start of a match to make it easier to control is also considered a practice that violates the ethics of the game insofar as it gives the bowler an unwarranted advantage. Bowling to the body of the batsman rather than to the wicket and seeking to intimidate or injure him or her is again considered not quite cricket. When the English team did just this in a match against Australia in 1937, the complaint of the Australians was that the English were not playing cricket (Blofeld, 2002). Such practices are violations of the canons of dialogic morality. Indeed, what is considered "cricket" is the canonization of the morality of dialogue—as C. L. R. James understood so clearly in his many writings on cricket (1983).

The Endgame

Once a game has begun and proceeds apace on its onward course, it has to come to an end. There are, of course, rigid, nonwhimsical and nonmalicious ways to close the game. This, however, is not the end of the dialogic game as such. There is another interaction after that: how do players—individuals and teams—conduct themselves in the immediate aftermath of the game? This may be termed the *endgame* (although this word has been used with other meanings), and how well it is played contributes to maintaining the morality of dialogue.

That is, once a game has been played and won and lost, there is still more business to be done. This is a moment of some embarrassment in most cultures. The issue is this: how does the winner disport himself or herself and how does the loser perform his or her role? Indeed, there is the final rule about how to win and how to lose. At the end of each game, in fact, both parties to a contest are obliged to do face-work rituals through which the players show how worthy the others are of respect and honor—whether they are winners or losers. Both parties participate in this process: the winners may compliment the losers for having played a good game—*face-making for the other as well as face-saving*—and indicate a symbolic reintegration between the parties.

The issue is so delicate that some cultures have taken steps to deal with it in a somewhat drastic manner. In one of the Trobriand Islands, the British missionaries introduced the game of cricket, and the members of the culture took to it enthusiastically. They, however, were forced to make a number of changes to the game. The home team always batted first. There was no limit to the number of players on each team—a gesture to include all the members of the community who wanted to play and to avoid having to make invidious distinctions. Every time a player was rendered out, there were celebratory dances by the fielding team. And, most significantly, the home team was always allowed to win, and if the score indicated otherwise, the game was continued until the decorous result was obtained. Yet the margin of victory was always kept small so that the guest team was not humiliated. The endgame, in fact, became a face-making and face-saving device, and at the end of the game, a feast was held to celebrate all faces.

In other cultures, where games are considered as essentially competitive activities, players and teams play with ferocious energy and antagonisms. But at the end of the game, there are many rituals of redress where the antagonists are united—however temporarily and superficially. Competing coaches at the end of football games rush across the milling players and officials on the field to shake hands with each other. In tennis and other court games, the loser walks over to the net and congratulates the winner and shakes his or her hand. There is a good description of this in the aftermath of the match between the aristocratic Baron Gottfried von Cramm and the American commoner described earlier:

> Gottfried, the noble loser, had to wait patiently at the net for me, the winner, to get up off the ground. I rose finally, bewildered, and rushed towards him. I tried to hug him but before I could, he stopped me and took my hand. "Don," he said, evenly and with remarkable composure, "this was absolutely, the finest match I ever played in my life. I am very happy that I could have played it against you, whom I like so much." And then he pumped my hand: "Congratulations." (in Baltzell, 1995: 298)

The endgame ends the agonistic dialogue and restores equilibrium, and until the next game, the winner is the champion and the loser acknowledges it.

It sometimes happens that the parties in a political or sporting contest do not play the endgame properly—that is, they violate the principles of the morality of dialogue—and resort to moves that, instead of creating a reintegration, create a schism or widen the one that already exists. In 1972, Honduras and El Salvador went to war because they were dissatisfied with the refereeing and the results of a soccer match. In recent years, international cricket—the game that gave the world the expression "it is not cricket" to refer to the violation of the morality of dialogue—has been the scene of a number of postgame disputes. In the international series between England and Pakistan, the latter fielded a couple of bowlers, Wasim Akram and Waqur Younis, who were accused of "ball tampering." In cricket, slight variations in the texture of the ball's surface can alter its manageability and the control of its delivery, pace, and bounce. As the game proceeds, the smooth surface of the new shiny ball wears off and the nature of the bowling and the fate of the game change. If a bowler can remove the glossy surface of the ball—for example, by using his or her nails to scratch it or by using sandpaper from his or her pockets—he or she gains an enormous advantage.

In this particular series, the English—the home of the former imperium, the people who invented the game and taught it to the colonies—were losing badly, due to the extraordinary bowling feats of Akram and Younis. The newspapers stated that Akram and Younis were "cheating" by tampering with the ball. Eventually, one of the members of the English team, Alan Lamb, accused the Pakistanis of "cheating." He was born and raised in South Africa and perhaps the sting of being beaten by Asians was too much for him to take. The newspapers—both progressive ones and the more overtly racist and conservatives ones—joined in the campaign and created an ugly national mood in England. It soon subsided, however, and Lamb and others were discredited when some other players and the umpires of the matches came to the defense of the Pakistanis. The defense took two opposite forms: the umpire said that he had examined the balls during the matches and found no tampering, and some of the players said that all the cricketers do this kind of tampering anyway (Searle, 2001: 23-35).

In playing cards with others—whether the game is poker or bridge—there are typically no referees. Each player watches out for the proper conduct of the others and ensures that the rules are followed. The order of the interaction is maintained in such games as it is in everyday life.

Nevertheless, in such games there is always the possibility that someone will cheat. This possibility invests the game—particularly when it is one for high stakes—with a great deal of dramatic tension over and above the one that is inherent to the game itself.

As one plays the game and watches the other to find data for one's own moves, he or she is also watching for signs of rule violation. If one does, in fact, see a violation what does one do? The honorable thing to do is to challenge the person then and there. This creates a series of problems:

I. Establishing beyond reasonable doubt that cheating has occurred.
II. Making the other player "lose face," if cheating, in fact, is established.
III. Losing face oneself if cheating is not established.
IV. The cheater's resorting to violence to deal with the loss of face.
V. Resorting to violence by the accuser and his or her fellow players to punish the cheater.

Each of these eventualities is detrimental to the dialogic morality of games. Cheating itself violates the trust that is an essential basis of dialogic interactions just as *unsubstantiated* charges of cheating are violations of the rules of the interaction order and the principles of the endgame.

The problems of the endgame are reproduced in the practices of electoral politics. In an election, two or more contenders enter a contest, and after a series of moves one of them is declared a winner because he or she has obtained a majority of the members of a defined group of people. Insofar as it is usually not possible to achieve unanimity about political matters, the principle of majority rule is put into practice.

George Thomson in a remarkable study of the processes of democracy in ancient Athens shows that once the "tyrants, who had maintained their control of the administration by filling the executive offices with their own nominees" (1973: 187) were disposed of, a new constitution was enacted. "The watchword of the new constitution was *isonomia*—equality of civic rights, equality before the law" (1973: 196). If such equality was to be enforced, an authority who could do that had to be established. The issue, however, is how such an authority is to be selected in keeping with the principle of equality? Not by virtue of heredity or ownership of property or force, surely. In the absence of an electoral system, the Athenians decided to do so by a lottery, notes Thomson.

The members of the New Council were the 500 elected by lot, and the same method was extended a few years later to the election of the highest officers of the state, the *archontes.* The use of the lot served the same purpose in the new democratic constitution as it had originally served in the democracy of the primitive tribe; it was a safeguard of equality (1973: 196).

Today we do not use the lottery to decide on our rules, but a commitment to the principle of equality has brought us to another principle: electoral procedures are instituted in which, after contests of one sort or another between the protagonists, voters decide by a majority who rules. Once the contest is over, however, attempts will be made to achieve a modicum of reintegration. This recognizes that rule by a majority is only second best to rule by unanimity.

The process of reintegration after a contest is a fundamental feature of electoral politics. Parties that are opposed to each other and fight an election unify to a certain extent and seek to allow an orderly government to be run by the party that won the election. This process is facilitated by the winning side's moving to the center just as the losing side will try to do. Pythagoras gave expression to this tendency with his doctrine of the "fusion of opposites in the mean." Deriving their doctrine from music, the Pythagoreans sought to apply it to a variety of arenas. In music, "the four fixed notes of the octave are represented by the numerical series 6—8—9—12 . . . The terms 6 and 12 are regarded as opposites, 8 is regarded as the sub-contrary or harmonic mean . . . and 9 is the arithmetic mean," observes Thomson. He argues that the emergence of a middle class, in opposition to the *monarchial* on one side and the *aristocratical* on the other side, made it possible for the middle class to be the harmonic. In their joint efforts, the two opposing sides ceased to be adversaries and found harmony by each supporting the middle class. In this way "an attunement of opposites, a unification of the mean, a reconciliation of dissentients" was achieved, in the words of Theon of Syria (quoted by Thomson, 1973: 201).

Bold as Thomson's thesis is, it is clear that at the end of various campaigns in today's electoral politics, opposites often move a fusion around the mean. The moves toward the center and the construction of a "harmony" or "unity" or a "semblance of a unity" after a political, philosophical, or musical contest or conflict are forms of the endgame. It, in fact, recognizes that life processes of all kinds emerge, develop, and progress toward a *telos* and then begin again. However, in politics, too, as in some gaming encounters, the rules of the endgame are often violated and lead to further conflicts and repression of the defeated side or the persecution of the winning side. One can mention various Fascist regimes being established after they failed to win a majority. Franco and the Phalangists fought a civil war to oust an elected socialist government in Spain. Augusto Pinochet in Chile used military action to oust a socialist government, too. In American politics, the conservative movement has systematically harassed elected liberal presidents and members of Congress in a gross violation of the morality of dialogue and decorum of electoral politics for a number of years in recent times.

The process of harmonizing after a contest is best described with Victor Turner's conception of "social drama." He argues and shows by various examples that societies enact what he termed "social dramas" in which "units of aharmonic or disharmonic processes," arise in conflict situations. "Typically, they have four main phases of public action," he writes (1974: 37–38). He identifies four stages of the social drama: "... breach of regular, norm-governed social relations," followed by "... crisis ... during which ... there is a tendency for the breach to widen ..." This, he continues, leads to "redressive action." In order to limit the spread of the crisis, certain adjustive and redressive "mechanisms ... are swiftly brought into operation by leading or structurally important representatives of the social system." Finally, Turner says, "There is *reintegration* of the disturbed social group or a *schism* between the contesting parties ..." (1974: 38–40).

In any case, the democratic principles of equality in civic matters and the moral principles of dialogic interactions are represented fully and systematically in games and allow participants to play them either vicariously or directly. The self's agency is informed by these principles and themes and becomes its *habitus* to be put into practice in a variety of arenas.

The "Game Ethic" as *Habitus* and Self

The quest for the moral life achieves a certain purity in the "game ethic" that was cultivated in the "public schools" of England during the heyday of the empire. These public schools were really private schools to which the elite in England as well as those on its fringes sent their sons to be educated to be both gentlemen and functionaries in the outposts of the imperial military and civil services. In these schools, the "games ethic" was inculcated into every student making it an aspect of his self and an essential element of his *habitus*. Here is a neat summary of this ethic given by one J. R. P. Sclater, who was both an educator and an Anglican clergyman:

> In the first place, we would rather lose a game than win it unfairly. In the second place, we would rather have respect to the spirit of the law than to its letter, in playing the game. In the third place, we would exact from ourselves and all associated with us a spirit of absolute obedience to the authorities set over us for the moment, never for a moment questioning the umpire. In the fourth place, we would, so to speak, play the ball where it lies—an entirely admirable attitude to have in respect to all life's difficulties. In the fifth place, we would desire to be among that

> company who, having started either in a race or a game, go on if we can, till we drop dead. In the sixth place, we would hope that that spirit would be developed amongst us which is not so very greatly concerned for itself, so long as the side on which we are is successful. (in Mangan, 1985: 52–53)

In seeking to fulfill the demands of this ethic, a young gamester is, of course, seeking an ethical life. He submits himself to a great discipline and self-restraint in playing the game and waits for opportunities to display these ethical principles.

The very structures of the games that the youngsters were encouraged to play embody the opportunities for the heroic quest. One can take rugby, football, and cricket—the standard public school games—to illustrate these claims.

In rugby football, the objective is to take an oval-shaped ball to the end of a territory marked as the adversary's and touch it down on the ground. It is a quintessential team game where each player weaves a network of relationships by making passes backward toward a player who is running behind him to one side or running forward with the ball and seeking to touch it down at the other end. While he is doing this, he will be challenged and tackled by his adversaries. The tackling must follow certain rules observed by all the players, too—that is, it must be fair. *In playing this game, then, an agent is simultaneously putting his own efforts—will, determination, courage, grit, dexterity and speed and tactical sense—into play as well as coordinating his moves with those of others.* Individual heroism is achieved, in the game ethic, by the coordination he achieves with his teammates. Win or lose, the heroic quest is rewarded, so long as one plays for the team and avoids self-centered moves and vainglorious gestures.

Cricket is another standard public school game that allows the same opportunities for the game ethic to be put into play. It is a game in which one lone player in the batsman's crease faces a bowler and tries to guard his wicket or prevent his hits from being caught by one of eleven fielders. The very structure of the game provides the opportunities for the heroic moment. The batsman is alone at the crease, and he has to use his own judgment, skill, tactics, patience, and perspicacity to score runs against the eleven arrayed against him. This is a wonderful opportunity for the commitment of self to the welfare of the team. Avoiding flamboyant and spectacular moves, the batsman, methodically and patiently accumulates runs in a long game and the more runs he scores, the more the team benefits. In this structure of facing eleven adversaries single-handedly, there are further opportunities for the ethical move: the last batsman sent in to bat is often the weakest, but often only a few runs are needed by this time to win the match. He or she, therefore, goes in with little expected of him or her. Often, however, he or she is able to rise to the occasion and claim a heroic role by scoring the necessary runs and winning the match for the team.

These ethical principles, it was recognized by the cognoscenti, were not merely virtues on the playing field but were the basis of the heroic life in the life after school. The players went into the military or political service of the country and fought many a battle with the game ethic as their guiding principle. This meant playing rough in mud and water and rain in the far-flung fields of the empire, doing one's duty, enjoying the challenge of adventure, and often sacrificing one's life or limb in pursuit of the good of the team—in this case Queen, country, and empire. One J. P. S. Daniel, a member of the Sudan Political Service of the British government writes:

> At school we learnt not to think of ourselves as a little tin god just because you were in the XI. In the Sudan, everyone was a hero outside it, but we were all really ourselves tested by the climate, plagued by the insects and disease, but from our physical training, we had learnt to look after ourselves in body and soul and to be loyal to, and proud of something more important than ourselves whether it was your House or your team or your school. (in Mangan, 1985: 86)

Noticeably in this comment, there is no loyalty claimed for family or kin: the "house" refers to the divisions in a public school to which pupils were assigned and became the basis of intramural competitions in sporting engagements.

These public school students, trained rigorously in the physical discipline of the games and the social disciplines of loyalty and self-sacrifice, would go forth and conquer an empire and help to maintain it, it was hoped, and they were viewed as heroes by their peers and significant communities. The equivalence of their roles to mythic heroes was never far from the minds of the cognoscenti. Here is one such identification between the mythic heroes and the real ones:

> Seen through the mists of time, Valhalla, its towers and battlements, uplift themselves, and from their places the phantoms of the mighty heroes of all ages rise to greet these English youths, who enter smiling, the blood yet trickling from their wounds. Behold, Achilles turns, unbending from his deep disdain; Rustum, Timoleon, Hannibal and those of later days who fell at Brunanburh, Senlac and Trafalgar, turn to welcome the dead whom we have sent thither as avante-garde of our faith, that in this cause is our destiny, in this mandate, our fate. (J. A. Cramb, 1900, quoted in Mangan, 1985: 50)

These smiling English boys achieved the heroic life they sought by falling in battle—death as the apotheosis of the team spirit, of sacrifice of self for the team. In rugby football and cricket, and in other team games, one faces injury and ill fate by seeking to do the difficult tasks of the game with equanimity and indifference, and then one goes on to fight the battles of the empire and faces death with the same spirit. These players who became imperial heroes, in minor ways as in major ones, were not forced into this quest. They were mentally colonized with these ideas and attitudes, and they grew up and then went forth to colonize whole continents.

Karmic Games

Religion has been defined in many ways, but we might claim that one of its fundamental features is to provide an agent with narratives about the social and the natural world and to provision his or her mediated imagination and existential curiosity. As such, it is essentially a form of art. Not only is it a narrative art, but it also provided the opening for all other forms that pass as art. These narratives seek to explain why the natural world and the social world are the way they are and why they should be that way. Further, these narratives give individual believers an explanation about their past and the future. Collectively, these features of religion enable agents to cognize an ordered and *causally sensible* natural system and relate their self-system to it in a disciplined way. Once again, a possible chaotic state is rendered into a cosmos.

One form of the order that religion creates for the human agent can be called the *temporal order*. Religion provides an agent with a narrative with which a presumptive past and an anticipated future can be conceived and lived with. Certain causal connections are made in the narrative and the agent is allowed to situate himself or herself into it: "virtuous" acts as opposed to "evil" ones would cause certain defined developments. These establish causal sequences and give believing agents the sense of temporal order in their lives. The agents can explain to themselves that the present predicaments in their lives are *consequences* of certain past events and that current events will create further *results* in the future. One such theory is the principle of karmic causation that both Buddhism and Hinduism, in their many variations, have propounded over the centuries as a comprehensive explanation for the world as it is, with its imperfections. Max Weber wrote:

> The most complete formal solution of the problem of theodicy is the special achievement of the Indian doctrine of the so-called belief in the transmigration of souls. The world is viewed as a completely connected and self-contained cosmos of ethical retribution ... Ethical merits in this life can make possible rebirth into life in heaven, but that life can last only until one's credit balance of merits has been completely used up. (1958b: 145)

In spite of its portentous cosmic significance, Karma is a simple enough concept that has been discovered in spheres other than the Hindu/Buddhist domain (Obeyesekere, 2002). Its central claim is well expressed in the Buddhist idea of "dependent origination." Stcherbatsky puts it this way:

> This term means that every point-instant of reality arises in dependence upon a combination of point-instants to which it necessarily succeeds; it arises in functional dependence upon a "totality of causes and conditions" which are its immediate antecedents. (1962: 119)

One of the point-instants is the very existence of a human being. He or she passes through these point-instants in a succession of instantaneous beingness, each of them caused by the previous moment. This point-instant can begin before birth and extend into the future after death. In short, all phenomena in the world are caused, and the cause of the present agent is the significance of a sequence of previous actions. This significance, accumulated over the myriad of past instants, is Karma. In Stcherbatsky's words, "Just as real existence is only a point-instant, just so a real cause is only this same point-instant. In other words, existence is dynamic, not static and it is composed of a sequence of point-instants which are interdependent, i.e. which are causes" (1962: 119).

Phenomena, in other words, have an origin that itself is dependent on an earlier point of origin in a chain of causation. The Buddha used such reasoning to explain the existence of suffering, birth, decay, and death in the world. In Surendranath Dasgupta's words:

> The question with which the Buddha started before attaining Buddhahood was this: [people] are born, they decay, they pass away and are born again and they do not know the path of escape from this decay, death and misery. How to know the escape from this misery?
>
> Birth, death and decay have causes but the masses are ignorant of them and the Buddha sought to discover them and teach them to the masses. (1962: 70)

The Hindu theory is different in some ways from the Buddhist one, but fundamentally, they are both theories about the causation of phenomena. Everything has a cause, including the features of a human life, in the preceding instants stretching backward, and every action one undertakes now becomes a cause of the next action or series of actions.

One ready vehicle with which the processes of karmic causation and the action of given individuals can be represented is the dice game. The essential process in a dice game is not so much the squares in board games into which the dice thrower takes the tokens of play, but what the dice represent and what the throwing signifies.

In Hindu mythology, time is conceived as a cyclic process in which one period, consisting of a certain number of years, is called a *yuga*. There are four yugas and each yuga succeeds another in a cyclic process. This fourfold pattern is also represented in the suits in cards and the latter may have originated from the system in dice. Each side of the dice is said to represent a yuga. The supreme Hindu god Siva is conceived as playing dice with his consort-wife Parvati. In other words, Siva is represented as playing with and creating time as such in which each individual soul is enmeshed (Handelman and Shulman, 1997).

In Hindu mythology, too, the dice game plays a critical part, and even here it is really a game that relates self to time. One may observe here parenthetically that the cards used in card games have a four-suited design—four-sided—and are also used to play with time. In the epic of all epics of the Hindus, the *Mahabharata*, the dice game is used as a device to relate the agent to time and is, in fact, a major plot device in the epic. In this epic, the dice game is used twice—once in the early chapter in which the head of the godly (dharmic) side plays with his adversaries and another in a substory regarding Nala and Damayanti. In each case, the turn of the dice is not a matter of chance but a sign of other forces (Handelman and Shulman, 1997; Hiltebeitel, 1987: 87–102).

The turn of the dice is taken by many to be a sign of one's Karma. *Karma is, after all, a sign-vehicle that puts the self in relation to time: actions from an earlier time period determine what happens in the current period and those in the current period will determine those of the future period.* At any given point-instant of the self's conscious existence, it has a memory of a past but can also wonder about the past beyond memory, just as it can anticipate/imagine a future beyond the earthly one. The doctrine of Karma places the self in this temporal sequence and in a causal sequence. And the games with dice are instruments without parallel for playing with time.

The relationship between dicing and time is represented very clearly in the primal Hindu epic the *Mahabharata*. In it, the key plot device is a game of dice between the good protagonists, the Pandavas, and the evil ones, the Kauravas. The leader of the Pandavas faces not the leader of the Kauravas but their agent, an expert player named Sakuni, and stakes his wealth, then his kingdom, and finally his brothers and their common wife and loses them all in succession. This sets in line a number of developments in the plot, eventually leading to the great battle between the two parties. What began as a contest between the agents with dice ended as a contest with arms. The roll of the dice was not a matter of luck nor was it based on the law of probability. Insofar as it always favored Sakuni at this stage, it was the karmic weight of his past actions as opposed to the ones of his goodly adversary that carried the day. The roll of the dice becomes a sign of Karma.

It is in the battle that concludes the epic that Arjuna, one of the protagonists on the good side, begins to entertain doubts about the wisdom and morality of killing one's adversaries. Krishna comes on the scene and instructs him about his karmic duty as a warrior.

This occurs in the poem in the epic *Mahabharata* in which two armies, one representing the moral order of both this world and the next and the other challenging it, are facing each other in the decisive battle. Arjuna, the moral leader, begins to have doubts about his calling as a warrior and questions the morality of killing his enemies. Krishna, Arjuna's friend and counselor, tells him:

> It is never born nor does it die.
> Nor once that it is, will it ever not be.
> Unborn, unending, eternal and ancient.
> It is not killed when the body is killed.
> (van Buitenen, 1981: 75)

Insofar as that is the case, and insofar as its being killed now is a fruit of its own past actions, Arjuna should perform his karmic action and kill it. It is all there is and the readiness to fulfill one's Karma is all, too.

In this text, one encounters both a battle between Arjuna and his enemies as well as a battle between Arjuna and his "conscience" in which he is aided by the god Krishna. The latter battle is one that every moral being has to wage in order to understand his or her predicament in this world. The goal of the Hindu-Buddhist eschatology in waging such a battle—contra Blaise Pascal's celebrated battle in his *Pensées* and his wager—is self-knowledge and understanding. In the confrontation between Krishna and Arjuna, *Arjuna's wager* is designed to understand his karmic responsibility and destiny: if I do this, what will happen? If I don't do this, what will happen?

The full philosophical significance of these ideas and their integration with other themes of Hindu civilization have been discussed in great depth by a number of Indological scholars (O'Flaherty, 1973; Hiltebeitel, 1987; Obeyesekere, 2002)—and is not being addressed here. The interest here is to examine the transformation of these ideas into the simple thoughtways of everyday life and the mundane practices of such a life.

The parallel between the dice game and the battle is neatly drawn in the epic—one begins the story and the other ends the story—but for an epilogue of reintegration. There is then the dice game as battle and dice game as a game insofar as the winner in both is determined by karmic forces, and of course, there is the battle of life, all of which can be very neatly represented in a simple board game. There are the dice, the roll of which will indicate one's Karma, and then there is the action of moving one's tokens to the right place and facing the consequences and rolling the dice again to see the results of one's past actions. Further, there is an antagonist ready to join battle sitting across the board.

These ideas have been translated in rather miniaturized forms into many lesser vehicles. Games played on segmented boards with dice are one such representation. These games are essentially racing games—an agent's token is raced along a path toward a goal in competition with one other player. In these games, however, there is a significant variation: one can move rapidly by landing in the space marked with a ladder—that is, move several spaces ahead—or move backward several spaces if one lands on a snake-space. The moving of the tokens is based on the throw of a die or a pair of dice. Simple enough as it is, it nevertheless encapsulates various themes of the theories of karmic causation and individual destiny as well as Hindu theories about the cosmos and the social and temporal order.

The Hindu game has many squares—from 32 to 132—each of them representing some religious/moral theme or an emotional disposition. Each of these represents causal principles. An agent who lands on a square as a result of throwing the dice pays the consequences of such a landing—either upward social/spiritual mobility or a downward slide. In the Hindu eschatology, everything is caused and the cause is one's Karma. It is, however, a cause that one does not know until the dice is rolled and he or she reads the meaning in the relevant square. He may land on a square marked "Greed" or "Anger" and move downward, while landing on "Compassion" may move one upward. This is, of course, the recording of the experience of the individual as he or she lives his or her life: one does not know one's Karma until its consequences are apprehended and experienced. Life is lived forward, but is understood backward.

One such game was *Moksha Patamu*—the path to heaven—and it contains squares representing vices and virtues—generosity, knowledge, asceticism as virtues, and drunkenness, debt, rage, greed, pride as vices. If a roll of the dice—that is, a practice, move, or act—landed one on a square marked "Rage," for instance, one slid downward and if it landed on "Generosity," one moved upward in worldly and spiritual success.

A more complex version has been published by Harish Johari (1975) under the name of *Leela,* which means "divine play." Johari notes that as the "player moves from space to space, he begins to see patterns in his own existence emerging with ever-deepening clarity as his understanding of the game broadens." He goes on to argue that as the play continues, the player's "sense of detachment grows as he sees each state as temporary, something to move beyond. And once the temporality of any space becomes a reality for the player, he can detach [himself] from that space, let it go as he seeks to discover even more about the wonder that is being" (1975: XI).

This game has 72 squares and is played with a single die. Each roll takes one to a square and it can either lead to an upward movement or a downward spiral. *The rapid movement of one's self, soul, world as a result of one's practices, either toward understanding, awareness and release from earthly tribulations, or the continuous experience of such tribulations is the essence of the game.* The die and its particular roll wonderfully summarize the ambiguity of the karmic doctrine: one's accumulated Karma will cause it just as one's own action will determine its future ambience. For instance, the Karma from the past can take one to violence, but how one handles oneself once on the square can redeem one and start the climb upward again.

The first square is called *Genesis*—the origin of the agent in the worldly life in this cycle of his or her existence. And from that moment onward, the agent moves onto squares marked "Maya" (illusion), "Anger," "Greed," "Avarice," as well as "Selfless Service," "Devotion" and so on. If the dice takes the player to selfless service, he or she will skip several squares and will arrive at a higher plane, whereas landing on the square of "Violence" will take one back to "Purgatory." One moves along these squares by one's own action, upward and downward, and if the sum of one's action reaches *satguna* (good qualities), he or she will reach *ultima Thule*—"cosmic consciousness—that is, an understanding of the self's place in the cosmos.

A slightly variant form of such games is the one known in the Tamil country of India as *Paramapadam.* This consists of 132 squares, and instead of verbal descriptions of virtues and vices, it contains various deities and *lingams* for the upward points—that is, the ladder—and empty spaces for the mouth of the cobra. If one lands on the deity's square, he or she is considered blessed by that particular god or goddess, and if one lands on the cobra-head, he or she will slither down. This game is played not to promote understanding of the passage of the soul or the theory of causation as such but as an act of worship, albeit worship with an understanding of causes and effects. One can play it then as a ritual, and there are sacred verses that can be recited as one plays the game.

In spite of its nature as an act of worship as well as a quest for enlightenment, *Paramapadam* does represent a narrative of the self as it moves from one act of worship to another, reaping its benefits along the way. Again, in Hindu theory, as opposed to Buddhist, one of the ways of alleviating the evil effects of one's accumulated Karma is by performing rituals and getting aid from various gods and goddesses.

The Tibetan karmic game called simply *Rebirth* was designed, it is claimed, by one Sakya Pandit in the twelfth century and has been retained in its original form by his descendants ever since. It is played with dice on a board, eight squares by nine squares. It is a complex game with various themes of the Mahayana School of Buddhism represented in it. Sakya Pandit explains his purpose in creating the game and how to play it in a series of verses. "Most living things find themselves neurotic and helpless. Continually dissatisfied, tossed by the waves of birth and death, and without the leisure or opportunity for the Doctrine, they build up only karmic causes of further strife and hardship." Having defined his view of the human predicament, he describes the value of playing this game: "Therefore, in playing this education game, they may become certain as to the effects of vicious and virtuous activity. It will then be possible for them to create good and improve their situation." He then describes the contents of the various squares in terms of Buddhist theory and describes them as steps in "the path to the pacification of existence" (Tatz and Kent, 1977: 11-12). The aim of playing this game, in contrast to the Hindu game *Paramapadam,* is not worship but understanding or achieving Buddha's style of "enlightenment." *Buddha,* in fact, means the "enlightened one," and the purpose of playing this game is to make everyone a Buddha if possible—or at least a quasi-Buddha.

The game board in fact represents the mandala—the ordered space of the cosmos. Human agents enter it by means of the token and participate in its dynamic processes. This is a cosmos that emerged out of the chaos—the *prabalaya*—that existed before. It is an ordered space, a managed system, under control and discipline.

The game is played by human agents who become actively engaged in it. They throw the dice and move the tokens as dictated by the numbers that come up. They are players of the game—whatever the game happens to be.

These agents are engaged with each other: The social systems in which they participate are interactional ones, and the processes in which they are active are social ones.

And finally, the game embodies a theory about the causation of phenomena: the dice may give a number that takes one to a particular square that makes one climb a ladder or slither down a "snake"—but each square is marked with a quality that causes these moves to occur. These games, plausibly enough, represents the vicissitudes of the self's journey through life and seeks to provide a moral and ethical understanding of these changes.

Calvinist Games

The Hindu game *Moksha Patamu* was taken by the English to England, and its essentially karmic ethos was converted into a Protestant one as *Snakes and Ladders.* "Generosity," "Knowledge," "Understanding," and "Renunciation" gave way to "Thrift," "Penitence," and "Industry." These moved the player up the ladder to "Grace," "Fulfillment," and "Success" while "Indolence," "Indulgence," and "Disobedience" brought one down to "Poverty," "Illness," and "Disgrace." The search for spiritual understanding characterized by renunciation, and so forth, which are features of what Max Weber called "other-worldly asceticism" has become, in the Protestant version, a search for "this-worldly" success and economic achievement, though tempered by divine grace. Indeed, worldly success—in the board game, as in life—was a manifestation of God's grace and this is neatly encapsulated into the game.

The game of Monopoly is obviously a game that encapsulates more directly and perhaps a little crudely the essential themes of capitalist enterprise. The original board game from which it is derived was invented by a Quaker, Elizabeth Magie, in the early years of the nineteenth century, to undermine the monopoly of land by various robber rentiers that was becoming rampant. Magie was a follower of Henry George who argued that the renting of land and the appreciation of its value over time profited only a few. He advocated a single tax on land alone to meet the costs of government and to erode the process of monopolization of land. The deleterious social consequences of monopolies in the essential services and in living quarters were the essential property of the Landlord Game.

Magie invented the game as a way of teaching ordinary people the evils of land monopolies. The properties of Magie's game were for rent only and could not be bought. The rules of the game claimed as its first principle: "The object of the game is not only to afford amusement to players, but to illustrate to them how, under present or prevailing systems of land tenure, the landlord has an advantage over other enterprisers and how the single tax would discourage speculation" (Wolf, 1976: 1).

The Landlord Game, it turns out, was not only a game for amusement but was *a critical game*. The Landlord's Game was taken up by many critical circles of the time and Scott Nearing, the early American socialist scholar, was a player and proselytizer of both the game and its ideas.

The game, however, was bought by the Parker Brother's concern, whose successors still own the monopoly on it. It has evolved into a game promoting ruthless capitalism and the acquisition of monopolistic control of the people's resources. The new game of Monopoly converted the Landlord's Game into a game for the nurturing of robber barons.

The central principle in the game of Monopoly is that players start with a fixed and equal amount of capital and on the throw of the dice encounter various opportunities to advance and make money by buying capital assets of many kinds and eventually becoming monopolists. The game inscribes one of the central claims of modern capitalism: everyone has an equal opportunity to succeed in life by taking the opportunities that comes one's way. However, in the game, each player starts with an equal amount of capital and no particular handicaps, and this is patently not the case in real life. No one, not the ones who become monopolists or oligopolists or those who fail to make a decent living, starts his or her life with the same amount of capital—economic, social, or cultural.

Rational calculation, ruthless service of the individualized interests of a single agent, studied indifference to the interests of other people, and studious pursuit of worldly success are the aims of this game. Various attempts have been made to invent other games that challenged the ethical principles of the monopolization of public resources by private individuals—for example, the game Anti-Monopoly developed by Ralph Anspach (1998)—but both the game of Monopoly and the processes of monopolization keep marching on.

Many other games also encapsulated these ideas as they developed over time. Various forms of the game of poker were, no doubt, played in a number of countries but during the heyday of capitalism, particularly in the American West, it became perfected as the encapsulated version of monetary investment, risk taking, and the handling of success and failure.

In poker, an agent essentially takes his or her assets and invests them in an enterprise that may or may not succeed. He or she does this, typically, not in a rash and intemperate manner, but after calculation and reflection—that is, in a rational manner. The agent will consider his or her hand of cards, estimate the challenges and difficulties he or she will face in the hands of the others, take some or all of his or her assets, and put them at some risk. Like any other entrepreneur, he or she may win or lose, win some and lose some, lose this time and win next time, and so on in an ongoing activity of investment and return. Poker, then, is a mimesis of the entrepreneurial social and political economy, Calvinist to the core, and the game itself evolved into its present form as capitalism expanded.

Forms of morality and ethics are incorporated into the structures and processes of the games that human agents play and have implications beyond the situation of play itself. Active and imaginative participation in these games provides the agent with "attitudes of the others" with which he or she formulates his or her self and conducts his or her life and the "sayings," "wisdom," and "commonplaces" with which the *habitus* is constructed. Further, the themes of the game are given validity and justification and become the operational ideology of the society.

Games, then, became structures of activity in which *habitus* and self-concepts are both cultivated and put into practice—that is, *practiced* and put *into practice*—and these habits of action and reflection seep into all other arenas of activity.

5

Toward a Heroic Life

In a study of the hero in myth, Joseph Campbell observes, "The hero ventures forth from the world of common day into a region of supernatural wonder: fabulous forces are there encountered and a decisive victory is won: the hero comes back from this mysterious adventure with the power to bestow boons on his fellow man" (1956: 30).

This claim becomes the key with which Campbell opens the structure of myths from far and wide. Campbell's hero, represented in myths, ventures forth from the world of common day to achieve something that bestows powers on him. No culture or civilization is excluded in Campbell's examination and in every one of them the hero emerges, though he may have a "thousand" differentiated "faces," to bestow boons on his fellow men and women. In such myths, the hero confronts the adversary and uses various strategies to overcome the adversary in combat and emerge victorious. The confrontation with an adversary—or with adversity—and the successful negotiation of such a confrontation is the essence of the hero with the thousand faces. In fact, a hero is an agent with many skills, if not a thousand, which can be put to the solution of one problem or another.

The Heroic in Play

Transforming Campbell's scheme of heroic action will get us: An agent stops one course of action, starts another, fulfills its demands successfully, then returns to the original course of action, empowered and with an enhanced sense of his or her self. The axial event in the performance of these tasks, too, is the confrontation with recalcitrant forces, manifested as resistance offered by another human agent or natural forces engaging in a struggle of varying intensities and overcoming adversaries or adversity to some degree or the other. The combat and adventure that are represented in myths are really exalted versions of the problem-solving processes of everyday life—the labored or ready adjustment of one's acts to the demands of the situation that one confronts in everyday life.

Confronting these demanding situations and overcoming them successfully create a hero. Heroic acts are those that enable an agent to face a problem and solve it. No doubt, some of these problems are more difficult than others and the degree of the difficulty and the manner in which it is overcome makes the heroism of the act vary in its significance. That is to say, some acts are more heroic than others while others are merely routine and ordinary—though they are not without significance for the esteem that the self is able to garner.

In such a life, an actor is called upon to perform a myriad of tasks—some of them of great complexity and challenge and others of a simpler form—successfully. Often he or she succeeds in undertaking these tasks with great skill and art and at other times fails to do so, with various points in between on this continuum. The fundamental structure of the heroic act is the successful accomplishment of a socially recognized and culturally valued task that possesses a certain optimum level of difficulty and resistance.

In the heroic myth, this form of activity is represented in an idealized and exaggerated form. The labors of Hercules in Greek myth or the adventures of Arjuna in Hindu myth can be considered as a representation of tasks of greater difficulty and challenge that each overcomes in his own way to become a hero. In everyday life, games become the surrogate for myths and the bridge between the ordinary tasks of everyday life and the challenging ones that demand greater mental and physical prowess.

Games are active or participatory myths in which the same structure that one finds in heroic myths is represented in neatly encapsulated forms. Indeed, the structure of games provides the perfect machine to display heroic qualities: In playing a game, an agent, whether an adult or a child, is offering his or her self voluntarily to a test of skill, character, perspicacity, acumen, intelligence, strength, emotional control and face-management, judgment, poise, and the capacity for dramaturgical presence and authority (have I missed anything?)—in short, successive instants in the full and critical presence of an other or others. Every such encounter without doubts is a quest for the heroic in which one wins and another loses, but he or she can certainly try again. Each such encounter transforms both parties to the transaction. Further, a game's limited duration enables a quick determination of victors and losers, and the winner's status is clean-cut and unambiguous. The standards by which winners and losers are determined are usually exacting as well as public. The game also provides a very powerful structure in which an actor can demonstrate his or her perspicacity, physical coordination, tactical skills, and in some games, team spirit. In putting his or her self into these myths, an agent leaves the secure world of everyday life, faces various challenges, and risks the status of his or her self. Often in these contests, the player wins and confirms his or her claims to the heroic; even after a loss, he or she can claim some status for having played well or stylishly or courageously.

Games are a structure of activity in which the action represents the myth of leaving, initiation, and return and of having to confront an adversary before the return. One enters the arena of the game—a board, a court, a field—and puts his or her self into the game, confronts an adversary, and returns to the original state, triumphantly. Or else he or she may lose the contest and return shamefacedly. This is the axial event in the quest toward a heroic life and in this quest—which can sometimes involve a long duration—an agent will seek perfection in the crafts and skills of the game, and through successful performances build his or her self, and win honor and esteem for it within given social circles. Such a quest is possible only to the extent that the craft of the game is successfully mastered over time.

The Quest for Perfection

In an essay, somewhat ironically titled "A Definition of Man," Burke in the end adds what he calls a "wry codicil": "rotten with perfection." He explains it thus:

> The principle of perfection is central to the nature of language as motive. The mere desire to name something by its "proper" name, or to speak a language in its distinctive ways is intrinsically "perfectionist." What is more "perfectionist" in essence than the impulse, when one is in dire need of something, to so state this need that one in effect "defines" the situation? … And in keeping with this view, we would state merely: There is a principle of perfection implicit in the nature of symbol systems and in keeping with his nature as a symbol-using animal, man is moved by this principle. (1967: 16–17)

Burke focuses on the uses of language as the instrumentation with which human agents seek this perfection—become "rotten with it." Every *use* of language, in writing and speaking, is an attempt to get something correct and to keep on rewriting, or changing a rough draft into a second and third draft in a quest for perfection. *There is, however, no need to confine this process to language as such; rather, all human acts, insofar as they are symbolic ones, are acts that seek perfection: there is always a good way of performing each act, a formally proper, effective, and efficient one in terms of purpose and means, and an aesthetically appealing one, too.* This goodness, effectiveness, efficiency, formality, and beauty of the act may never be fully realized, but the human agent will strive to achieve it, at least the next time or the time after that. Such strivings may not be ubiquitous but are rampant, nevertheless, in all areas of life. This quest for perfection, to become eventually rotten with it, is really to strive toward a heroic life, a quest that always only approaches success without ever fully realizing it.

In everyday life, a human agent is always undertaking acts that are never perfect but, nevertheless, become exercises that will enable him or her to do the act better the next time. In other words, every act is a *practice* for the next act. This may be done consciously and deliberately—as in various professions like medicine and law—or callings like music and teaching, but are, nevertheless, features of the ordinary acts of everyday life. Practice may not make for perfection, but it is an essential aspect of the quest for it.

This question for perfection is manifest in the demand that the acts performed in everyday life should be, as far as possible, felicitous ones. J. L. Austin, in his famous study of "performative utterances"—in producing which agent is "doing something, rather than saying something"—claimed that sometimes they can result in "infelicities." Such infelicities arise if "certain rules, transparently simple rules, are broken" (1970: 237). In fact, in everyday life, agents strive to ensure that these rules are not broken and that their utterances as well as their acts are felicitous ones. This demand for felicity is manifested very strongly in the rituals associated with religion. Stanley Tambiah observes, "Ritual is a culturally constrained system of symbolic communication. It is constituted of patterned and ordered sequences of words and acts often expressed in multiple media, whose control and arrangement are characterized by varying degrees of formality (conventionality), stereotypy (rigidity), condensation (fusion), and redundancy (repetition)" (1985: 128). Goffman (1967) showed that the acts and utterances of everyday life, too, have to conform to the demands of ritualization. The greater the extent to which one's acts and utterances are ritualized ones in this sense, the greater the chances that the agent's identity will be accorded the status of normalcy. When such felicity of action becomes extraordinary and striking, he or she will often be given exalted status—indeed, made into a hero.

Games, particularly the physical ones, share nearly all the properties of rituals that Tambiah has described for rituals, and that Goffman has claimed for the interactional order of everyday life, and that Austin has claimed for the value of utterances. Further, the quest for perfection is an essential ingredient of the playing of games.

From the moment a child is born, it is cast into the acquisition of various skills and subject to evaluative judgments by the adults around it. The smallest steps toward maturity and mastery of self and body are noticed and analyzed and made into both anecdotes for the family and friends and part of the record of the child. Once the voluntary moves are taken by the child in this direction, various objects and aids are introduced to the child with which it has to once again demonstrate mastery and win esteem. Toys, puzzles, and conversations become elements of these challenges. For the child, there are opportunities to show his or her developing skills and practice them to achieve improvement. Every such step is, in fact, a record of achievements that move toward the child's development into an adult, and the involvement of various significant others in the child's life. Indeed, both children and adults need demarcated structures of activity in and through which the relationship between a significant other and a dependent can be conducted so the child can receive the approval necessary to stave off fundamental anxiety.

Games are also structures that permit a child to demonstrate mastery of a variety of skills, both physical and mental, and to win approval from his or her social circles, and to subject himself or herself to assessment. The acquisition and mastery of these skills occur in inescapably social and interpersonal contexts. Indeed, games of all kinds are magnificent instruments with which a child can articulate his or her quest for perfection: physical coordination, eye and body relationship, grace and style of movement, judgment of distances and time, tactical skills, control and management of emotional states, and interactional processes. Every game, whether it is a serious game or merely a preparatory one, is a version of the "practice, practice, practice" that is the road to perfection.

This quest for perfection becomes very evident in games in which one performs alone against another. Boxing is a game in which more than one's self is at stake: one's body can get injured, and often boxers are crippled or killed. However, it is not a game in which one player practices violence against another *weaker* player. In this game, no player has a decisive *a priori* advantage: steps are taken to ensure that they are evenly matched. Nevertheless, the essential quality of boxing is not the aggression, but making punches and receiving them according to a very finely coded technique. It is a technique that demands footwork, balance, disciplined use of one's left arm and hand and right arm and hand, ducks, feints, thrusts, and attacks and retreats. The craft of boxing and the even matching of the players make it more than just a "fight" or a "brawl." A boxer in such fights is able to "give" as well as "take," attack and defend. Becoming a successful boxer is then accomplished by reaching for perfection by training, body-discipline, sexual continence, and mental training for the management of emotions. The boxer may not win too many of his contests, and may get injured in some of them, but the point of a boxer's life, as Loic Wacquant shows in a masterly analysis of the game and its players, is to seek to master a craft, live according to its codes, and fashion a self and a life around it (2003).

The Heroics of Record

The quest for perfecting a craft often manifests itself as a quest to create a record. While the quest for the heroic life in and through game playing is undertaken in such a way that the rewards are available in the immediate moment and soon thereafter, there are other consequences as well. Some achievements in game playing provide an agent with a more enduring status as a hero. One becomes an "immortal" sports icon by achieving various successes in sporting and gaming events. The word, in fact, is used to describe players who score 100 runs in their very first appearance in a test match in cricket. Such immortals are found in all sports and games. These players undertake vigorous training programs and devote themselves to meeting an extraordinary standard in their chosen game. These achievements are recorded in some form or another and, indeed, become spoken of as "records." Alan Guttman (1978) has, in fact, argued that sports have been transformed from being "rituals" to "records"—with the quest to achieve a recordable standard becoming the goal of training and discipline and performance. In other words, in addition to the constructing of heroic moments in the course of one's life and enjoying its perquisites, gamesters also aspire to create *heroic reputations* that will endure after their gaming days are over. Raymond Schmidt and Wilbert Leonard have discussed this in terms of the "post-self"—the self that persists after the active phase is over. They observe: "We conceptualize the post-self as the concern of a person with the presentation of his or her self in history. The post-self is paradoxical in that it blends the future with the past from the perspective of the individual in the specious present. Individuals ponder the mark that they will leave in time" (1986: 1088).

Such a post-self is constructed in the present by a series of steps that involve training, discipline, and performance. The quest for a heroic life, then, is undertaken in anticipation of having both heroic moments and celebration by the significant others at the moment of victory and of being remembered later in life. The post-self exists in terms of reminiscences, records, memorabilia, and enshrinements in so-called halls of fame. These halls, before the American sports industry gave it a concrete manifestation, were a metaphor for signal achievements. Their origins are probably in the Arthurian legends in which the hall of fame was in fact the knights' meeting place at the roundtable, and to achieve entry into this hall, an agent had to have performed feats of valor in combat—performed them successfully, for to have failed would have meant loss of life.

In modern American sports, there are, indeed, real halls of fame into which players who have had successful careers are admitted after being evaluated and selected by panels of other professionals—sports people. In these halls, the player is memorialized in the form of plaques and other memorabilia. To gain this distinct honor, a player then has to conduct his or her sporting career with exemplary form over the years and have a few significant records to his or her credit. In addition, nowadays, one must also have certain moral qualities: Pete Rose, among all recent baseball players, could be said to have won a life-long quest not only for the heroic life but also for the heroic enshrinement in the Hall of Fame of baseball. Nevertheless, when it was discovered that "gambling was going on," that he, in fact, bet on games in which he was a player, he was deemed ineligible for presence in the heroic hall. This issue, in fact, became a contest between the down-to-earth and rural game of baseball as it has been played for a long time and the new high-toned, corporate-capitalist game it had become over the years. This tone became heightened when Bartlett Giametti, a classical scholar and former president of the quintessential institution of the American aristocracy, Yale University, was made the commissioner of baseball. Rose had only a record of good baseball to offer against an adversary who had so much moral power. Rose was disqualified and remains outside the hall though the commissioner from Yale University has long departed. Rose's heroic quest was fulfilled in that he achieved a notable record, but it lacked the final consummation and consecration. On some scores, Rose was deemed imperfect.

Many of these seekers after a self that is remembered after the achievement may not live long enough to see the full impact of their achievements. It is, however, not the future self as such that is at stake here, but the fact that the winner and his or her social circles will *define* him or her as a historical hero that is relevant. In the specious present, the winner (and the record maker) is defined not only as a hero for the moment but also as one who will be a hero for a time in the future. It is the winner's imagined self as it will be taken in the future that qualifies the present and makes the heroic quest a source of esteem and honor.

The Aesthetics of Play

In playing a game successfully one not only masters the craft of the game but often manages to bring an artistry to it. Players are often recognized as stylists and praised for aestheticizing their performances. Paul Ziff has observed, however, that the aesthetic dimension is absent in most sports and that in any case such a dimension is irrelevant to the success of the player in the game (1974: 45). David Best concurs with this view and advances the notion that the purpose of each sport can be specified independently of the manner of achieving it, while in artistic endeavors this cannot be done (2002). This view has been challenged by many other philosophers, and Drew Hyland, after surveying Best's writings and that of his critics, concludes: "In virtually all sports we praise the outstanding athletes for their gracefulness, beauty, creativity, elegance—we praise them, that is, in the language of aesthetics" (1990: 115). This is, no doubt, true, and the beauty of execution of a move in a game like tennis or cricket or baseball can, nevertheless, be an object of an agent's quest. These qualities give an additional element to the claims for the heroic that a given athlete or gamester can make, and, indeed, some athletes become "rotten" or "ripe" with them.

> Although form does not figure in its scoring, tennis has at least on occasion considerable aesthetic appeal. A flat forehand drive executed with perfect form from the baseline is a graceful stroke ... Generally speaking, it is a fact that improving one's appearance, making one's movements smoother, more graceful, is likely to upgrade one's performance. Making sure that the forehand is hit with a long fluid follow-through will not add grace to one's stroke but it will increase one's control while adding considerable pace to the ball. (Ziff, 1974: 45)

The aesthetic and the efficient are nicely merged in such a stroke in tennis. Such a stroke is achieved after a great deal of practice, self-appraisal, and coaching. To play well and successfully is heroic enough, but to do so gracefully is an added quality of the heroic life.

In the playing of games, there are two fundamental stages: learning the essentials of the game and then achieving mastery over them. These goals are achieved by practice. The mastery involves the art and craft of the game as well as its techniques and rules. A baseball announcer comments about a pitcher: a good pitcher is one that has control over "velocity" and "location" and then has his own "stuff"—the latter a reference to the *particular* skills and techniques he is able to bring to the act of pitching. This stuff can include not only the efficiency of the delivery but also the grace and style of his movements. Among baseball batters, Joe DeMaggio was considered a graceful player as was Reggie Jackson. Consider here the description of a cricketer and the particular way he stood at the pitch to strike bat to ball to perform a particular stroke called the "cut":

> It was study for Phidias to see Beldham rise to strike, the grandeur of the attitude, the settled composure of the look, the piercing lightning of the eye, the rapid glances of the bat were electrical. Men's hearts troubled within them, their cheeks turned pale and red. Michelangelo should have painted him.
>
> Beldham was great in every hit, but his glory was the "cut." Here he stood, with no man beside him, the laurel was all his own; it seemed like the cut of the racket. His wrist seemed to turn on springs of the finest steel. He took the ball, as Burke did the House of Commons, between wind and water—not a moment too soon or late. (quoted in C. L. R. James, 1983: 15–16)

James reproduces this passage about an eighteenth-century English cricketer and gives a description of other local cricketers in the Jamaica of his youth who could also cut. They were not famous outside the club circles, but spectators and passersby would stop to watch and appreciate the cut as performed by Arthur Jones or W. S. Hill.

Such acts of heroic style are to be found in the play of famous players no doubt; but they are also to be found in the performances of nonfamous and local players as well. This is nicely put by Keith Andrews, discussing cricket: "I am sure every batsman young or old, talented or otherwise must dream at sometime of playing the ultimate innings, dispatching the greatest bowlers to all parts of the ground with a glittering display of strokes" (1992: 9). Such "ultimate" innings are, of course, rare and never come within reach for the ordinary player, but he or she can still participate in the quest for it, seek to become "rotten with perfection."

The opportunities for individuals to achieve an aesthetic presence for their selves that sporting structures provide are similar to the ones in artistic enterprises. An agent is able to perform in the sporting complexes as he or she would in a play or, for that matter, in rituals. In such playing, he or she is expected to accede to certain formal properties of performances as well as to seek certain goals. Indeed, the playing of a game resembles dramatic performances closely. The claims made for ritual by Ron Williams and James Boyd apply with equal force to sports: "Ritual is akin to an artistic masterpiece. An artistic masterpiece is that which rewards attention over time" (1993: 140). Games are, in fact, carefully constructed structures—before they are actually played—and carefully performed ones as they are being played—in which an agent becomes both an artist and at times a hero.

Heroic Acts and Esteem

In everyday life, each agent has some claims to certain levels of honor and esteem in his or her social circles. Such honor may be lower than that of the others in the circle, or brighter, but each person strives to achieve it, maintain it, and introduce its calculus into his or her acts and lines of action. Such honor and esteem is, needless to say, based on the caste, class, and gender stratifications of the society in question, but it is possible to transcend them, too. Nevertheless, such honor and esteem are *won* and *maintained* and are a function of the attitudes offered by the other in one's social circles. These attitudes themselves are functions of the nature of the act that elevated them.

Insofar as every act and every line of action carries a self with it and are instrumentations of the self, it follows that they have the capacity to either enhance the esteem of the self in its own eyes and that of the others, or diminish it. *Esteem for the self, in other words, is not something that is garnered only from support and validation by significant others and social circles, but from the significance of the acts and the sequence of acts that elicit such validation and support.* If one is told after a shoddy performance in a structure of acts—tests, examinations, games—that one had done well, and one is given a high grade, the recipient, being a self-conscious and knowledgeable actor, will know it to be an empty assertion and attitude and refuse to use it to claim honor and esteem—at least in his or her own eyes.

In everyday life, performing a task, performing it with dispatch, visible competence, and grace can contribute to enhanced esteem. The construction of esteem for the self depends not *merely* on the approval and approbation of significant others, but on the approval received from others on the successful and competent performance of a particular task or line of activity. While everyday life allows for many opportunities to perform successfully, there are some that can stand out. For children and young people, successful outcomes of examinations and class work can contribute toward higher esteem and toward a heroic life.

Everyday actions can be classified as difficult ones and easy ones. The former demand a greater level of skill and competence and even more composure of one's self and emotion than the latter. If one accomplishes the easy ones on a routine basis, one is living a normal life and, indeed, the substantial majority of a life consists of such actions. Periodically, however, one is asked to face difficult lines of action—to go forth and face an adversary, slay a dragon, clean the Augean stables—and to bring to them extraordinary skills, but the rewards from one's significant others are also bigger. The business of accomplishing these tasks of greater difficulty—I must stress that this is a relative category in terms of the age of the performer, his or her previous experience in the task at hand, the quality of the antagonist, human or material, that he or she had to face—can be said to be elements of the heroic life. In undertaking these difficult tasks, an agent is also engaging in what Alicia Cast and Peter Burke call "self-verification." They note, "Self-esteem is an outcome of, and necessary ingredient in, the self-verification process that occurs within groups, maintaining both the individual and the group. Verification of role-identities increases an individual's worth-based and efficacy-based self-esteem" (2002: 1041).

This process of self-verification works as follows: one has already developed a more or less firm self-concept, and when an occasion presents itself, it is put to the test; to the extent the demands of the test are met, self-esteem is maintained, reinforced, or even enhanced. And to the extent that these tests are public and socially witnessed—or at least socially validated—the self's esteem and honor are supported and reinforced. Esteem, in other words, is not something that is given freely and uncritically but is offered on the basis of an examination and evaluation of given performances, the accumulated social meanings of which become the self of the actor.

Insofar as such esteem for the self grows and accumulates on the basis of performances in concrete occasions, it is obvious that such occasions must be available—or be made available— to actors. An actor can use the occasions that come his or her way fortuitously and perform in them and achieve esteem, or he or she may have to seek occasions in which it is possible to face a challenge and achieve distinction. From childhood onward, actors find such opportunities that are suitable to their age category, perform accordingly, and acquire esteem from the support and validation of their primary groups. There are feats of physical prowess that one can master and display just as there are mental tests—both formal and informal—that are available for an actor to use to achieve validation of self and esteem from significant others. These achievements, in fact, allow an actor to proceed toward a heroic life—success, periodic if not consistent, in the significant lines of action that one undertakes: not certainly, a knight errant or a warrior prince, but a hero nevertheless. Such knights and princes have to meet challenges that are appropriate to their age, reputation, skill, and status in various dimensions, just as the nonknights and nonwarriors do.

In any case, it is clear that such processes of action that lead to outcomes that either enhance the self or diminish it need occasions in which the actor and his or her self can be allowed to act, to perform—through instrumentations by which the performance can be judged and evaluated—and some value, vague or specific, be given to it. Esteem for the self is achieved by situated activities that are culturally accepted and socially and interactionally valued.

The self-assessment does not occur in isolation. It is accompanied by assessment and validation by significant others. In fact, significant others are always observing the tasks that an agent happens to be performing and subjecting it to assessment, as an index of the agent's competence and character. In Harry Stack Sullivan's (1953) original formulation, a child develops a self-system in order to avoid feelings of anxiety that may occur if the child displeases the significant other. One can develop skills and competencies, not necessarily those of the routine sort, in order to win the approval of the significant other—the more the better; the more the approval, the better the sense of well-being. To achieve these competencies and achieve them in social contexts, there is a need for various objective structures.

The conceptualization of a self and the garnering of esteem for it cannot be done in the abstract, nor is it enough merely to receive the rapid approbation of others—significant or generalized. Rather, selves are constructed and esteem achieved by performances in concrete arenas that the relevant others can use to confirm an aspect of the self and an esteem for it. And the recipient of such confirmation will recognize it as such—in contrast to empty and *unwarranted* praise and approbation. Indeed, concepts of self and esteem for it have to be warranted and justifiable structures and processes that both the individual and his or her others constitute jointly.

Self-esteem, far from being an abstract and unidimensional concept, can be concretized as *competence* and *worth*, as Victor Gecas and Michael Schwalbe (1983) have argued. Competence is defined in terms of "efficacy"—self-efficacy—the extent to which actors define themselves as efficacious. The worth dimension of self-esteem is defined as one's perception of oneself as a being of some value—tautologous though it may seem. It may be surmised that one's sense of worth is a result of displaying competence in one line of activity or another. In other words, one's sense of esteem about one's self will depend on the outcome of an act or series of acts that he or she has undertaken and the evaluations to which they are subjected.

Games of every sort are instrumentations with which an agent can manifest certain skills, face an adversary, and engage him or her as well as the natural environment—rain, snow, lay of the land, and so forth—in combat and display a quest for perfection and at times achieve it as well as win the game. *In games, one finds an organized structuring in which it is possible to seek the heroic life in a systematic manner.* While in the rest of the act-structure of everyday life, one has to wait for the right moment for an act to occur in games, there is a ready-made structure where acts to which one is answerable can be performed and subjected to all the possible evaluative criteria necessary. The acts are then and there, the duration is short, and the judgments immediate and readily and lucidly given.

Such esteem or honor for the self can be achieved even in the playing of a simple game. Consider the following Thai children's game that is played as follows: minimal number of players, two; game equipment, five pebbles of equal size.

First step: The player lets go of the five pebbles on the floor. He or she picks up one as the throw pebble, throws it in the air, picks another one up from the floor, and hastens to flip the palm up to catch the throw pebble before it falls on the floor. He or she picks up the rest of the pebbles one by one.

In the second step of the game, the player picks up two pebbles on each throw of the throw pebble. In the third step, he or she picks up three pebbles, and then in the fourth step, all four pebbles are picked up after the throw of the throw pebble.

In each of these steps, should the player make any pebble move other than the one he or she intends to pick, he or she is dead. His or her turn in that round of the game is over. Whichever turn he or she misses will be taken in the next round.

The fifth step is the score-making step, after success in the preceding four steps. The five pebbles are held in the open palm of the hand. The player throws them into the air and tries to catch them on the back of the hand. Those caught are again thrown into the air and those finally caught in the palm of the hand are then counted. Should the player fail to catch any pebbles, he or she is dead. The one who catches the most pebbles in the last maneuver wins the game (adapted from Anderson, 1980: 245–58).

This game, played in many other parts of the world besides Thailand, has an intricate structure. It provides the players with a sequence of moves that are successively more difficult, in an interactional context, that calls for manual dexterity and disciplined maneuvers. Each step holds the possibility of defeat as well as the chance to continue the game. There is a final complex step undertaken by all the players who have arrived at the stage that determines the winner. *As one plays, one is subject to continuous self-assessment as well as assessment by the other.* This is a game that is played without rackets or balls or courts, but with pebbles on the sandy yard in front of the house; nonetheless, it has a structure that is similar to tennis. One serves and then forfeits the serve to the adversary and then gets it back again, and if no winner is found, a final stage is played to break the tie.

The availability of games of all kinds in which various actors can participate provides opportunities for the acquisition of elements in which selves can acquire esteem and approval just as they provide opportunities for the actors to merge with others and interact with them in significant ways. In both cases, the selves are validated and allowed to sustain themselves. Such a *jamming* of selves is necessary, indeed, for their continued existence as vital presences to themselves. It is, then, not the professional gamester or athlete alone who is enmeshed in a search for the heroic moments in a life, but everyone who plays a game. A game is the microcosmic representation of the world's activity, a machine for achievement, achievements in small doses that can accumulate to a big win, an encapsulated structure with unambiguous and concrete signs of victory and defeat and organized as a quest for perfection.

For players, games are objective structures in which their selves can be put to the test and various evaluations and judgments made about themselves both by themselves and by others. For, to begin with, a performer can and must and does evaluate his or her performance based on the distance it is from reaching perfection. Every gamester strives to master the rules, skills, graces, and nuances of the game, not by reading about them or listening to talk about them, but by practicing them at every possible opportunity. He or she practices and practices, performs on a selected occasion, assesses his or her play on all relevant variables, and then practices again selectively to improve on the deficiencies discovered on the earlier occasions. Such self-assessments can lead to further attempts at practicing to overcome the deficiencies—in other words, the search for perfection. One can seek to achieve the perfect drive, the most beautiful "late cut," a fine forehand, the perfect serve, the best curve ball and keep on searching for it.

The Vicissitudes of the Quest

Gary Alan Fine, in his study of Little League baseball players, does not directly address the issue of self-presentation and the acquisition of esteem as a result of success in the playing of the game. Nevertheless, he does present some information that can be used to infer the presence of selves and the emergence of esteem in children's activities. Performance in the field seems to determine the way the players are treated by the other members of the team and "labels of villainy" and "heroism" are offered on that basis. Consider the case of Tom Mayne. His status was defined by the nickname "Maniac," playing on his name and the fact that he was awkward as a player and generally a failure on the team. The following season he became a very popular member of the team—based on sociometric rankings—and got a new nickname, "Main Eye," because he was now one of the best batters on the team and a successful third baseman. He has now emerged as a hero.

Fine reports other cases where the "villain" of the team became a hero by his performance in the game. One example is very telling because it illustrates how a single act can transform one's status in the group and the self of the performer. "Smell-ton" was the nickname of one baseball player on a team. However, notes Fine, "During the first week of the season, much to everyone's surprise—his own included—he hit a grand slam home run for his first little league hit. This nickname Smell-ton was forgotten and for the rest of the season, his teammates called him Jim. Status is one determinant of nicknames, although nicknames label a boy and solidify his status as well" (Fine, 1987: 135).

Nicknames determine and solidify not only status, but are also signs of the self, the conferment of an identify through the looking glass of one's peers. In the case of Maniac and Smell-ton, their selves were changed into heroic ones by the successful accomplishment of a socially recognized and culturally valued task; they achieved esteem in the eyes of their peers and, no doubt, in their own as well. Furthermore, their achievements were in structures of activity—games—the performance of tasks that were culturally established and difficult at the same time.

Arnold Palmer became a very public hero in later life, but before he became a champion, he also achieved many heroic moments. Palmer was one of the greatest of the gold players; his personal qualities, the open, cheerful smile with which he presented himself to the world, and the confident stride with which he walked the greens endeared him to millions of fans. We can select from his autobiography various encounters in the trajectory of his career that were heroic moments leading successively toward a heroic life—moments in his career when he was still an amateur and beginner. Here is Palmer describing his first junior tournament and his defeat in it:

> I watched Jack hit his first drive off the tee, a blast that sliced straight into the trees, and smiled. I was so cocky that I was sure I already had him beaten, especially since my drive found the beauty of the fairway.
>
> Off we went, with Jack in trouble and me already feeling the matter was mine. A few hours later, Jack waltzed me 4 and 3 and I learned one of the most valuable lessons of my career: Never take any opponent for granted on a golf course. (1999: 41)

Later in his career, he described his encounter with more celebrated players:

> The highlight of my freshman year was beating Harvie Ward and Art Wall ... to win the Southern Conference Championship. I am sure many of the reporters considered it a major upset—Harvie after all was considered by many to be the best collegiate player in the country—but I never had any doubt in my mind that I could beat him or anybody else ... I came home that summer bubbling with confidence and with a college-boy spring in my step and won the Susquehanna Amateur and reached the semifinal of the North and South Amateur. (1999: 54)

Soon, however, he was brought down by another match:

> That summer I flew to Memphis, Tennessee and met a man named William Barrett, Jr. in the first round of the United States Amateur Championship at Colonial Country Club. I felt pretty confident about my chances ... As strange as it sounds, perhaps I was both awed *and* cocky—I failed to play as well as I should have and was beaten fairly handily, 6 and 5, by the much older Barrett in the first round. I took losing hard, mentally kicking myself for a number of missed opportunities. (1999: 55)

In these early encounters, Palmer is experiencing a number of heroic moments as well as giving play to certain emotions. He is elated and cocky, awed and proud, and later when he loses, he "takes it hard" and is "kicking himself." Games are, in fact, the best structures in which such emotions can be put into play and the presence of a self felt and cognized.

In golf, the quest is a lonely one, pursued on the course all by oneself with the ground, the weather, the wind, the hazards of the game, and another player or players as adversaries. In contrast, football in high school, in particular, provides for many the perfect structure in which the heroic life can be pursued. It is a game in which the values of "manhood"—strength, determination, indifference to pain and physical injury, a stoicism and composure under pressure—are promoted. Playing it successfully as a young man gives him the opportunity to claim a particular self in his formative years. In addition, it is a game that is highly valued by some fathers who want their sons to display these qualities.

Here is the story of Don Billingsley, whose father had been a star football player for his high school. The father was divorced from his wife, and Don had been living with his mother in another town. In his sophomore year, he left his mother and went to live with his father because he wanted to play for his father's high school. Eventually, he became the starting tailback for the high school—his father's position. Here is H. G. Bissinger's description of Don's first move:

> With [his father's] eyes focused on him, the ball popped loose from Don's hands without anyone touching him. He went after it on his hands and knees desperately trying to recover it and redeem himself, but he couldn't get to it. A groan went up from the crowd and El Paso came up with the ball. (1990: 84)

He fumbled his chance toward a heroic life and never recovered after that. The fullback was injured and Don expected to be asked to fill in by the coach, but an untested junior named Chris Comer was put in, and he played the entire second half as fullback. Bissinger describes the scene: "It was Comer's first game ever ... he had talent but they were wary of him ... But these concerns began to lessen when Comer took the ball early in the third quarter at the 50, lingered behind the line for a split second until a tiny alleyway developed, turned the corner, broke past two defenders with an acceleration, dashed down the sideline for a touchdown" (Bissinger, 1990: 87).

Comer made another touchdown and moved toward a heroic life of his own. Comer, a black player, would get all the touchdowns, all the attention, all the glory, and Billingsley would get the aches and pains of being a blocking back. Here is Bissinger's description of Don Billingsley's predicament: "So the injury to the [fullback] hadn't made a damn bit of difference. As he later looked back on it, it seemed that the minute one black player got hurt, there was another to take over. 'I didn't get to carry the ball' was the way Don Billingsley sized it up. 'They moved up another nigger to carry the ball'" (Bissinger, 1990: 88).

Don Billingsley's quest for the heroic life, his desire to be like his father and impress him, was thwarted by somebody else's talents and became a very bitter experience. He suffered his defeat at the hands of a black man. In the racist community in which Billingsley had lived, this was a double failure.

Football, in fact, has a special place in the relationships between fathers and sons in some segments of American society where the son seeks to become a hero to his father. In addition to becoming a medium through which fathers and sons can interact comfortably with each other, described well by Malcolm in his work *Fathers, Sons, and Football.* The game also becomes the perfect instrumentation with which the son can display the values of a masculinist, muscular, and "Protestant" culture fully. Fathers, as significant others, will demand satisfactory performances from their young sons to receive their approval. Here is a poignant example of a young man who wants to win esteem for his self by winning the esteem of his significant father. Joe is a member of a high school football team that is about to play a championship game. A reporter talks to him:

Reporter: Has it been hard for you, your dad driving you so hard?

Joe: Yeah, there were days when we didn't talk to each other. I just sat in my room and avoided him ... I am going to take the final ball and give it to him. (*The Crusaders,* 2002)

A young man is driven to work hard and work toward success, and the offering of the "final ball" becomes a measure of his success on the field as well as a way of winning his father's approbation.

Boxing, like golf, is a game in which an individual agent is alone in the arena and provides the opportunity-structure for vindication and verification of self without aid from anybody else—except, of course, coaches and seconds. The quest for a heroic self is clearly the foundation of the boxing life as described by Loic Wacquant. He observes:

> Fighters conceive of boxing not as a springboard for aggression and an exercise in violence, but as a skilled bodily trade, a competitive performance craft requiring sophisticated technical know-how and an abiding moral commitment that will enable them not only to improve their material lot but also, and more urgently, to construct a *publicly* recognized, heroic self. (1995: 501)

The boxing arena enables the agent to shed his other identities as he enters the gym and the ring and focus on a new one where his physique and talent are used as artful instruments for the construction of a new self. Win or lose, this self becomes an instrument for the "ontological transcendence," in Wacquant's phrase, and achieves a heroic moment or series of moments.

Boxing is wonderfully suited for these transcendental moments and selves. The agent is alone in the ring facing an opponent who is there to hurt him physically, to begin with, and emotionally later. As one fighter put it, "It is up to the fighter to fight Louie: *cain't nobody make me fight!* You come in there with d'understanding of whatever y'know, you gon' do. If you ain't prepared, that's your *fault"* (Wacquant, 1995: 501).

Alone in the ring, the fighter assembles a series of punches and moves and responds to his own moves as well as those of his opponent. He is in charge of his acts and the physical pain and the emotional strain—a little bit of fear, a little bit of anger, a little bit of frustration, as well as a little bit of joy—and the emergence of a dialogue with punches and responses in the quintessential myth of combat that will, indeed, enable a self to give itself a heroic coloring.

Often the quest for the heroic life can go awry and lead to extremes of conduct and a conception of self that can make life difficult for the heroes as well as for others to be around. In the ethical system of ancient Greece, the concept of *hubris* or *hybris* was used to describe a particular failing in the conduct of individuals. In the comprehensive survey of the complex meanings of this term, Douglas MacDowell notes that "hubris is always bad. It is an evaluative term, not an objective one." He proceeds to define it: "Hubris is having energy or power and misusing it self-indulgently. English expressions that could be used to translate the word, in some contexts at least, are animal spirits, exuberance, ebullience, bumptiousness, and egotism; but *hubris* is a much harsher word than any of these" (1976: 21). Kenneth Dover adds another dimension to this: "Hubris is behavior in which the citizen treats a fellow citizen as a slave" (1974: 147). In Athenian society, the display of hubris was considered a crime and punished by law. In Greek mythology, too, heroes were punished for their hubris.

This hubris is manifest in the sporting life in many ways. Such conduct, in fact, detracts from the heroic stature of an agent and, indeed, indicates a failing hero, though typically they do not suffer the fate of the heroes of Greek mythology. One of the most common ways in which hubris manifests itself in an aggrandizing self is in the interaction between the sexes. In Athenian society itself, David Cohen observes, "From the standpoint of Athenian law... two particular categories of the usage are of relevance: physical assault against free person and conduct related to sexual violence, sexual aggression or to violations of sexual honor" (1991: 173). In contemporary society, too, the aggrandizing self that athletes are allowed to cultivate in both the institutional settings in which they operate and the primary groups in which they function allow also for the emergence of hubris. This often results in attacks on women. The bonding that occurs in certain games—football, basketball, and hockey—has been suggested as one of the reasons for these occurrences of attacks on women. It is, however, more than that: the sense of hubris that occurs in an athlete is an essential component of his self—the adulation of the crowd, the unqualified support of institutional structures, and the fact of standing out from the simple and ordinary people in the high school or the college cannot but lead to the emergence of hubris in football players, basketball players, and hockey players. Local heroes all, they must cultivate hubris and an aggrandizing self and show it, and one of the surest ways of doing this is to attack women sexually. The manifestations of hubris are truly an attendant feature of the heroic life in certain institutional and social contexts, and often, no more than in earlier years, heroes fall from the pedestal on which they were placed—for example, the boxing champion Mike Tyson.

This does not happen, however, often enough. Indeed, in some cases, the hubritic offender has been rewarded with more honor and prestige—at least among his peers—for having successfully treated a woman as a slave, to use Dover's terminology. In the culture of college fraternities, for example, where sporting success, too, is highly valued, Martin and Hummer observe, "Inter-fraternity rivalry and competition—particularly over members, intramural sports, and women—encourage fraternity men's commodification of women" (1989: 457). Loyalty to a fellow member who has displayed sexual-male hubris is the other side of admiration for fulfilling one of the aspirations of the fraternal male role.

Patricia and Peter Adler have studied this phenomenon of hubris in college settings and described the emergence of what they term the "gloried self"—a result of aggrandizing moves by a gamester that really lead to a "conflict of self." "The forging of [these] reflected selves began as team members perceived how people *treated* them; subsequently they formed reactions to that treatment," observe Adler and Adler (1989: 301).

This treatment and the reaction on a more or less continuous and systematic basis, leads to the emergence of "constricted self," which the Adlers describe very well as follows:

> The gloried self is a greedy self, seeking to ascend in importance and to cast aside other self-dimensions as it grows. It is an intoxicating and riveting self, which overpowers other aspects of the individual and seeks reinforcement to fuel its growth. Yet, at the same time, its surge and display violate societal mores of modesty in both self-conception and self-presentation. (1989: 300)

This quest for the heroic life, which manifested itself initially as a drive to succeed in a chosen game and mobilized players' emotional, social, and physical resources to achieve it, eventually leads to an *aggrandizing self* that often violates societal rules of modesty and decorum and becomes consumed by a greed and an ambition that can also lead to "conflict between their desire for recognition and flattery" and the socialization they had received to fight these feelings and impulses (Adler and Adler, 1989: 300).

The failings that the Adlers describe can be considered as failures of character. There are also other more direct examples of the fallen hero: The fact that games consist of many heroic moments also implies that the possibility of failing in these moments, with disastrous consequences to the self, also exists. Many games have a moment that is so crucial that the outcome of the entire game depends on it. These are moments in which an already established hero is given the chance to reinforce his or her status, or a new player is given a chance to become a hero. In American football, such a moment occurs when the score is tied and there are only a few seconds left in the game and the placekicker gets the chance to score three points. The entire stadium and every player and the coaches and the officials are focused on this play. The competing sides take their appointed positions, the ball is given to the quarterback, and he positions it quickly for the kicker to send it soaring between the goalposts while the opposing team is rushing toward the kicker to stop him. The whole maneuver with the ball is a smooth and graceful one and the entire fortune of the team depends on it. There is nothing like it in all of sport for the sheer focusing of enormous responsibility—responsibility for the team, and for the state or country or city that supports the team. The drama is intense and the chance for a heroic moment unique: it is for the kicker to win or lose the game all by himself. In a game in which the placekicker stands or sits on the sidelines for most of the time, he is now singled out to emerge as a hero or loser. There are many tales of placekickers who did, in fact, put the ball between the upright goalposts and win for the team. It is, however, the tales of those who failed that are instructive here. They gather a post-self characterized by unwelcome memories. If the kicker is given the chance and he fumbles it, he will be remembered as a failure, it appears, not only for the season but for long afterward. Consider this report:

> The University of Washington's Chuck Nelson had kicked a NCCA record of 30 straight goals going into his 1982 game against rival Washington State. But in that game, he missed a key 33 yards that led to the Huskies losing in what was considered a tremendous upset. Nelson would eventually be known throughout the Pacific Northwest as "Wide Right Chuckle." (Freeman, 2002)

Indeed, notes Freeman, kickers who miss are given nicknames that represent such misses. He reports the case of Sam Mowry, who became a successful federal prosecutor. Years after he missed a kick, people would walk by him and say, "What's up wide right?" And even a convicted felon to whom he was giving a plea bargain asked him, "Hey, ain't you wide right?" (Freeman, 2002). The defeat will remain a major event in the immediate life of the player and may continue to haunt him or her for a long time. As Billy Jean King, a victor in many games on the court and a failure, too, at times, observed sagely, "Victory is fleeting, but a loss is forever."

In many national and international soccer championship events, the penalty "kick-out" is used to break a tie at the end of the overtime period. Five players are selected initially to stand at the penalty spot and kick the ball between the goalposts, with only the goalkeeper to defend the goal line. It is in every sense a duel with only one thrust allowed to the kicker and one parry allowed to the goalkeeper. Nevertheless, the odds are stacked in favor of the kicker: he or she has more room to maneuver and more moves and strategies at his or her disposal. Still, he or she can fail to score and one miss is enough to decide the game. Here, the defeat is not so much at the hands of the other team as such, or the goalkeeper, but a set of circumstances over which the kicker has great control. Nevertheless, if the ball ends up in the hands of the goalkeeper, the loss will be hard to bear and will haunt the kicker for the rest of his or her life. One single move, one solitary mistake can end a season, lose a championship, and make one's team or country or the nation dejected for a year, two years, or four years—until the next championship season.

This was the fate of many kickers in soccer—but some of them take it very hard. The English kicker Stuart Pearce, in the penalty shoot-out against Germany in the semifinal of the World Cup in 1990, broke down in tears as did the Italian kicker Franco Baresi in the final of the World Cup in 1994 against Brazil. Their performances received negative comments from the press and sports commentators on television, particularly Pearce's conduct from the British press. It was not quite British, you see, to cry over a failure.

The heroic self can be won and maintained through games but perhaps they may not be remembered for long unless one has created a "record." Various games have such heroes but none so secure in his heroic status as Roger Bannister, who was first to run the mile in less than four minutes. Others have to face the prospect of their records being broken unless they slip away from "fields where glory does not stay," as A. E. Housman's Shropshire lad did:

> The time you won your town the race
> We chaired you through the market-place
> Man and boy stood cheering by,
> And home we brought you shoulder-high.
> Today, the road all runners come,
> Shoulder-high we bring you home,
> And set you at your threshold down,
> Townsman of a stiller town.
> Smart lad, to slip betimes away,
> From fields where glory does not stay

And early though the laurel grows
It withers quicker than the rose.
(in Williams, 1952: 486–87)

Games, then, provide both the structure and opportunity for one agent to put his or her skills and competence into play, face the resistance of both other players and objects involved in the game, and emerge victorious—indeed, a hero. The myths of conquest and combat that one finds in the literature are essentially exaggerated versions of the problems and possibilities of everyday life. Games are mimeses of these problems and possibilities, myths in which various themes are enacted in the flesh and in the spirit, combats staged in various forms of elaboration, with opportunities for agents to become heroes—or fail in the attempt.

6

Reflexive Catharsis

Emotions are volatile experiences. At a particular moment one can be feeling placid and unconcerned, and suddenly someone else utters a sentence or two, and one becomes incensed and is ready to strike a blow against that someone. The person utters another sentence or two clarifying the meaning of the first utterance, and one's anger subsides. The emotion of love may take longer to kindle, but it, too, can begin quickly, flicker away, grow stronger, and again decline in time, or it may follow some other sequence. Emotions then, occur in time: fear, awe, reverence, are given play by the self, experienced in their kindling and their flaming and their dying—and perhaps at times in their rekindling and reflaming. It cannot be doubted that the self experiences its ongoing presence in an interactional world of other selves and material objects through the constant play of emotions.

Arlie Hochschild has introduced the notion of emotions as capable of being "managed." She observes, "I use the term emotional labor to mean the management of feeling to create a publicly observable facial and bodily display; emotional labor is sold for a wage and therefore has *use value.* I use the synonymous terms emotional work and emotion management to refer to these same acts in a private context where they have use value" (1983: 7). This approaches emotions from a radically new perspective: to allow that emotions are *managed* or subject to *work* is to claim that the actor has some measure of control over the emotions and can choose to give them form and presence. This is, indeed, what Hochschild's research supports: Flight attendants are trained to display pleasant, friendly, and supportive emotions to their passengers, though they may "actually" be irritated and angry at them. They, Hochschild claims, are practicing "surface acting" in this drama of human relations: putting on a front, creating a behavioral manifestation on the surface. In contrast to this, when these flight attendants go home to their spouses, lovers, and children, they manage their emotions by engaging in "deep acting" and show their love, affection, and so on—or perhaps even anger and hostility, too—to their associates.

The concept of the management of emotions must, however, be advanced a little further. It is not that they are managed so much as that they are *put into play*. That is, an agent, an actor, a self, finds himself or herself in a situation and a context and opts to put one emotion or one set of emotions into play in the situation and reap the consequences. In the case of the flight attendants, we have the following situation:

The agent: a self-conscious actor, aware of the role as a flight attendant, an employee of the corporation, trained to act in a certain way and committed to the economic and social consequences of playing this role.

The act: He or she smiles, jokes, and accepts the, at times, rude and provocative and demanding behavior of the passengers, with equanimity.

This could be described as putting the emotions of "joyfulness" and "pleasure" into play in the situation and constructing a social act with particular characteristics with the passengers. It is, of course, the case that the flight attendant is not committed to this particular emotion but is, nevertheless, putting it into play.

At home, too, with spouse and children, he or she can be said to be putting certain emotions into play but is, in this instance, committed to them. Nevertheless, it must be admitted that even in this instance, the attendant may be only partially committed but is giving the emotions full play, just to create a particular social act that is relevant at the moment. The implication of Hochschild's work, then, is that the actor usually has some measure of control over his or her emotions. One can, in fact, claim that a human actor, with varying degrees of control and reflexivity, gives play to various emotions in situationally and personally appropriate ways.

The fundamental feature of these moves is their *reflexivity*: the self, situated in time and place and interaction and conscious of its responsibilities to itself and to others, acts in a certain way and is able to simultaneously assess its own performances and the emotionality that accompanies them. This play of emotions that the self experiences can occur through the acts of others by their meaningful indications, suggestions, and innuendos, inducing one to anger, jealousy, love, hatred, and so forth. When these inducements are forthcoming, it is possible for the recipient to refuse the inducement and allow himself or herself to be indifferent to them. The recommendation that one should do this has come from religious leaders from the Buddha to Jesus Christ. The Greek philosopher Epictetus puts this nicely: "If you do not wish to be prone to anger, do not feed the habit; give it nothing which may tend to its increase (quoted in Harré and Parrot, 1996).

Similarly, envy and jealousy can be handled by the self, which can give it play or obviate it so that it dies before it gathers momentum. Or else one can redefine the object that is causing the feeling of jealousy or envy. This is the essential theme of Aesop's fable regarding the fox and the grapes, which became sour after the fox failed to obtain them.

These plays occur as moments in ongoing sequences in which the individual finds himself or herself in moments that he or she expects to evolve into new moments. In other words, emotional plays occur in narratives in which the individual puts himself or herself. It is a reflexive placement of the self in anticipated emotions, ploys that bring a heightened sense of the self's presence.

The situations in which an actor finds himself or herself experiencing these various emotions can occur because the other is engaging in acts that provoke them. Or else he or she can go in search of opportunities in which various emotions can be put into play. One searches for love by taking various steps, utters various sentences, and so forth, in seeking to engender the emotion of love in self and other. One also seeks adventure, puts one's self and body at risk directly and thereby puts one's emotions into play. Racing-car drivers, mountain climbers, stuntmen and stuntwomen, sky-divers, and so on are people who seek the opportunities in which various emotions can be put into play. Duelists, soldiers in combat, and various other professionals who police, guard, and defend people and territory, too, put their lives on the line and in doing so experience the play of various emotions: fear, anxiety, and awe at one's own temerity. In such enterprises, though there is ostensibly a threat to one's life, the chances of getting killed are small or else the activity would have been abandoned. Nevertheless, there is some risk—a loss of one's life in some instances, but a loss of esteem for one's self in all such challenges. Indeed, in extreme activities as in standard ones, it is the self that is put to the test. In many of these exercises in the narrativization of emotions, there are real risks involved: In pursuing an object of love, one risks his or her self-esteem and reputation; in driving a car at high speeds in races and climbing mountains, one risks one's life. However, when one seeks love or adventure, the risks are counterbalanced by the anticipation of increased esteem for the self and enhanced reputation. At the fulcrum of the act when any of these risky moves are contemplated and put into practice, the actor, too, must feel ambivalent emotionality—fear and anxiety, the thrilled anticipation of success and adulation of interactional and significant others, and so forth are all mixed together. The emotions are felt and put into play, once again, by casting oneself into one narrative or another: romantic story, heroic tale, the adventure yarn, the myths of conquest and combat.

Acting and putting a self into play are, then, *simultaneously* a rational and emotional process. Indeed, in putting the self into play, an agent puts his or her emotions into play. Emotions, too, are not static feeling systems that reside in the mind or body of the individual but are dynamic processes that come into play in the self of the individual and manifest themselves in acts both internal to the mind and external to it. Human individuals actively feel their emotions as ongoing processes and seek various ways of experiencing them, controlling them, disciplining them, expressing them, and reciprocating them.

If one, therefore, begins with a human actor as an agent, an actor in his or her own right, then one must perforce enlarge the theory of the emotional structure of participation, directly or indirectly, to include enacted events. Such a theory must be inclusive enough to consider not only theatrical events but also events in which an actor is a participant as a direct agent. The emotional process of *watching* a play or a football game or a film and the act of *participating* as a player in a game of golf, tennis, football, poker, or bridge must have something in common and demand an encompassing accounting. The responses of audiences to such events have been generally described as "catharsis." Indeed, in order to develop both as coherent and complete a theory as possible, one must eschew the word *catharsis*—however hoary and respectable its provenience, and substitute the concept of emotional *play* or the play of emotions in its stead. Yet, insofar as that word is an essential part of our critical vocabulary today, we must perforce retain it but expand its meaning to indicate emotional *activity* that includes more than pity and fear.

Catharsis as Act and Experience

Catharsis, from Aristotle's early commentary on it to the more elaborate discussions of it since then, has been considered as the reaction of an audience to an enactment of a tragedy on a stage or arena. Summarizing this view, Gerald Else notes:

> The usual interpretations of catharsis are too numerous to list but they all have in common a focus on the pity and fear which are aroused *in the spectator.* They are to be somehow "purified" (reduced to beneficent order and proportion) or "purged" (expelled from his emotional system) by the play. (1970: 98)

Two questions are raised by this interpretation of catharsis: One, insofar as the purification and purging occur at the end of the play, at the resolution of its plot, what is the status of the spectator *before* he or she is purified or purged? Two, does the performance of the tragedy have an effect on the players? One can conjecture that long before the purging occurs, the spectators will be involved emotionally with the play, and not merely with the emotions of pity and fear. If the play is any good, they will feel a variety of emotions as they become cognitively engaged with the plot. The emotion will be exercised, given shape and form and even the body will be made to cooperate with these exercisings. These emotions, besides pity and fear, can include love and hate, awe and disgust, and so on. Insofar as the spectators came voluntarily to the theater to see a play, and paid money for the privilege, it can be said that they came to feel these emotions and, indeed, came to experience these emotions, to give them play.

The players who enact the tragedy, however, are immune to these feelings. They may feel exhausted physically and emotionally at having to perform the same part over and over, but there is no record of their experiencing pity and fear or any other emotion. They are hired hands with a certain talent, no doubt, paid to perform these roles again and again. Actors who performed in medieval passion plays are said to be exceptions to this. Typically, however, actors who enact tragedies are not affected by the content of these plays. Aristotle's notion of catharsis—"through pity and fear, bringing about a catharsis of such emotions"—conceives it as initially a passive process that is based on a repressed or controlled state of emotionality that is "relieved" by exposure to a dramatic presentation. This is based essentially on a hydraulic or an alimentary metaphor for the mind and self of a human being: as he or she moves in the world of objects and other selves, he or she accumulates various "substances" that build up and need to be purged—no doubt to be ready for the next series of accumulations. Such a view is based on a conception of the human being as a passive entity: he or she is essentially one who is acted upon, a victim of unseen as well as seen forces in an unequal society of a few masters and many slaves who attract humiliations and collect resentments that are eliminated periodically by exposure to dramatic tragedies or tragic dramas.

One can, however, challenge this view of the human being and substitute for it one who is an agent of his or her actions, an actor who, whatever his or her position in class structures or power structures, is able to mobilize moves of his or her own, voluntary gestures and acts that bear the stamp of his or her identity. No doubt, the frequency and strength and originality of these moves may vary, but the capacity for such actions does not. It is universal to the species.

Indeed, the experience of catharsis is not limited to the various passive forms such as watching a tragedy being performed on stage. One set of active moves that induce catharsis is the various religious rites that various agents perform. In such acts, emotions, far from being distanced or repressed or sublimated, are given *expression* and allowed to play on the self and in interaction. One of the most ubiquitous of such ritual acts is the practice of sacrifice, and a close examination of sacrifices across the spectrum will show that they are acts in which emotions are given play, experienced as manifestations of the self of the participant, and the consequences of which are garnered as signs of the self. These rituals are acts in which the themes of "mortification and its variants" are given manifestation. In this "sacrificial motive" are included "suffering and victimage which are basic to tragic conflict" (Burke, 1959: 364).

One must, in fact, expand the meaning of catharsis to include not so much the "release" of repressed or controlled emotions, but the giving of systematic play to a variety of emotions and the expression of emotion in and through a variety of acts. This view of catharsis is similar to Benedetto Croce's theory of the aesthetics of poetry. He has a take on catharsis that is different from the Aristotelian one, claims Burke: instead of works of art, such as tragedy's inducing a "purge," he contends that they allow "expression"—for the spectator as for the writer. He expands on this as follows:

> Unquestionably, the symbol-using animal experiences a certain kind of "relief" in the mere act of converting any inarticulate muddle into the orderly terms of a symbol-system. There would be at least three major critical points in such a process: the poet is one way "cleansed" of his "extra-poetic materiality" when he hits upon his theme and starts to track down its implications; he is cleansed in another way when he becomes so deeply embedded in his symbol-system that its effect takes over and in a new quality or order of motives emerges from it; and he is cleansed in still another way when the goal having been reached, a fulfillment is complete. Corresponding stages may be ascribed to the reader, or to the work itself, as with the different qualities of beginning, periphery, and end, analyzed without reference to either reader or writer. (1959: 364)

A poem—or any work of art—is an expressive form, a concrete and tangible manifestation of the artist's emotions, and the act of creation is an expressive act. Such acts have a beginning as a conception and mature into a performance and lead to a resolution—all the while giving play to ideas, emotions, and attitudes. Such acts of composition with one kind of medium or another—paint, plaster, stone, sound images, or words—leading to the expression of emotions, attitudes, and ideas, are not confined to consciously artistic enterprises. They occur in everyday conversations—or, at least, frequently in such conversations. Freud discovered this in the course of his early work and, characteristically, attributed it to the "release" of repressed emotions—thereby missing their compositional and narrative qualities. Indeed, it is not obvious that any unconscious forces are being released at all. Rather, the only phenomenon for which we have evidence is that an agent is putting together in words, with a certain coherence and narrative sequentiality, with vivid imagery and allusions, an account that evokes given emotions and displays certain attitudes. Consider:

> We found, to our great surprise at first, that each individual's hysterical symptom immediately and permanently disappeared when we had succeeded in bringing clearly to light the memory of the event by which it was provoked and in arousing its accompanying affect, and when the patient had described that event in the greatest possible detail. (Breuer and Freud, 1966: 4)

The patient describes the event that caused her the trauma "in the greatest possible detail." The description is not available to us now, but one can surmise that the description followed some narrative conventions and was, above all, a recollected and recounted one. Such narratives were subject not only to the vagaries of selective memory, prejudiced emphases, characterization of self and other, and an economy of words and management of the plotline. In such narratives, the actor is not so much describing an actual event, but in the telling itself, he or she is putting various emotions into play, not only for his or her own benefit and fulfillment but also for winning the attention and interest of his or her audience. It is such play of the emotions, of giving them expression and form and coming to a resolution that becomes cathartic. Not so much a purging or a cleansing then, but a performance situated, seen and heard and perhaps even applauded. What exactly happens in such a performance? Or, for that matter, what exactly is "talk"? In such talk, or in relevant writing for that matter, an agent gives coherent symbolic form to his or her emotions, attitudes, and ideas and constructs a narrative of his or her self.

In composing a poem—or for that matter, a novel or play—the author himself can be cast into the narrative. Using the concept of identification, Burke argues that Milton, in composing his epic poems on Samson, was, in fact, identifying himself—his blindness, political tribulations, and betrayals—with those of the heroic Samson and experiencing some emotional satisfaction and relief. Burke sums up his thesis as follows:

> It is almost a kind of witchcraft, a wonder-working spell by a cantankerous old fighter-priest who would slay the enemy in effigy and whose very translation of political controversy to high theologic terms helps by such magnification, to sanction the ill-tempered obstinacy of his [own] resistance. In saying with fervor, that a blind Biblical hero *did* conquer, the poet is "substantially" saying that he in his blindness *will* conquer. This is moralistic prophecy, and is thus also a kind of "literature for use" at one remove, though of a sort that the technologically-minded would consider the very opposite of use, since it is wholly in the order of ritual and magic. (1969b: 5)

The composition of the poem, the putting together of the narrative in its details of plot and imagery and character, is a magical act, a spell, in fact, by which Milton was exorcising his own emotions of frustration and defeat. He does this not by crying and weeping or being silently sad or depressed, but by actively participating in a symbolic construction.

Burke is describing a state of feeling, an emotional exercise in which an agent is able to *actively express* his or her emotions instead of passively watching a performance and feeling "pity and fear" at the fate that has befallen the protagonists in a tragedy. In the mode of catharsis that

Burke is describing here, the agent is able to select the symbolic means by which he or she is seeking to "cleanse" his self and mind of various emotions by performing them. By selecting a theme and starting to work on it, the poet is able to transcend his or her own materiality and corporeality. Once this proceeds apace, he or she is able to immerse himself or herself in the creation and construction of new forms and combinations of the symbolic system that he or she has chosen to use. Finally, once the project is finished, there is the sense of closure and the "sense of an ending," in Frank Kermode's (2000) phrase, a fulfillment, an orgasm.

Lest one is tempted to think that Burke's argument is a mere literary conceit, consider here an anthropologist's account from the field of a bereaved young woman handling her sorrow. The key emotional process here is the symbolic transformation of a private sorrow into a public medium, a medium governed by cultural rules about language use, composition, meter, rhyme, metaphor, and so on. A young woman from Bali, Suriyati, has been in love with a young man and was expecting to marry him. He, however, dies of tuberculosis, and she is quite inconsolable, and, although she soon marries someone else, she carries her sadness with her. To "find a way out of her sadness," she wrote poems. Her culture provided her with a form and an expressive mode, and she transformed her sorrow into verse:

> My love ...
> This life on earth is laced with deceit
> Now you are free of it.
> No longer does it make its demands on you
> You are free ... pure ... cleansed.
> My love ...
> I am overcome with sorrow
> To see the emptiness of your bed
> Abandoned we are, I, father, mother, your brother and sister.
> My love ...
> Tears sprout
> As I lay the blossoms of my sorrow
> On the ground of your resting place.
> I cling to the last trace of you
> embracing at the very moment we part.
> I move without touching the ground.
> The blossoms of my sorrow fall to the ground.
> All has turned empty, lonely, still, and dead.
> But he who went away
> leaves a million thoughts,
> a million loves
> and a million visions, haunting a poor body
> And stirring in the black night.
> (in Wikan, 1990: 196)

Again, the key process is the transformation of private feelings into public forms and their eventual communication to others. Such processes, however, are not confined to writing or singing or speaking, but they can be found in other forms of expression as well. Dancing is another medium in which feelings are transformed into ordered movement, shapes, and patterns.

These "compositions" enable an additional fruit to emerge: the satisfaction of having done a good job, admiration and acceptance of self for having done well or well enough. Indeed, this cathartic consequence is suggested by Pierre Corneille's approach to catharsis. He advanced the view that tragedy induced admiration and awe at the heroic actions of the protagonists of the tragedy. For example, Oedipus's act of self-blinding when he realized the enormity of his misdeeds can induce such admiration and awe in the audience, rather than pity and fear. Other writers, outside France, began to develop Corneille's argument and used it to develop the concept of "heroic tragedy." Moses Mendelssohn, defending such a view of tragedy, argued that the "noble ethic" contained in it encouraged "ambition" and "self-assertion" and would make the spectators "more virtuous" (in Rubidge, 1998: 4). In other words, watching the various protagonists on stage displaying courage, bravery, steadfastness, loyalty, generosity, and discipline would induce admiration in the audience and lead them to a virtuous life as well. Such a "virtuous life" or at least a life in which the "noble ethic" is put into practice, was a feature of the life of the aristocracy at certain periods in history and was particularly well suited to those who adopted the military vocation (Rubidge, 1998: 4).

Games and Catharsis

Playing games—physical ones or mental—is another medium through which emotions are given shape and form and, indeed, given play. Games as they are played give a sense of control and power to the player, and in social environs in which many actors feel powerless and estranged, the playing of games becomes a way of symbolically transforming one's sense of alienation and other sorrows to frameworks of action and movement and progress and quick resolution. Playing a game, among other things, is an act of symbolic composition, with some games as tightly structured as a sonnet—for example, chess—and others, long and elaborate like a novel—for example, baseball. In these games, as in a sonnet or a sonata, an agent, acting with others, constructs a symbolic form in which emotions and attitude and self are put into play and brought to a resolution.

The playing of games incorporated the "noble ethic" into its framework. The program of action that a player puts into effect induces responses, not by invoking pity and fear, but by providing avenues for the assertion of self, to indulge in acts and emotions that are manifestations of one's intentions and desires. Such assertions of self typically involve courage and steadfastness, emotional discipline, and studied patience—the successful execution of which will induce admiration, not only from an audience but from the protagonist himself or herself.

The social psychological process involved in the moves that an agent makes in the playing of games is essentially that of both constructing and confirming an *identity* as an ongoing process. In this process, the agent, within the compass of the game, is able to construct himself or herself as a courageous, deft, assertive, and emotionally controlled entity, one who is in charge of his or her lines of action and able to execute them at his or her will. This occurs both when he or she wins in the gaming encounter and when he or she loses—provided that he or she lost while playing the game as he or she was supposed to play it. Courage and skill and control can be asserted, a self presented, even if the final score is not in one's favor. In such exercises in which mind, body, self, and other are involved, it can be said that an agent is able to experience *performative ecstasy*—that is, a stepping out of an old self into a new self that is acceptable and admirable in some ways. Such a state of ecstasy is achieved *reflexively*: turning one's intentions into organized systems of actions that, in turn, influence the presence of one's self. Thus, the self experiences a *reflexive catharsis*. In experiencing performative ecstasy, an individual steps out of his or her self, the one he or she has constituted in the routine life and to which a commitment has been made over the years, and experiences a sense of momentary liberation. Its major quality is its active and voluntary nature: one seeks out the experience; commits mind, self, and body to it; and then deliberately undertakes various moves to consummate it.

In experiencing performative ecstasy, then, a player steps out of a mundane self into another enriched one and lives with it, for a while at least. Nevertheless, the fruits of such ecstasies, the residues of the emotional play that was experienced, make it easier to live with the mundane self once one returns to it.

Games—in addition to their cognitive and interactional features—enable participants to experience various emotions and to give them play. Different games, however, provide different types of structure in which emotions can be experienced: soccer and basketball are games that move fast and have an accelerated pace, and the emotions come fast and often rise to a crescendo as the game proceeds. There is hardly any respite, and people as they play them—or watch them—feel rushed into extreme emotionality. Golf, on the other hand, is slow, methodical, and evenly paced and allows for the play of a more cultivated and measured emotionality. American football, too, is a staccato game with many interruptions and does not admit the fluent emotional development of soccer or basketball.

The pacing of the game, and the timing of the action, in other words, affects both the intensity and the depth of the emotions that players and spectators experience.

In this regard, games become theatrical events: they present actions, organized as episodes between agents, that cumulatively develop a theme as well as a variety of emotions in temporal frameworks. In other words, games are theatrical events as well as storytelling events. In playing a game, an agent is engaged in a performance: he or she uses various skills and talents he or she may possess to put his or her mind and self and/or body into some sort of activity that he or she controls. Such performances are addressed to another who is a fellow performer and are often addressed to spectators as well. These performances require meticulous attention to the rules and regulations of the game. The players of games bring both a discipline of the body and a control of mind and self to the game.

In an extensive study of the "theatrical event," Wilmar Sauter (2002) cites Terry Gunnell, a Swedish theorist, to claim that "text" must meet three criteria to be considered drama. They are:

1. The text contains characters who address each other.
2. The action occurs in the "present tense."
3. It is representational (no narrator is necessary).

From this perspective games can, in fact, be termed theatrical events. In Gregory Stone's felicitous phrasing, games allow for both "play and display" (1971). They are dialogic in character insofar as each player interacts with the other then and there and puts himself or herself on display. Further, they represent within their own performatives a "version of reality"—indeed, a mimesis of a version of the selves of the participating agents within an interactional framework—in a story that is created by the performance.

It is in enacting these theatrical features of games that an agent is able to experience reflexive catharsis and performative ecstasy. To play a game with a reasonable degree of efficiency, one gives one's self its demands—to follow the rules and the ethos of the game, to give it both intellectual commitment and emotional involvement, to play to win, and to care enough about the resolution. Such processes enable an actor to escape from his or her routine, everyday self and to move into a heroic and acting self: to become an agent in charge of his or her acts, leading these acts to a resolution. This is performative ecstasy—the process of stepping out of one's self through performance. Game playing then enables an agent to find surcease from alienation and angst, boredom and nausea, fear and trembling, anxiety and dread—at least for a while, by immersing himself or herself in games.

The emotional play in games is essentially a reflexive activity. The dictionary describes reflexivity as "of or relating to an action directed back upon the doer or the grammatical subject." While such reflexivity informs all actions, as G. H. Mead argued (1932), it achieves particular prominence in the playing of games. The structure of games demands that the activity of playing occurs in small compasses of time and space with every move being monitored by self, others, and at times a referee, with each move in the game, and the game itself, resolved then and there. Games are continuously reflexive processes inasmuch as the success or failure of every move is judged immediately in the presence of at least one other and the meanings thereof "directed back upon the doer." Further, in game playing, the response from the other is immediate, quick, crisp, and admitting of little ambiguity or uncertainty of signification, which is another sense in which acts are "directed back upon the doer." That is to say, one judges one's own actions and allows such judgments to influence the self, and these actions are further directed to the actions of the other player. Such an immersion in the game revolves back on the self, permitting it to undertake a number of reflexive exercises and garnish or adorn one's self with the products. Winning will do this and losing with dignity, losing after a good fight, losing in a controlled manner, losing without cheating and unsportsmanlike conduct are all capable of garnishing the self and creating various cathartic effects.

Every move, insofar as it is an assertion and expression of self, becomes a reflexive move: a player has to assess the risks involved in making it, the chances of its being a fruitful one, and the immediate consequences of its success or failure. While certain elements of the acts of making a move in a game may become habitual, the larger problem of every move must be thought through and calculated, each one reflexively constructed in terms of its implications to the self in the short term and in the long run. The control that a player has over his or her acts and the sense of initiative that such control infuses into the self, the reflexivity that such acts demand of the self, confer a cathartic effect—the catharsis of expressivity and, at times, admiration and acceptance of self.

These reflexive acts enable the player to continuously put his or her self into play and experience the emotions that emanate from the acts of the game. These emotions, to the extent that the move is successful, will be ones of joy and satisfaction and the resultant adoration. If the move is unsuccessful, one, at least, can feel that he or she did his or her best, played fair and well, and can derive satisfaction from that.

In playing a game, an agent is able to gain unique control over the ball—or other objects—and guide and move it as one may wish. These are moments of power and agentic mastery of the act. The symbolic composition of such acts and the emotional performatives that are involved in such composition allow the processes of reflexive catharsis to emerge.

Consider here Richard Giulianotti's description of soccer playing: While emphasizing the player's position in a collective enterprise, he, nevertheless, acknowledges the agentic power involved in the game as well:

> Players are locked into structured relationships which emphasize the collective over the individual . . . Even in receiving the ball the players pursue the collective interest and follow the procedures, "clearing the danger" in defense or passing to team-mates. Yet in doing so, the "actor" is required to *select* from a number of options—who exactly to pass to, at what speed or angle and with what accompanying instructions. (1999: 127, emphasis added)

Not only does an agent have control of the ball, he or she is also able to dictate the next move. Expressive action and emotional involvement are combined and given play in the next move, with a succession of such moves enabling a catharsis to emerge. This process of active construction of moves that bear a narrative relation to each other and lead to a resolution can be found in all games. In fact, playing a game is a form of symbolic composition, willfully and artfully managed by the player, intent on taking the narrative to a particular conclusion.

Consider again Mia Hamm's description of one of the central acts in a game of soccer:

> You can call it trapping, collecting, receiving or controlling but whatever name, it is still the most important skill in soccer. During a game, the ball comes at you in a hundred different ways at a hundred different speeds and a thousand different angles. Oh, yeah, and it is spinning too. You have to be able not only to control the ball but at the same time prepare it in the best position to make your next move, whether it is a pass, a dribble, or a shot. (1999: 61)

Once a player has trapped the ball, he or she is in control of the ball and is able to execute the next move. In undertaking these procedures, watched by at least the other players on the field, the agent gets to perform an act which he or she has to assemble—indeed, compose, however momentarily, and execute at the same time. During the course of the game, the player will get many chances to do this, and in the end, they all constitute a composition in unison. Herein lies the expressive cathartic event, the various acts of assembling a "theme" in soccer.

If in team games one can find the opportunities for assertion of self and implicit admiration of self, such opportunities are abundant in individuated games. Here is an example from bridge where a famous bridge player obtains gratification from the game itself and from an unexpected opportunity. Sontag, who was playing against a Forquet and Sharif partnership, described it as follows:

> Despite appearances, it turned out that the Lancia team was not as calm and composed as they wanted us to believe. Alan Truscott of the *Times* described what happened: "There was considerable tension ... This tension took its toll on the very first deal when there was an opening bid out of turn. Instantaneously, an opponent came to the rescue. 'Let us re-deal it,' he said. But there was a twist to this scenario. It was Forquet, winner of 15 world titles, who opened out of turn. And it was Sontag playing for the first time against one of the world's all-time great players who waived the penalty. He could, of course, have called the director who would have enforced the law: Sharif would have been barred from bidding and there would have been a lead penalty in addition."
>
> Permitting Forquet and Sharif to play a new deal won me "Sportsman of the Year" award from the international Bridge Press Association, but my action was not motivated by generosity. I did not want to win on a technicality ... Taking advantage of a technicality would have proved nothing especially to myself.
>
> It was satisfying that the great Forquet took us seriously enough to suffer from a case of nerves. (Sontag, 1977: 18–19)

Sontag and his team eventually won the match against the Italian team after several days of play. Sontag observed, "I was not sure we would win until the second to last hand. It was then that Belladonna banged his massive fist on the table and shot a murderous look in my direction, a look that was almost regal in its anger. He was so unused to anger" (1977: 37).

After Sontag's team won the trophy, he noted, "After a few drinks at the hotel, I took Kathy to Alfie's for a steak and some good red wine. It was marvelous. Then we went to a discotheque" (1977: 38).

In Sontag's account of his experience, there is, to begin with, the heroic gesture, indeed, a sacrifice of a chance to begin the tournament with an unexpected advantage. It received the admiration of others, and no doubt, he was pleased that he made the gesture: he was sportsman of the year as well as the one who kept the challenge of the game alive by refusing to win on a "technicality." He brought his wife into the account and celebrated with wine, bread, meat, and dance.

Such cathartic effects of participating in games are fully realized in games where one single antagonist faces another in single combat and is able to engage the other with total dedication. Boxing is one such activity, and it has the added advantage of being a game in which the players are able to experience physical pain with every move. Mind, self, and body become equally involved in the cathartic process.

Boxing, to begin with, is a game in which the agent is able to experience the full weight of his power and agency and experience the resistance of the other in one fell swoop.The power to act and to mobilize the body and assert oneself is a cathartic act. It is a manifestation of power and energy and control and often provides the self with narrative intent and expressive voice that is often lacking in other aspects of one's life. Here is a description of this process:

> I mean, to be able to stand before a man, a massive man an' he punches you an' he goes through efforts to hit—an' harm you, an' he's unable to even touch and an' you're no more than (whispering excitedly) twelve inches away from him: that, that it takes art to be able to do that ... That's to be able to have *your rhythm,* to put forth your own individual *style,* and have it portrayed and presented to the public, uh to be able to, I mean *have an art,* and have it appreciated you know; it is very beneficial. (in Wacquant 1995: 506)

This sense of power that a pugilist experiences is enhanced by a special quality of the boxing game: one can feel this sense of power and participate in self-admiration and self-acceptance as well as in eliciting the approbation of significant social circles, even if he loses in the end. Wacquant describes this very well:

> The *specific honor* of the pugilist, like that of the ancient gladiator, consists in refusing to concede and kneel down. One of the visible outward signs of that much-revered quality called "heart" said to epitomize the authentic boxer is the capacity not to bow under pressure, to "suck it up" and keep on fighting, no matter what the physical toll. (1995: 496)

A good pugilist goes the whole way and receives admiration from others as well as from himself: he didn't surrender, he fought on, he showed heart, a claim that is insistently attested to by the physical pains and aches that he would be experiencing for a few days afterward. He has, in fact, cast himself into a heroic narrative and proved himself worthy.The cathartic effects of such a process are attested to by the comments of another boxer: "When you get out to the gym, you feel like a brand new person. Some people like to get high an' *that's my high* ..." Another pugilist observes, "That's a great feelin', that you are in shape an' you live a disciplined life, there is nothin' like it in the world—you're on *cloud nine*" (in Wacquant, 1995: 511).

The art of boxing is not merely a violent physical attack on the other with jabs, hooks, crosses, upper cuts, feints and parries, pivots, and blocks. Rather, observes Loic Wacquant, "a fighter must also develop the ability to combine and integrate these elements afresh during each bout to resolve the practical conundrum posed by his or her opponent's repertoire of physical, technical and tactical tools" (1995: 503).

For boxers, such a composition of the acts of boxing into a coherent scheme can also, simultaneously, "carve out a margin of autonomy from their oppressive circumstances" and can be useful for "expressing their ability to seize their own fate and remake it in accordance with their inner wishes," observes Wacquant and he concludes, "That is why, in spite of all the pain, the suffering, and the ruthless exploitation it entails, of which fighters are painfully cognizant, boxing can infuse their lives with a sense of value, excitement and accomplishment" (1995: 501). The boxing arena enables the agent to shed his other identities as he enters the gym and the ring and focus on a new one in which his physique and talent are used as artful instruments for the construction of a new self. Win or lose, this self becomes an instrument for "ontological transcendence" in Wacquant's phrase, and achieves a redemption of sorts.

Authenticity of voice, management of one's mind, self, and body in harmonious acts of power and creativity and emotional expressiveness in a disciplined manner, and its submission in a narrative that leads to a fulfilling *telos* and an engagement with an other are all combined in this much maligned art, science, and social activity. The act of getting into the ring and duking it out with another well-matured agent is a form of compositional activity. One can see here the authentic voice of the pugilist and his own understanding of its artfulness and empowering significance.

In the boxing arena, the working-class young men, many of them also black or Hispanic, thereby facing a double alienation in the society, find an opportunity to both assert an autonomous self and manage a symbolic transformation of ideas, attitudes, and emotions into an organized repertoire of punches, jabs, feints, and ducks, and thereby experiencing reflexive catharsis.

The sense of *acting* successfully and controlling the situation and outcome as far as possible and gaining joy out of it is more common in individuated games like boxing and tennis than in team games. Here is Don Budge's description of one such moment in tennis:

> Each time [he hit] gave me the chance to employ my new strategy. I moved up for the second serve. And located there, as I figured, I was able to catch his second serve before he could bounce up and away. I hit each one back, hard and deep, putting Gamm on the defensive and myself at the net. Each of the four points I won were made exactly the same way with a well-placed net volley on my second shot. I had the break I had to have and I was back to 3–4. (in Baltzell, 1995: 296)

The description of the event that Budge gives here fairly reeks with self-satisfaction. The abundance of the first-person pronoun and the acknowledgment of the success of his strategic thinking indicate the admiration he was to feel for his performance. During the course of play, his body, mind, and self were involved in undertaking a creative and powerful series of acts, and afterward, his happiness is almost palpable. He described the scene in the stadium after he had won his game:

> I suppose it was an hour or so after the match before I was able to dress and leave the locker room. I think it was nine o'clock by this time, but the midsummer sun was not down yet. I walked out and glanced at the stands and I was shocked because there were still thousands of people there clustered together all over the stadium. It did not seem to me that they were talking much to each other or moving around. They did not seem to be ready to leave. It was as if they wanted to stay there where they had watched the match. I have never seen anything like it before, or since, just all those people standing there and remembering, long after I had dressed and gone home. (in Baltzell, 1995: 298)

The audience's admiration, even awe, at the game they had just witnessed between Budge and von Cramm reinforces Budge's own joy and allows him to give play to various shades of emotion, and admire himself to boot.

Basketball has a certain iconic status in high schools and colleges, and even professional teams elicit extraordinary loyalties from fans. Some star players also become heroes in the culture. It is a game that is played widely in American society and allows for participation by people of varying talents—from players of extraordinary ability to ordinary players who join pickup games. Its quickness and its capacity to change rapidly from a winning score to a losing one enable agents not only to put into play a variety of emotions but also to experience them in rapid succession as alternating waves.

Pat Conroy describes a number of scenes from his life that support, in many ways, the thesis about catharsis that is being advanced here. Conroy is, of course, a renowned writer, a master of composition and reflexivity, and this may skew the argument in favor of the thesis. Or else, it may express and support the thesis with great clarity and panache. He notes:

> As a boy, I had constructed a shell for myself so impenetrable that I have been trying to write my way out of it over thirty years ... No outsider I have ever met has struck me with the strangeness I encounter when I try to discover the deepest mysteries of the boy I once was. Several times in my life, I have gone crazy, and I couldn't tell you why. The sadness collapses me from inside out and I have to follow the thing through until it finishes with me. It never happened to me when I was playing basketball because basketball was the only thing that granted me a complete and sublime congruence and oneness with the world. I found joy, unrecapturable beyond the realm of speech or language, and I lost myself in the pure, dazzling majesty of my sweet, swift game. (2002: 3–4)

It is, of course, capturable in speech and language, Conroy's disclaimer notwithstanding—at least up to a point—and he does capture it in this book. Noticeably, the book is entitled *My Losing Season* and is, in fact, mainly an account of his failures as a basketball player. He describes one such episode of failure and gives a fine rendition of the alternating currents of emotion, indeed, the span of emotions, that occur in watching a game from which one has been excluded.

> "I rotted on the bench" is the most accurate phrase I can think of. I also felt putrefaction settling in as I watched the games go by without my participation ... I had to surrender my dreams of that season to the sure knowledge that my position had been taken from me, fair and square, by a far superior athlete. Even though I would not play this year, I still had to shoulder responsibilities to my teammates ... And I could cheer, yes cheer my ass off for the good of my team ... I cheered Tee loudly and then silently offered a prayer that he would break both his legs. Horrified, I would right myself and scream support for DeBrosse, then quietly pray that his pancreas would fall out onto the floor. This despicable pattern of applause and indefensible prayer got me through the second half of the Wofford game. (2002: 160)

He does, however, have some moments of success and the consequent joy. Here is a description of one such event:

> I returned to my teammates, overflowing with a strange exhilaration. I could not suppress the confidence I felt, or deny it, or hide from it, or lose it or dig a hole for it to burrow in. I simply had it in aces and spades and I gloried in it and strutted around the court and stuck it down Davidson's throat. (2002: 326)

Throughout Conroy's narrative, one gets such instances of performative ecstasy and reflexive catharsis. He is, of course, describing several years later, his emotions at an earlier time, and in a prose that has achieved a certain refinement since he felt those emotions—but that is no reason to discount the complex emotionality of the scene he is describing. Furthermore, he is lucky: he was able to experience these emotions as they occurred several years earlier and recollect them in varying levels of tranquility years later to achieve compositional ecstasy just as John Milton did.

The efficacy of game playing as a means of achieving reflexive catharsis becomes clear when one considers the case of those who lose the game they happen to be playing. It is possible to lose a game in many ways: one such way is to lose very badly and be thoroughly humiliated. This, however, rarely occurs insofar as most people play against those who are a "match" in skill, talent, age, strength, and so on. When players are evenly matched—achieved by a variety of social conventions and more formal rules like handicapping and "seeding" and "ranking"—a player loses after having put up a good fight. In such a game, a player gets the opportunity to show "grit," "determination," "heart," "guts," a "fighting spirit," a "never-say-die attitude," "willingness to take punishment," and other qualities of character that will enable him or her to elicit the admiration of others as well as his or her own.

Further, in such instances, the losing occasion, while not, of course, providing joy or satisfaction of the ordinary sort, nevertheless, provides opportunities for the experience of other deep emotions—albeit sorrow or rage. To feel some emotion, any emotion, to feel saddened or awed by one's own performance is to be alive in a world of others and to obviate any feelings of alienation and nothingness.

Indeed, feeling sorrow and rage, frustration, and even terror is not something that human agents routinely avoid. Rather, many actively seek it. Consider mountain climbers: they know that this is a dangerous enterprise and yet put their lives at risk in pursuing it. Bungee jumping and other forms of "extreme sports" are other examples of activities in which agents seek certain emotional experiences—in this case, adventurous terror.

Gambling and Reflexive Catharsis: Reflecting with Money

To understand the full extent of the cathartic process involved in gambling, one must recapitulate the earlier comments about the significance of money in the interactional life. It is, *par excellence,* the instrument of power and domination in one's relationships with others. It can be used in one way or another to influence, control, and dominate the other. In a capitalist society, it is a measure of an individual's self, a metric of his or her place in both the current interaction and the community at large. Furthermore, in such a society, every adult is expected to have some money on him or her in every public arena, ready to undertake small monetary transactions as well as to understand and cherish its value—both economic and social. One must pay for his (or her) drinks, buy a buddy a drink at times, pay the bus fare, be parsimonious, bargain when undertaking monetary transactions, and so on—all indices of full membership in a community. Money is a reification of the powers of the individual, variable and quantifiable. George Simmel observes:

> The tremendous importance of money for understanding the basic motives of life lies in the fact that money embodies and sublimates the

> practical relation of man to the objects of his will, his power and his impotence; one might say, paradoxically, that man is an indirect being. (1990: 211)

First, the power that money represents is really the power of the self on the one hand and the measure of the self on the other. It is a double-edged sign that represents the self while its quantifiable aspect measures the self. The relationship of money to the self is that it is used to define the self's connection to the other. One can work for another and get his or her self validated in a more minutely calibrated way by the amount that is received as payment. A cut in pay, however small, will diminish the self, just as an increase will enhance its worth in one's own eyes, just as in those of one's relevant others.

Second, by having more money and asserting overtly or covertly, the power to use it in one way rather than another, an agent defines a self and the selves of others with whom he or she has a relationship. The use of money in an interaction allows the self, in Goffman's words, to maintain a socially proper *demeanor* and expect—or even demand—the proper *deference* (1967). In everyday transactions, an adult or near-adult can be properly demeaned and be given suitable deference only if one has possession and control over sufficient money—except in special circumstances.

Third, an agent, by asking or not asking the other for money, defines himself or herself just as he or she defines the self of the other. The asking can be of many kinds. To begin with, one can ask the other for a loan, with or without interest. Or else, he or she can ask for a gift or a donation or for alms. If it is a loan the other's willingness to give it will be based on the agent's capacity to pay it back. In gambling circles, one gives a "marker," a promissory note whose value and the value of the self issuing it depend on the other's willingness to accept it. The applicant for this loan can be often heard to say, "I am good for it. You know I am good for it." In any case, once such transactions are begun, the recipient becomes a supplicant, with commensurate effects on himself or herself, and the giver becomes the dominant one.

In everyday social life, money plays a central role and one can use it reflexively in many ways. Putting it at risk is one such way, and a common way of doing this in a simple and direct way is to gamble with it. When a person gambles—that is, stakes his or her accumulated resources—what is being staked is his or her self. The money, in fact, is a token of the self of the player. By putting it at risk, he or she is also exercising his power and acting to give play to his emotions. In the moments of the gambling transaction, the player experiences a variety of emotions. The cathartic element in such a transaction is not so much in the experiencing of these emotions, but in the manifestation of one's encapsulated power and the willingness to risk it. It is the control, the competition with other selves, the chance to best the other in knowledge, cunning, intelligence, and ruthlessness that provide the reflexive catharsis. The reflexive as well as the active process involved in acts of gambling indicates to the player that he or she is not entirely powerless in the world, nor is he or she without resources that he or she can readily put at risk. The acts of play thrust him or her into patterns of meaningful dialogues with others. Even if he or she has nothing to say to another in ordinary circumstances, he or she can say enough at the poker table with his or her money. In face-to-face gambling—as opposed to betting on horses—there is both addressivity and answerability that are focused almost exclusively on a token of the self. The selves of the participants become fully involved with each other through the process of addresses and answers that, in fact, is the fundamental activity of the game.

The supreme example of this phenomenon is the "potlatch" practiced by the Native Americans of the Southwest, made famous by the studies of Ruth Benedict and Franz Boas. There are many interpretations of this practice in which valuable objects are given away in a rather competitive spirit and, in extreme cases, put to the fire. Boasting and shaming the other in addition to dealing with objects of value were also part of the potlatch, as Benedict (1959) noted, leading her to the conclusion that the entire configuration indicated a culture in which "megalomania" was a dominant characteristic. Melville Herskovits (1952) considers potlatch a form of conspicuous consumption, agreeing with Benedict, who had made the same observation. Others consider potlatch to be a struggle for achieving and maintaining rank. Homer Barnett (1938), for example, considered rank as the key process in the potlatch, where people are invited as witnesses to the phenomenon of achieving rank by displaying property. A more recent analysis claims that "the central characteristic of the potlatch is that it represents the most formal and elaborate of exchange processes in the societies in which it is found. Like all types of exchanges, it defines relationships both within and between groups" (Rosman and Rubel, 1972: 659).

One can consider poker as a form of the potlatch. In playing poker, an agent both displays his or her wealth and puts it at risk and, more often than not, loses it. The abandonment of one's accumulated resources, in large gamblings or small, as a public display can be considered a definition of poker. The "structural" explanations and the "psychological" explanations— "rank" and "megalomania" —are both involved in the gaming with cards for money, as in potlatch.

The process of reflexive catharsis, in fact, reaches a kind of apotheosis in the game of poker. In poker, not only is the agent in complete charge of the moves, but every move is fraught with deep uncertainty. In a very condensed moment, victory and self-assertion or defeat and humiliation are both envisaged as possibilities, and every such moment is pregnant with emotionality. The game of poker is, in fact, structured more than any other game, as a successive series of such condensed moments. Furthermore, in such moments, signs condensed of the self become deeply involved. In these games, winning and losing money are mere by-products of the playing while the acts of putting self and emotions into play are the main products.

When money—a scarce resource valued by all but the religious retreatists—is involved, its capacity to create excitement for the self is measurably increased, insofar as money and its surrogates can, in fact, be *measured.* Putting money into play is "where the action is," to use Goffman's (1967) expression, one that is actively in use among poker players. Johnny Chan, sometimes described as a "legendary player," observes, "I love this game. We all do. We want to be in the action all the time. The only time we aren't in the action is when we are sleeping" (2004: E-5). Such "action," of course, is no ordinary action but one freighted with the significance of the self's weight and worth encapsulated in a "moment." Another legendary player, Howard Lederer, observes, "I know I am in a tournament and am going to lose ... But you have to be in the moment. I was having a mediocre day at cards, but I was doing my best. You can't think about the meta, about the past, about the bad beats. You have to play the cards in front of you" (in Chan, 2004: E-5). Indeed, the action is in the exquisite merging of moment and self and its ecstatic presence in the tokens that are wagered to the unfolding of the next moment.

In playing poker, a player engages in the various megalomaniacal moves that Benedict discussed. Boasting and shaming the other, needling and humiliating the other verbally and gesturally, are common place—often playfully, but maliciously more frequently. Basil Browne observes, "Needling is a direct attempt by players to annoy or upset fellow players. Needles are personal comments aimed at another player's ego" (1989: 13). Such needling and the money that changes hands, in fact, change the rank of the players in relation to the others and in their relationship to those outside the game itself—like spouses and children of those who lose consistently more than they win. Some games are organized as a struggle for rank, as in the fictional poker game discussed in the novel and film *The Cincinnati Kid.* There is an aging poker player, Lancey, who is being challenged by the *kid* from Cincinnati. The aging player is referred to as the *man,* and if the kid wins, he will be the new man. In the event the kid loses, Lancey remains the man. In the real world of poker, too, there are tournaments arranged for the best players to meet and test their ranks—described nicely by Alvarez (1983): "Poker playing is also conspicuous consumption: one displays a certain indifference to the money, pretends losing or winning does not affect him or her that much."

Andy Bellin observes:

> Professional gamblers ... lose an understanding of the value of money ... A hundred dollar chip here, a thousand dollar raise and a million dollar

> prize there, it knocks the sense out of them. But just as a doctor needs to be able to overlook the humanity of his patients to be effective, a gambler needs to disregard the monetary value of money. Otherwise he would be ineffective. (2002: 161)

This important measure of the self, which is hoarded and cherished and exchanged with extreme care and regard, is treated in a different way in poker. To put one's wealth at risk—trust it to the luck of the fall of the cards and one's own undependable skills and the uncertainty regarding the distribution in someone else's hand—is to display a cavalier and profligate attitude. This is an attitude that manifests power and control as well as the freedom to assert it with the most potent of signs in a money economy.

The poker player takes this cavalier attitude about money to the table and performs with it. It becomes a prop to his or her presentation of self and each move he or she will make at the table is a construction of a narrative, a symbolic composition and a continuous transformation of self. He or she calls his or her bets, picks up the needed cards, bluffs and threatens and shows his or her courage, and displays his or her bravado and his or her skills in agonistic dialogue with various antagonists at the table. In such tasks, he or she is able to manifest a self, give it play, engage emotionally with others, and even admire his or her performance as the game proceeds.

The reflexive as well as the active process involved in acts of gambling indicates to the player that he or she is not entirely powerless in the world and is not bound by the utilitarian attitude to money. He or she is not without resources and can readily put himself or herself at risk, while entering into patterns of meaningful dialogue with others.

Insofar as playing poker is a move in a strategy of giving play to the self by addresses and answers, thereby experiencing various emotions and a sense of control and power in an interactional situation, whether one loses or wins becomes of no great relevance. The action is the name of the game, the act of putting one's self into play and exercising control over the self and the situation. The cost of the action—if one loses consistently—is the fee for the participation, the means for experiencing performative ecstasy and catharsis. The game gives the player the chance to construct and perform sequences of action, admire his or her skills whenever appropriate, or revel in contemplating his or her audacity and cunning.

To sum up, catharsis is not a hydraulic process but a reflexive one in which self, act, and meaning are involved. The cathartic effect of playing games is created by a variety of factors. To begin with, there is the sense of power and control that the playing gives the player. He or she is in charge of the act; it is his or her voice that is expressed in the coordination of mind, self, and body that is game playing. Secondly, these moves are addressed to the other, eliciting answers that enable a dialogue to be constructed. In games, the emergence of dialogic process is guaranteed: unless there is addressivity and answerability, there is no game. The action sequences and the dialogicity enable a variety of emotions to be given play. It is not so much a "purging" of the emotions that game playing provides but a systematic and concerted expression of emotions, a series of acts that give play to them in narrative sequences, with fundamental emotional variations, leading to persuasive denouements.

7

Gaming Ideologies and Playing Utopias

The concept of ideology has undergone many variations in its usage over the years since it was first used by French theorists in the eighteenth century. Noting that the concept's growing popularity has been matched only by increasing obscurity, Willard Mullins (1972) observes that the main problem has been that it has been used without adhering to the strict maintenance of boundaries between it and various other related ideas like "myth" and "utopia." Similarly, the concept of utopia has received a number of commentaries. The history and development of the concept itself has received scholarly commentary from a number of authors—Frank and Fritzie Manuel (1979), Krishan Kumar (1987), and Paul Ricoeur (1986). Individual utopian texts, too, have been subject to detailed commentary—for example, Stephen Greenblatt on Thomas More's work (1980).

In any case, when agents play games—or for that matter participate vicariously in them—they are both gaming ideologies and playing utopias. *To game an ideology,* in the usage here, is to give it expression and performative presence and to systematically indicate its essential features, wittingly or unwittingly. And *to play utopias* is to perform selected features of utopian conceptions with awareness and interest.

Ideology and Utopia

It was Karl Mannheim who coupled ideology with utopia in a celebrated book of the same title. Ideologies, he argued, should be distinguished into "particular" ideologies and "total" ones. Particular ideologies refer to the "more or less conscious disguises of the real nature of a situation, the true recognition of which would not be in accord with [an individual's] interests. These distortions range all the way from conscious lies to half-conscious and unwitting disguises; from calculated attempts to dupe others into self-deception" (1960: 49).

The concept of total ideology, Mannheim argues, "calls into question the opponent's total Weltanschauung (including his conceptual apparatus) and attempts to understand these concepts as an outgrowth of the collective life of which he partakes" (1960: 50).

On utopia, he comments: "A state of mind is utopian when it is incongruous with the state of reality within which it occurs ... Only these orientations transcending reality will be referred to by us as utopian, which when they pass over into conduct tend to shatter, either partially or wholly the order of things prevailing at the time" (1960: 173).

Elaborating on this, he notes that utopias "transcend the social situation, for they too orient conduct towards elements which the situation ... does not contain, but they are not ideologies, i.e. they are not ideologies in the measure and insofar as they succeed through counteractivity in transforming the existing historical reality into one more in accord with their own conceptions" (1960: 176).

For Mannheim, ideologies, both particular and total, determine the mental components of individuals and their conduct—though in different ways. They function to "disguise" interests, on the one hand, as well as to provide a whole worldview in which individuals get submerged without realizing its detailed operation, on the other hand. Utopia is again a meaning-system that transforms current reality into one that agents desire. It is an agent's or subject's "state of mind" and presumably influences his or her understanding of current reality and future aspirations as well as the actions he or she may prosecute.

The most striking feature of Mannheim's comments on ideology and utopia is that he is indicting its social-psychological and situated character. Eschewing grand and macroscopic versions of these concepts found in the work of others, he is arguing that these thought-ways are manifest in conduct. He refers to "his interests," "conscious lies," calculated attempts to "dupe others," as well as "self-deceptions" as elements of particularistic ideologies. Even the total ideology—the Weltanschauung or meaning-system—for Mannheim manifests itself as an individual's system as he "partakes" in "the collective life."

Peter Berger and Thomas Luckmann (1968) took this argument one step further by arguing that all "reality" is "socially" (and symbolically) "constructed"—indeed, constructed "conversationally." Ideology thus became something that permeated the consciousness of all agents living in given societies and as such could be put to different uses. Berger and Luckmann essentially gave a phenomenological and interactional cast to the whole issue of ideology: ideologies are generated interactionally and manifested interactionally—though in this they took what was implicit in Mannheim and made it explicit in a more detailed and philosophically enriched way.

The direction given by Berger and Luckmann has been followed by others to cast it in a more microsociological framework. In my own study of the uses of astrology in Jaffna, Sri Lanka, I tried to show how various general religious and philosophical concepts or "epistemes" were brought down to the ground in the conversations that an astrologer conducted with his clients. Karma, for instance, became an actual discursive concept with which both the astrologer and client sought to understand the text of a horoscope reading. Sitting face to face with the client, an astrologer would present a narrative of his or her life—either a complete one that began in a previous incarnation and extended to the current one and to a future one, or a truncated one about this incarnation alone—in which a causal connection is made with the accumulated Karma and certain events and experiences in this life. Further, the ruling myths of Hinduism are used to reinforce these claims and illustrate them (Perinbanayagam, 1982). More recently, Gary Alan Fine and Kent Sandstrom have argued that one must avoid overtly "abstract conceptions of ideology, divorced from individual actors" and they have sought to link abstract conceptions to "lived experiences and to social interaction" (1993: 36). In essence, Fine and Sandstrom conceive of ideology as processes that occur in instances of situated action. Marc Steinberg (1993) has offered an extension of this view by introducing Mikhail Bakhtin's work into the discussion, arguing that ideology occurs in dialogic processes between actors. Ideology is presented as implicit and explicit elements in the language of the discourse that occurs between actors.

If one may seek a common thread running through these latter works, it is this: Ideologies are manifest as discursive and practical *performances.* No doubt, if a performer in one of these is pressed, he or she will be able to produce a discourse in a dialogue replete with addressivity and answerability, but as a situated action, it is merely an incarnate ideology. Ideologies, then, are not held in abeyance in the mind as "consciousness" nor are they mysterious forces that operate in invisible or inaudible ways; rather, they are put into practice in the acts of everyday life, spoken, given manifestation in discourse and dialogue, subject to the grammar and rhetoric of performances, and above all, addressed to another, as to the self, in situated interactions. Our concept of these performances must include, also, actions that are purely "physical" or "practical" without benefit of immediate discursive articulation. For example, a husband beating a wife, routinely and habitually, and I suppose, periodically, is performing the ideologies of patriarchy, male-dominance, women-as-chattel property, and so forth, without giving it explicit discursive and dialogic articulation. In doing performances, an agent's mind, self, and body are simultaneously put into operation, usually with an other, as a co-participant or an audience, in such activity. In the playing of games, then, agents are, in fact, performing ideologies—indeed, gaming them.

One can say this of utopias, too. These are textual constructions that are presented as fictions or treatises and are meant to be read by the populace. Nevertheless, they also influence actions in everyday life and are often transformed into programs of action—socialism and Owenite utopias, for instance. Most utopias are texts, written for reading, study, and contemplation, produced at a particular historical moment to speak to certain theoretical issues and practical problems that are current. To this, one may add paintings, sculpture, and architectural units: many of them depict idealized states of being much to be desired, but not that easily achieved. The paintings of the Impressionists, for example, can be taken as a manifestation of the processes of democracy, argues Virginia Spate. Many of these works depict the joys of leisurely life, free from the oppressions of work and labor in the emerging commercial civilization. She observes that the work of the Impressionists' paintings—singling out the work of Claude Monet, in particular—overloads "the pleasurable" while rejecting "the alienating, the reifying processes of contemporary urban capitalist society . . . It constructs the 'other' of modern, urban life through a series of images which cancel out the unresolvable contradictions of the capitalist city" (1987: 102–03). Utopias have been imagined by architects, too, and many utopians have also imagined architecture, observes Miles Lewis. Even here, then, the aim was to escape the harshness of the current world and live in an idealized one (1987: 108). The many versions of the perfect human form created by sculptors—Michelangelo, for instance—were also utopian forms.

Games, too, insofar as they receive continuous constructions and reconstructions, are sociohistorical phenomena that are produced as "texts" and speak to certain issues and problems that are relevant at that time. However, unlike most utopias, enshrined in texts, games are performed and they put into behavioral practice various utopian constructs so that both players and spectators can experience the ecstasy of participating in a reality that is different from their everyday one. Further, games are such complex and multifaceted activity-systems that they can simultaneously be used to articulate both ideologies and utopias. They could even be included as a category in the broad approach to the sociology of knowledge developed by Doyle McCarthy (1996) where knowledge is considered as "culture." Clifford Geertz has already shown that games—cock fighting in Bali—are indeed a part of what he calls the "cultural system" (1973).

Ideologies of Action and Identity

Insofar as games are activity-systems in which agents initiate and consummate various forms of action with the concurrent construction of an identity, they can be examined for their ideological valences. Nelson Foote (1951) and more recently Harrison White (1992) have argued that identity and action-systems are intimately related to each other. Foote claimed that identity generates "motivation" and, consequently, actions. White claimed that identities are the instrumentations through which agents seek to control their relationship with others. He wrote, "Identity is any source of action not explicable from biophysical regularities, and to which observers can attribute meaning." He continued, "Identities add through contentions to the contingencies faced by other identities. Social organization comes as a by-product of the cumulations of these processes (1992: 6).

Yet, it seems to me that these sequences can be reversed: particular social organizations can foster specific identities just as specific identities can cumulate into given social organizations. At least it can be claimed that there is, in fact, a dialectical relationship between identity and action. Identities are defined by given actions, and action-systems generate given identities in cycles of performances. One performs an action-sequence, and it confers a particular identity, and the acceptance and validation of this identity then impel further performances of the relevant acts in recursive sequences resulting in particular social organizations.

These identities are performed with the full involvement of not only the mind and self but often the body, too. Examining the relationship between athletes and dancers, Noel Dyck and Eduardo Archetti (2003: 10) observe that "what physical action produces on the playing-fields and dance floors is selves" and note that the "self is embodied in performance," citing the work of Nigel Rapport (1998). One performs a self that is embodied, no doubt, but it is really an aspect of a complex system that is put into play—that is, a selected identity of the self. In any case, the performances in games are truly activities of an embodied identity.

In any enterprise, feudal or capitalistic, peaceful or warlike, serious or playful, it is important to have agents who will take responsibility, provide leadership when necessary, and perform their appointed tasks with commitment and the required alertness and attentiveness. Such performative qualities will bear fruit for the enterprise in question as well as the agent himself or herself. These qualities, however, are hard to find in the ordinary activities of everyday life. There is often laziness, indifference, boredom, and emotional withdrawal in the performance of the many tasks of the world.

The ethic of working with full dedication and developing skills in a chosen craft or occupation is an essential part of the social psychology of everyday life. In all cultures, steps are taken, in one form or another, to ensure that children from early on are taught the skills necessary to be able to participate in the world in which they live. These can be instructions in hunting or cultivation; or in reading, writing, and arithmetic; or in constructing objects and structures from metal, stone, masonry, and brick. The fundamental feature of these attempts to train the young—or, for that matter, the old, too—is the demand that they work hard at the chosen tasks, practice with dedication and commitment, and subject themselves, in their own eyes and in the eyes of others, to certain evaluations with which identities are ascribed.

In certain cultures such a set of demands—its Weltanschauung—was tied to success in this worldly life as well as in the next world. This is true, famously, about Protestantism. The religious systems of Buddhism and Hinduism, too, were based on a theory of action, albeit one with different consequences. The fact that these religions made a philosophy or theory of action central to their recommendations for the ethical conduct of everyday life attests to their significance in the study of everyday life itself. Different religious systems assigned varying significances to action and differentiated its importance to success in this world.

The Protestant theory of action insists on the "causality" of action to the extent that it leads to determinate consequences, on the one hand, and to its origins in the intentionality of the agent, on the other hand. In everyday life, action-sequences need to be managed by an agent in order to achieve certain goals. Furthermore, one needs to undertake these moves as an essential aspect of his or her identity as a Christian of a particular sort. One can use Weber's own work to illustrate these claims. The acceptance of the identity of a "Protestant"—Christian—is also to accept the performance of actions involving the following features drawn from one of Max Weber's principal sources—Benjamin Franklin. He listed "13 virtues," five of which were:

1. Temperance: eat not to dullness; drink not to elevation (that is, practice a disciplined *moderation* in acts involving eating and drinking, or, by extension, any other activity).
2. Silence: speak not but what may benefit others or yourself; avoid trifling conversations (that is, be *parsimonious* in acts of speaking and conversation—and any other kind of activity).
3. Resolution: resolve to perform what you ought; perform without fail what you resolve (that is, give free and dedicated commitment to whatever you do).
4. Frugality: make no expense but to do good to others or yourself (that is, be wise and efficient in the use of your resources—whatever they may be).
5. Industry: lose no time; be always employed in something useful; cut out all unnecessary actions (in other words, undertake actions that are efficient, parsimonious, and thrifty of time and effort).

The rules drawn essentially, though not exclusively, from Protestant theology were for Weber a contributory cause in the emergence of capitalism. Commenting on Richard Baxter's work on the emergence of English Puritanism, Weber writes: "Waste of time is thus the deadliest of sins. The span of human life is infinitely short and precious to make sure of one's own election. Loss of time, through social ability, idle talk, luxury, even more sleep than is necessary for health ... is worthy of absolute moral condemnation ... [Time] is infinitely valuable because every hour lost is lost to labor for the glory of God" (1958a: 157-58).

To labor for the glory of God—or for anyone else's glory for that matter—is to engage in purposive rational action. Indeed, a proper deconstruction of "labor" as it appears in the Protestant documents cited by Weber leads to but one conclusion: a good Protestant must conduct his or her waking life with a series of purposive rational actions—albeit ones that lead to economic returns just as they proclaim the glory of God and become acts of worship.

This ideology of action can be contrasted with the Buddhist one. The Buddha in his many discourses set out what has come to be known as the "Four Noble Truths" and the "Noble Eightfold Path."

The first noble truth is that birth is suffering, old age is suffering, illness is suffering, and death is suffering. This has been expanded with more details to make eight "paths."

The second noble truth argues that illusion and desire are the cause of suffering. If, therefore, one eliminates illusion and desire, one can eliminate suffering.

The third noble truth is that with various ritual practices it is possible to extinguish this suffering.

The fourth noble truth is that by following certain paths it is possible to eliminate suffering.

The aim of the good Buddhist life is to eliminate suffering, and to do that, the Buddha recommended the eightfold path. There are actually two eightfold paths—one for the secular life and one for the enlightened ones. I will give the ones for the secular life here:

The Right View: The right understanding of the law causes four noble truths, particularly the four noble truths and its enunciation of the doctrine of suffering and its causes.

Right Thinking: To think right is to think without craving, anger, passion, or hate. If one understands the law of causation (the right view), then the will to right thinking will follow suit.

Right Action: This doctrine is expressed in the negation: do not kill, do not steal, and avoid improper sexual activities.

Right Living: In obtaining the necessities of life, one must follow proper procedures. One must be committed to his or her work. This also includes a disciplined daily life: when and what and how much to eat, to study, exercise, rest, and entertain.

Right Effort: This has four divisions: working to prevent evil; working to reduce evil; working to produce good; working to increase the good already created.

Right Memory: This means being always careful, clearheaded, and attentive.

Right Meditation: This refers to thinking about the four noble truths and seeking spiritual enlightenment and peace of mind, thus diminishing the importance of thought and action (Rahula, 1959: 16–50).

Right Speech: This refers to avoiding lies, slander, malice, and words that hurt others, and to refrain from idle chatter (Rahula, 1959: 50).

The fundamental thesis of these truths and the recommended paths is that earthly secular action must be limited, and above all, the craving to excel, to develop ambition and seek to compete against others, to triumph over them, is not the path to the good Buddhist life. The craving for gratification of one's desires is caused by blindness and illusion about the nature of human existence and should be eliminated.

Such a minimalist approach to existence and the theory of action that goes with it is not an ideology that will lead to a striving for earthly success and this-worldly achievement—particularly in the area of work, the accumulation of wealth and the practice of investment—indeed, in the pursuit of what Weber called "this worldly-life" (1964: 267).

The flight from the world could not lead to the emergence of an economic ethic of this-worldly activity, and by derivation, to the kind of ethic—or ideology—that would lead to the pursuit of this-worldly activity encapsulated in gaming. By contrast, the Protestant ethic of this-worldly activity and the recommendation of how much an ethic should be practiced were reproduced in the game ethic and given rampant expression in the public schools in post-Reformation England.

The Puritans were opposed to all manner of sporting activities and amusements—so much so that James I and Charles I of England had *The Book of Sports* written to counteract Puritanism (Weber, 1958a: 166). Nevertheless, their theory of labor as purposive rational activity would be inscribed in the games that human societies have devised, just as the various other theories and elements of their ethic were. Indeed, it is a great historical irony that the ethic of action that the Puritans enunciated in opposition to leisure activities like game playing should find its most striking presence in the field of organized games.

The ideology of ambition, hard work, and the success and worldly accomplishment that they gave rise to as signs of God's grace is encapsulated in the structures of various games. In playing games, an agent is expected to have the desire to play well and win, whatever obstacles the structure of the game and the moves of the opponent may put in his or her way, to strive and push toward winning. The games, in other words, represent in a systematic form the ideology of working hard to master certain skills in order to get along in life.

Games are structures of intense activity conducted within given durations and in delimited spaces in which agents perform continuously with commitment. In the absence of such alert commitment, there is no game. In playing a game, an agent must commit his or her self as fully as possible to the proceedings, become emotionally involved as well, and undertake actions that are both vigorous and subtle. Every game demands such a performative commitment and it is systematically cultivated—whether by coaches or by the self-discipline of the player. The gaming situation is the arena where the dictum "anything worth doing is worth doing well" is fully realized even for such intrinsically fruitless activities like putting a ball into a hole in the ground or hitting a ball out of certain boundaries. Every player strives to do things well in the duration of the game as well as in the practice sessions that he or she undergoes before the actual playing.

Insofar as both industry and the military need agents who can bring such a performative structure to their tasks, it can be said that the gaming practices were attempts to inculcate the ideologies of action into their selves. In games, in fact, the ethic of hard and committed work, deferred gratification, emotional discipline, and physical endurance came to full expression.

The perfect marriage of the Protestant ethic and the spirit of gaming occurred in what came to be called "muscular Christianity." Concerned that the nineteenth-century Protestant Christianity was oriented too much toward sentimentality and passivity, many churchmen tried to move it toward "action, rather than reflection, aggression rather than gentility," as Clifford Putney put it (2001: 18). Christians were also enjoined to practice self-discipline and lead a strenuous life. The entire sporting complex became, then, an effective structure of activity in which such aims could be realized. Games—even on Sundays—as well as bodybuilding, scouting, and other forms of outdoor activity were strongly advocated and were also taken into the schools that the church controlled (Putney, 2001).

To enter a game as a participant is to accept willy-nilly the sequences of action that are necessary to play the game satisfactorily. Indeed, games are ideological embodiments of the ethic of everyday life that Weber identified with certain strands of Protestantism.

To begin with, to play the game, an agent must commit himself or herself fully to the routines of the play. Half-hearted and uncommitted moves, those without "heart" and passion are doomed to fail. Learning the game, and being coached in it, is to acquire the habits of hard and dedicated action-sequences—indeed, the "work ethic."

Secondly, the ethic of game playing demands a parsimonious management of energy, emotions, and acts. The "thriftiness" that Calvin and Luther recommended to their respective followers did not involve only monetary matters, but it involved also a parsimony regarding time and effort and emotion: "nothing in excess." In playing games satisfactorily, the careful rationing of a player's energy is of paramount importance: if a tennis game is a five-set affair, a player should take care not to waste his or her energy in chasing after impossible shots. A long-distance runner should harness his energy and endurance in such a way that he or she does not "run off steam" in the final laps of the race.

Emotions are an enduring feature of all social acts, and in games, their parsimonious management is of paramount importance. To be passive and affect-less in the performance of the acts of the game will only produce defeat, just as becoming too emotional and involved will produce erratic and uncontrolled moves. In game playing, the Zen dictum "float like a leaf on the river of life" would be very inefficient. Rather in Mohammed Ali's advice about boxing, "One must float like a butterfly, but sting like a bee."

Finally, the acts in a game must be subjected to a discipline in which the maximum effects are achieved by the execution of acts that expend minimum effort and energy. The elegant stroke play in cricket, the management of "batting basics" in baseball, and the careful coordination of body, feet, and hands in tennis are designed to achieve this parsimony.

In getting children and, eventually, adults to play these games, certain strong ideological themes are being rendered into their selves and the horizons of the world in which these selves will operate. The construction of such selves, described as "character-training," was undertaken in a variety of settings, but most vigorously in the schools to which the elite, first in England, then in the United States, and in England's far-flung empire, sent their boy-children. One of the latter, Chester McNaughten, principal of a college in India for the sons of the feudal chiefs, attached the "utmost value to games as a training in character . . They developed energy, promptitude, judgement, watchfulness, courage, generous emulation, appreciation of the merits of others and the brightest standards of truthfulness and duty" (quoted in Mangan, 1985: 133). On another occasion, he wrote to one of his pupils during vacation, "Be temperate and pure and do not be idle ... Take plenty of outdoor exercise—riding, running, walking, cricket, lawn-tennis, shooting" (in Mangan, 1985: 134).

In McNaughten's case, he is arguing that the very playing of games will help in building a particular "character." It behooves us to go further and see that the very structures of the game and the demands that they make on the player ensure the emergence of this particular self-concept. Agents with their "character" forged in the public school systems of England, particularly in its sporting arenas, went forth into the outposts of the British Empire and put their training into practice. One such agent, R. J. S. Thomson, opines:

> My schooling was an excellent preparation for my career in the Sudan Political Service. From an early age, one was taught to be self-reliant and to accept responsibility. The virtues of self-discipline and physical fitness, both essential elements in public school training, were to prove of inestimable value as also was the exercising which one gains from being a house and subsequently a school monitor. (Quoted in Mangan, 1985: 86)

The capacity to accept responsibility and practice "self-discipline" can be obtained in many ways, but one principal method was through the playing of games. Consider the game of cricket: The essence of good cricket is to be patient and persevering in the accumulation of runs while, at the same time, playing in such a way that the interests of the team are kept uppermost in the player's moves. Every ball that is delivered by the adversarial bowler or fielder must be judged and handled with care: if it is a ball that is too dangerous to be driven or hooked or cut or swiped, it should be left alone or blocked without the possibility of a run being scored. The player should wait for the next ball to be delivered and the one after that to attempt a scoring move. Furthermore, depending on one's place in the batting order, again one must play with care and calculation or be a little rash if the interests of the team demand such behavior at that point of the game. These are, of course, elements of the ideology of action described elsewhere as "temperance," "self-discipline," "resolution," and "industry." One must work at the game with emotional control and steadfastness toward a purpose and consideration for the larger goals of the playing.

The association between these ideologies of action and identity were enshrined in other games, too. In all court games, this ethic and ideology are enshrined in the very structure of the game and its scoring system. Tennis, the mother of all court games, has been played in England for at least 500 years, but it became a systematized game only in the aftermath of the industrial-capitalist revolution and bears striking marks of its provenance. The rules that were formalized and put into written form have one theme in common: an individual, or a partnership of two, faces various obstacles and restrictions and is expected to strive to overcome them. One can analyze the rule-structure and the scoring system as well as the performatives of the game and see this structure in operation.

The game begins with a serve of the ball by one player into a court that has been marked in a very systematic way. Once the game has begun, a scoring system is put into play. Each player serves toward winning a "game" that consists of 60 points counted in units of 15. A server may win point after point, and when he or she reaches 60, he or she wins the game; however, there is a catch here: the player must win by at least two points. If the score reaches an even 45 points for both players, it is declared a "deuce" and they keep playing until one party wins by two points.

Each player then accumulates games this way, and once he or she gets six games, he or she wins the "set." However, even here he or she must win by two points. If it is five games for both parties, the players play on until one party has a margin of two games over the other. This often leads to long duels taking a great deal of time and was deemed unsuitable in the modern game. It interfered with the organization of the tournament, the spectators' travel plans, and above all, the broadcast of the games over television. A manner of deciding the winner was introduced called the "tiebreaker." According to this method, each player gets to serve twice, after an initial single serve by one of them, and whoever reaches seven points first is deemed the winner. However, once again, he or she must win by two points. The entire scoring structure of the game is organized in such a way that not only must one party win decisively, but the other party is given every chance to fight back at every possible turn in the game. *The upshot of the two-point margin that is put into practice in games and sets is to create a structure of activity and a paradigm of a contest in which each party must display grit, determination, and perseverance in order to be a champion, and display them in the various instants of the game, in the nowness of the moves.* No room here for doubts and uncertainties, for retreats and meditation, and certainly not for the existentialist angst of Alan Silitoe's long-distance runner who reached the finish line first but refused to cross it. Do or die, fight back, strive, keep emotions under control, and, as they say, keep one's eyes on the ball.

In rugby football, for example, players have to play a rough game facing injuries as each one strives to move forward by forward-running and backward-passing, facing the resistances of the defenders. Perseverance, "pluck," courage, and an indifference to physical pain in the interests of the team are essential features of satisfactory playing. These features of the playing are given expression in a verse written by the headmaster of Harrow, Edward Bowen. In the last verse, he describes the acceptable player, Tom:

> Who follows up till he drops,
> Panting and limping and sore? Tom!
> Tom who with scuffle and sprawl, too,
> Knows where he carries the ball to;
> Ankles and toes! Look how he goes!
> Through them and out of them all, too!
> (Quoted in Mangan, 1985: 47)

One can conclude this examination of the determined and disciplined self manifests in games by focusing on the training and match play of the *Crusaders,* a high school football team.

Very systematically, the various coaches and the fathers of some of the players convert what is a game into a structure of activity governed by the work ethic, personal discipline, and a single-minded determination to succeed. The coach, Stengel, tells his team:

> It is going to snow tonight. I do not know how much is going to come down. No matter what happens—even if the world comes to an end—we are going to practice at 2:00 o'clock. There are no excuses. If you have to rent a dog-sleigh, come. (*The Crusaders,* 2002)

The adversities that a player has to face, the suffering and pain he has to undergo notwithstanding, he is told: get on with the job, keep the action going, work hard. In addition, the idea of doing one's best, of putting one's best foot forward, is systematically played throughout the course of the training and in the course of the game—for one's own sake and for the sake of the team. Here is the coach talking to his players on the day of the game: "I know I will get the job done—but I don't know how well I will do it. But I want to go and help the seniors win the game and State championship."

A father of a player expands on this theme of hard work and dedication: "In the long run, that's what it takes. Anything you do in life is worth doing well. There is no easy way. That's what I have taught my son." The son takes this advice, but confesses that it has been hard on him. There were days when he even avoided talking to his father.

The ideologies of action, of doing things in a disciplined and systematic way, as well as the ethic of work are distilled and put into practice systematically in and through this game of football. This is a game that is well suited to the practice of these ideologies insofar as it is both a team game and one in which individuals can demonstrate initiative and entrepreneurship. One coordinates his or her moves with others, but the coordination is a result of the initiative, enterprise, and governing intelligence of each individual player.

Versions of Manhood

These ideologies of action when put into practice generate typical identities—and, of course, once they are generated, they become sedimented into the consciousness of an agent and lead to a new series of typical actions. One noted identity that was generated by these ideologies of action was one or more of what Michael Oriard has called "versions of manhood" (1993). The game ethic insofar as it was a complex and multifaceted one was able to generate a variety of identities—all of them legitimately named "manhood" or "manliness"—even perhaps the rather elusive phenomenon known as "gentle-manliness."

In a study of manhood in America, Michael Kimmel (1996) has argued that conceptions of manhood have influenced every aspect of social, economic, and political life—business, education, family organization, war, sex and companionship, and even sports. Kimmel's study is a truly compelling one. However, one can reverse the equation here and ask not so much how conceptions of manhood influenced sports but how sports was used to foster certain forms of manhood.

These ideologies of action fomented variations on the theme of gender identities—for example, on notions of "manhood" and "manliness."

For example, one can discern one version—the rough, hard, unflinching and unyielding identity manifested in many versions of football, and an equally pervasive version of the "gentlemanly" manhood deployed in cricket and tennis.

The football that emerged in American society from the latter years of the nineteenth century systemically sought to advance one extreme version of manhood. Oriard quotes a description of the game given in 1892: "To bear pain without flinching, and even to laugh at one's wounds and the scars of a hotly contested game, is very good discipline and tends to develop manliness of character" (1993: 189).

This particular version of manhood needed to be cultivated with great care in the game situation because various changes in the economy and society had created a sufficiently large number of young men, who, instead of growing from childhood into the rough-and-tumble of work and the hard, sweating labor that went with most work, were now being sent to college. From childhood into a soft, young adulthood was unlikely to create the manliness necessary for the emerging industrial social order. Football, with its programmed system of "necessary roughness" was deemed the new medium to achieve this manliness. Oriard notes, "Football offered the American youth a rite of passage into manhood. The very fact that college-aged players were neither clearly boys nor men but boys at the critical stage on the threshold of manhood, undoubtedly contributed to football's cultural power" (1993: 193, 198).

The rules of the game were changed periodically to ensure the presence of the necessary roughness and physical challenge, but sometimes the rules had to be rolled back when too much roughness appeared. Indeed, the game elicited political interference at various stages to ensure that it remained a rough game but without exceeding certain limits. Teddy Roosevelt, Oriard shows in a perceptive analysis, was to intervene in various ways to influence the structure of the game and to explicate its relationship to America's manifest destiny. When the game became too rough and some players were becoming maimed for life and even killed on the field, Roosevelt was there to run interference against criticisms and expressions of concern. In various essays that he wrote, he claimed that the playing of rough games raised up the nation's natural aristocrats, developed good "American citizens," and ensured the prominence of the Anglo-Saxon race, Oriard notes. Roosevelt argued that games became too brutal and dangerous only if the contenders were ill matched. Oriard quotes from Roosevelt's essay "The American Boy," that games "were fraught with danger when they become one-sided and unhealthy," and continues, "has, beyond all question, had an excellent effect on increased manliness" (1991: 19).

The masculinist ideology that is contained here and its relationship to not only national issues but also civilizational issues was found to be in all games, but it is particularly strong in field games played by a team.

The fact that these games were analogues to warfare and combat in general may be responsible for this accentuation. As in the warfare of the times, male bonding, organizational interdependence of the players/warriors, and unflagging and unquestioned dedication to a common purpose were essential features of these games.

In the cultivation of such attitudes and performances, the bounded structure of players—the "team"—needed an other with the help of which it would be able to define itself and develop cohesion and purposefulness. Two such others were available for these male teams: the *other team,* on the field, and the fundamentally differentiated *other gender,* off the field. Women—their identity, their social and biological characteristics, attitudes, demeanor, powers, and capacities became the other with which the masculinist identity of the team as a whole and of its individual members could be defined. Such definitions were accomplished by word—discursively, conversationally, allusively—and by deed—performatively and behaviorally.

Studying the everyday culture of rugby players, Steven Schacht, in fact, concludes that there is not only male bonding but an active misogyny on and off the playing arena:

> Rugby players' social reproduction of gender, ultimately grounded in misogyny, allows these men at the individual level to psychologically and sometimes physically dominate women. At the societal level, rugby, like many sporting practices, both reflects and supports a hierarchical ideology of masculinity and the subordination of women. (1996: 550)

The powers that be always recognized the connection between sports and political/military systems—though during different periods, different games were thought to be important. At a time when wars were fought with bows and arrows and the individualized skills of the marksmen were very important, the coordinated movement of players on a field was not considered relevant in warfare. Not surprisingly, then, Edward II banned football in 1314 on the grounds that it was interfering with archery practice, notes Giulianotti, citing Stutt (1999: 94); James I of England upheld this ban in succeeding decades. The emergence of a rationalized army, based on disciplined formations and strict bureaucratic controls, was more akin to organized team games played on fields; and in these games, the ideal of forceful and aggressive masculinity, national political goals, and military efficiency formed a nice logical interdependence. Heroic combat was no longer necessary, but the team games as the new warfare allowed for heroes to emerge nevertheless.

Football, then, as with all team games played on the field where both team coordination and adversarial relations with teamed-others were the organizing principle, coupled with the need for physical activity calling for both strength and courage and the likelihood of injury, became the perfect instrument to socialize men into an ideology that was politically necessary and culturally valued.

Nevertheless, all games did not prosecute the ideology of a manhood characterized by a necessary roughness, violence, and stoic indifference to pain and injury. Tennis and cricket can be considered structures of activity that promoted another version of manhood—the "gentle" and well-mannered bourgeoisie, who played these games for "sport" and not for profit or income. These versions of manhood have been on the wane for a number of years, but one can still say that the versions of manhood represented in certain games are gentler and less rough, violent, and aggressive than in the various versions of football.

The lively commentator on the gentlemanly traditions of tennis is Digby Baltzell, a gentleman from Philadelphia himself, tennis player, and sociologist. He gives his show away in the opening sentence of his book on tennis: "I began this book in 1984, the year Jimmy Connors and John McEnroe disgraced themselves and the country by their crude and rude behavior in the course of losing to Sweden in the Davis Cup Final Round in Gotenburg" (1995: XI).

He chronicles the decline of the values of civility and decorum that characterized the game in its early years and equates the latter with the "gentlemanly code of honor"; Connors's and McEnroe's offenses were that they did not behave like "gentlemen." This gentlemanly code of conduct is not given any neat description by Baltzell, but he cites approvingly a paragraph from C. L. R. James's book on his cricketing life:

> I never cheated, I never appealed a decision unless I thought the batsman was out, I never argued with the umpire, I never jeered at a defeated opponent, I never gave to a friend a vote or a place which by a stretch of the imagination could be seen as belonging to an enemy or a stranger. My defeats and disappointments I took as stoically as I could ... From the eight years of school life, this code became the moral framework of my existence. (Quoted in Baltzell, 1995: 4)

This gentleman was a cricket-playing Jamaican—a scholar and a revolutionary, and English to the core. Baltzell uses this citation to illustrate the code of the gentleman and then goes on to describe how this code was cultivated in the elite schools of old England and New England. In these schools, various elements of the code were inculcated into their wards chiefly through the playing of games—tennis, cricket, and rugger. From the schools, these gentlemen moved to the clubs and eventually took over the leadership of the country, and Baltzell argues that codes of sportsmanship and gentlemanly decorum were in practice in political and economic life.

A good illustration of this ethic is an incident from the Davis Cup Final of 1921, written by Bill Tilden. The article itself was entitled "Sportsmanship in Tennis." He begins: "There is a difference between amateur and professional sport. The former insists upon honesty, generosity and fair play among its players; but although there is a desire to maintain an equally high standard in professional athletics, it has been found that when money is a consideration, fair play is bound to make a hasty exit from the scene."

He then mentions that the games of golf and tennis "grip their followers in such a manner that all are loyal to the sport and to all the high standards sportsmanship signifies." And then he provides a stinging comment in parenthesis: "Can we say that of baseball?" (in Baltzell, 1995: 211-12).

After this preamble, he gives a striking example of gentlemanly and sporting manhood. It was the final set in a match between J. C. Parke of England and Norman Brookes of Australia and was one that would decide the tie. Here is Tilden's description:

> Parke was at his best, an occasion when he played superbly. It seemed apparent to all that he had Brookes beaten. He was leading two sets to one and match point in the fourth. Then it was that he drove Brookes far out of the court with a deep drive, and immediately followed it to the net. Brookes lobbed but he lobbed short. It meant the match for England if Parke won the point, quite possibly the Davis Cup as well. Parke swung hard into the ball and drove it through Brookes' court for a kill. But his racket, flowing through in a long downward flight touched the net ever so slightly that none of the officials saw it.
>
> "Game, set and match, Parke" called the umpire.
> Brookes came forward, smiling, hand extended in congratulations. Parke remained where he had hit the ball, his face turned to the umpire. "Mr. Umpire, he said, I hit the net." "You are sure, Mr. Parke"? came the reply. "Quite," he answered. Brookes stood silent, still ready with congratulations. "The point is Mr. Brookes' deuce," called the umpire.
>
> Play recommenced. Parke lost that game. Brookes, quick to seize his last chance, could not be stopped. The match, and ultimately the Davis Cup went to Australia. (In Baltzell, 1995: 212-13)

This long citation gives both the drama of the occasion and as neat a summary as one could want of the version of manhood that Baltzell would call the gentlemanly one. The "gentleman" is one who sticks to the code of conduct so strictly that he even calls a point against himself. This match and the one between McEnroe and Connors and the Swedish Davis Cup team that irked Baltzell so stand on opposite ends of both styles of play and an era: the gentleman player and the rough, commercial entrepreneur.

Yet, McEnroe, Connors, Nastasy—the so-called bad boys of tennis—are the exception rather than the rule. Though one cannot imagine any of today's professional players going to the extent that Parke did, there is no doubt that tennis and cricket as such—its recent developments notwithstanding—enabled the emergence of a different version of manhood than the various forms of football.

Playing Utopia

In an early essay, Michael Holquist sought to show how chess was an approximation of utopian constructions and that, in playing it, one was, in fact, playing utopia. He wrote:

> Utopia has in common with chess, first of all the general characteristic that it is a simplification, a radical stylization of something which in experience is of enormous complexity, often lacking any apparent symmetry. Chess substitutes for war, utopia for society. In each case what was rough is made smooth, what was chaotic is made orderly. The chess game has *rules*, utopia, *laws*. (1968: 110)

Insightful as these observations are, they do not go far enough. ***It is not just chess that is a mimesis of utopia, but all games are such representations.*** All games represent the deliberate construction of smooth, orderly, symmetrical, and rule-bound structures of activity that are spatially contained and temporally transformed, in which human agents put their selves into play—just as they do when they read utopian novels or write them; it is not chess that is a mimesis of war, but, as already argued, all games are representations of complex systems of interaction—war itself being a subset of such systems. War is a form of relations between two structures of associates who face each other and seek to outdo each other. Indeed, Kenneth Burke has called war "the ultimate *disease* of cooperation" (1969b: 22). One must, after all, persuade a sufficiently large number of people to cooperate with each other and form an army to fight the enemy army.

One can, however, follow Holquist's (1968) lead and delineate further parallels between utopian programs and games:

a) Utopias are spatially set apart from the current society: utopias are "nowhere" in Thomas More's original formulation and in subsequent writing, too.

aa) Games are set apart spatially from the rest of the world: arenas, courts, "diamonds," "fields," "links," "courses," "boards," "tables," and so on.

b) Utopias are set apart temporally: they existed in the past— "Golden Age," "Eden," or will exist in the future— "Paradise," "Communism." Leon Trotsky, in fact, combined the two and wrote: "A Paradise in This World."

bb) Games are played in a time that is separated from the real time of everyday life. The time of actual play is determined ahead of time in all football games. In court games and board games, there are no limits imposed, but, these games are, nevertheless, played in times that are demarcated as "play time"—and separated from work. They, too, have a certain beginning and an end, at which time the players return to real time.

c) Social relations will be reconstructed in utopias toward greater equality and harmony: Robert Owen; Karl Marx and others; "communism," for example.

cc) In games, there is an insistent focus on the equality of all players and various steps are taken to ensure that, *on occasions of play,* the principle of equality is maintained. In team games, this is taken further and a harmonious relationship among all players is cultivated.

d) Economic relations: In utopias, everyone is entitled to the goods of the society and share in them. There will be no want and no avarice: "To each according to his needs, from each according to his ability."

dd) In games, the contribution of every member of the team is equally valid and important. No playing position is undervalued within the playing of the game. Every member is expected to make his or her best contribution and receive the same rewards within the framework of the game.

e) Sociopolitical roles may be reversed: "the last shall be first"; "dictatorship of the proletariat."

ee) In games, it is often the case that the "underdog" gains the upper hand. Such underdogdom has two dimensions—one the social-economic underdog, and two, the sporting underdog. In the former, a member of an oppressed class or race rises to the top of the game and dominates it. And in the latter, a player who has been failing in the sport in the immediate past or one who has never won against a star player wins a contest.

f) In utopias, work and leisure are redefined: work is undervalued and leisure is elevated as the higher good. Play becomes the dominating theme of such utopias, and the human agent is redefined as "homo luden" (Marx).

ff) The games define the human agent as players who obtain joy and esteem from the mere act of playing—though winning occasionally will help, too. There are agents in modern society who play all the time—"ski bums," "surfer bums," and "tennis bums." The ludic life provided by games must exclude professional players for whom gaming is work. They often retreat from their professional performances to engage ludically in other games: professional baseball players play golf in their leisure time, for example.

g) Political systems will be reconstituted: justice and procedural efficiency will be maintained. Reason and rationality will be the guiding principles of action. The emerging utopian order will be a social contract.

gg) The very definition of games is that they are strictly rule-bound activities in which every move is governed by established principles and procedures. These rules have, in fact, evolved into forms that are both substantively and formally rational, and the entire basis of the game is a social contract among all participants.

Among these many parallels between utopian constructions and games—which are both textual and practical constructions—one can select two themes as crucial to a consideration of games as utopia: 1) the rule-bound nature of games and their utopian significance; 2) the doctrine of equality in many forms that informs utopian constructions as well as games.

Utopia and the Social Contract

In a comprehensive survey of utopian thought in the Western world, Manuel and Manuel observe that the two major characteristics of utopian writing are: 1) a clear intent to break with the past, and 2) a preoccupation with describing a place, a history outside of space and time (1979). In such texts, there is also an implicit critique of existing or past societies and the presentation of alternative societies.

The most significant feature of such utopian forms that are outside "space" and "time" is that they are written texts in which various strategies and techniques of composition are used to construct an imaginary social order. In these texts, then, one finds descriptions of possible worlds. In such a writing of utopias, the significant feature is to construct new rules for interactions and relationships. To put it differently, what is involved in the functioning of the new society is the observation of rules of interaction and relationships *vis-à-vis* each other as well as in terms of property, honor, and status. Such utopian writing is always a writing against the grain and constitutes a rejection and an attack—overt or ironic and satirical—on the existent state of affairs. Such a writing, far from being disconnected from the historical process or the sociocultural context, is, in fact, actively engaged with them. Utopian texts are, in fact, an element of the "cultural poetics" of the period that produced them (Greenblatt, 1980).

If this is true of literary works by Shakespeare or Marlowe or More, as Greenblatt has argued, then it is also true of the games that each culture produces and allows its members to play. Furthermore, the changes the games—in their organization, rule-structures, and audience-form—undergo as time passes also reflect the changing sociocultural milieu. Phillip Sidney's opinion that a poem was "a speaking picture, with this end, to teach and delight" can also be applied to utopias—which are written pictures intended to teach and to delight (Manuel and Manuel, 1979: 2). And so are games—written, spoken, and performed pictures—intended to instruct and entertain. In playing games, human agents are playing utopia, performing an idealized and miniaturized possible world.

Utopia is above all a textual construction of a desired state of affairs in social, economic, and political relationships between human agents. In the texts that are so constructed, an author, an agent in his or her own right, and a participant in the processes of his or her society and culture at a particular historical moment, depict a desired state of affairs. The word "utopia" itself was first used by More to describe a social order that was literally "no-where" except in the imaginative text that he constructed. However, the concept of an ideal and/or idyllic society is much older than the sixteenth century when More composed his own. His work was not the only medieval version of utopia.

It is not customary to treat what Hobbes wrote as a utopian construction. In Manuel and Manuel's survey of utopian thought in the Western world, they do not include Hobbes, though they do make passing references to his work—in one place acknowledging that Hobbes's work was, in fact, utopian (1979: 335). It is, indeed, the case that the state that Hobbes conceived was an orderly one with no invidious distinctions and surplus oppression of one agent by another, with judicious magistrates and procedural decorum—albeit a society based on a fear of the sovereign. This state of affairs as constituted makes human beings of a certain sort superior to both "natural man" and "beasts" because "it is not merely the nature of man that makes him worthier than other living creatures, but the knowledge that he acquires by meditation and by the use of reason in making good use of rules for his future actions (Hobbes, 1968 [1651]: 35).

In making his case, Hobbes posited a "state of nature" before the social contract emerged. This was a hypothetical premise on which he builds his argument and describes such a condition in which "every man is Enemy to every man; the same is consequent to the time, wherein men live without other security, than their own strength, and their own invention shall furnish them withall." In such a condition, he continued, there would be no "industry," no "culture of the earth," "no navigation," "no commodious building," "no knowledge of the face of the Earth; no account of Time; no Arts, no Letters, no Society. And the life of man, solitary poor, nasty, brutish and short" (in Parsons et al. 1961: 100).

Here in Hobbes's speculations, there is a neat paradigm: there were no laws at one time in the past, when there was no "society" and then laws were created, and "society" emerged and life ceased to be nasty and brutish and short. The construction of such a state of order, in which power was given to an entity to enforce the laws of order, is truly an early instance of utopian thinking. Human agents, by their own efforts and rational calculations, created an orderly world that was neither nasty nor brutish, and where people lived a long time.

For Hobbes, the imagination of a state of nature where there was war of one against another was a means to come to a conclusion about the importance of a "lawful"—a law-enforcing—state. In constructing this "state of nature," Hobbes did use certain contemporary versions of the society of the Native American that were available in England at that time. In this he appealed, says Richard Ashcraft, to "anthropologic evidence and to the commonly held cultural prejudices of his readers ..." In effect, through Hobbes, the savage and the anarchist became synonymous labels to be applied to any enemy of the order and "civilization" of English society (Ashcroft, 1971: 1077). Needless to say, the societies of the Native American were neither without laws nor were they without a civilization of their own.

Hobbes's "civilized" society, as orderly and harmonious relationships between individuals governed by rules that are exercised by an instituted authority, was a version of utopia without empirical references. There is, however, one system of practices in which Hobbes's first premise is neither imaginary nor an arbitrary construction created to induce a particular conclusion: the history and formalization of various games. Football—in all its manifestations—can be viewed as the construction of a social order and a Leviathan from a "state of nature" in which there were random practices, violence, artlessness, and brutishness.

Norbert Elias and his disciples have argued that the developments in the football system were part of a larger sociohistorical process they called "civilization" (in Dunning, 1999). This is no doubt true. Nevertheless, it is necessary to focus more specifically not only on the management of emotions and interpersonal etiquette and bodily activities as the Elias school contends, but also on the emergence and systematization of the playing of games by constructing rules. The fundamental theme of the rules, as they progressed through the years, was to make the game more orderly, predictable, and sociable and less brutal and individualistic.

Consider here a description by a contemporary observer of the consequences of playing one of the ancestral versions of football called "hurling": "When the hurling is ended, you shall see them returning home, as from a pitched bataile with bloody pates, bones broken and out of joynt and such bruises as serve to shorton their dais; yet all is good play and never Attorney or Crowner troubled for the matter" (Carew, 1602, quoted in Dunning, 1999: 86).

Of this game, Dunning further comments, "There was no limitation on numbers of participants, no stipulation of numerical equality between sides and no restrictions on the size of the playing area." Hurlers did not play on a demarcated field but on the territory between and surrounding what were agreed on as goals of the two sides . ." (1999: 86).

This gave way eventually to the emergence of written rules and various instructions to manage the game and referees and umpires on the fields of play themselves—the coming, indeed, of the "attorneys" and "crowners" of Carew's formulation.

The evolution of the modern games of "soccer," "rugger," and "American football" with a strict rule-bound structure and authoritative institutions like referees and organizations managing the games, is similar to the emergence of any law-bound and contractual social order. This generalization can be applied to all modern games: over the centuries, they evolved into more systematically organized and contractual systems managed by "attorneys" and "crowners"—that is, enforcers of the laws and agents of the "crown"—the word "crowner" itself evolving into the modern "coroner."

As rational structures were constructed for games and they were submitted to the ethic and etiquette of social contracts, these games were also constructing a version of utopia: out of chaos, disorder, nastiness, brutishness, and indiscipline, an orderly and civilized system was created.

In the long run, the game that became rugby football or "rugger," or football played according to the rules established by the football association, or "soccer," was an organized state of affairs in which life was much less nasty, brutish, and short than it was in the early centuries.

If one considers the development of American football—"Ameri-ball," it could perhaps be called, recognizing the U.S. claim to exceptionalism and manifest destiny—one can see the same process occurring in a game that is about 100 years old.

The indiscipline and violence on the field in American football in its early years, too, was decried, and the concept of a strictly rule-bound game was advocated by its champions. Concepts like "spontaneity" and "gentlemanliness" were now being bandied about—concepts that can be taken as the opposite of Hobbes's nastiness and brutishness. To be a gentleman and sportsman is really to be bound by certain rules of conduct. Caspar Whitney, albeit being a defender of "the necessary roughness" of football, also derided its excessive violence and brutality in its early years and considered "slugging" an opponent "ungentlemanly" and "unsportsmanlike." He even went on to denounce "foul play" in striking terms and distinguished it from a "fair fight":

> Every man of decent spirit likes a fair fight; if it were an understood part of football to punch your opponent, every player would necessarily be on his guard, and a blow well delivered a part of the skill that we might

> appreciate—if we fancied that sort of sport. But, in football, strange as the statement may read, to the average on-looker, striking an opponent except with your body is not permitted—or, rather, is permitted contrary to the rules. (1894, quoted in Oriard, 1993: 212)

These rules were put into place earlier but were not strictly enforced, and Whitney and other commentators of the time took the umpires to task for their failure to enforce the rules and bring order out of chaos. The game became reorganized in such a way that these ideological elements were to a degree muted by means of various rules. In fact, one can see the evolution of a social order through the means of a contract in the history of the game: from being a nasty and brutish game, it became a well-regulated and orderly one, with a Leviathan of referees and linesmen and officials controlling excessive individualized aggression and aggrandizement.

This is nicely summarized in the phrase that is used to designate a violation of the rules: "unnecessary roughness." This makes a distinction between a "roughness" that was necessary and one that was deemed unnecessary. In early games of football, this was a nicety that was not accorded much attention, whereas nowadays the eagle eyes of the many officials of the game are out watching for and penalizing those who cross the delicate boundaries into roughness, unsportsmanlike conduct, and illicit tackling.

Even after the institutionalization and formalization of football—that is, the construction of a "social contract"—the games continued to be refashioned to meet new demands and solve emergent problems. David Nelson, the historian of American football observes:

> The kicking sport of soccer has not changed its basic rules in two hundred years, but United States football in a little over one hundred years has been a sport in transition. The original rules of 1876 numbered sixty-one. Today, there are 738, with twenty changes a year in the last two decades. (1994: 21)

These changes were intended to make the game more efficient, that is, rational in Weber's sense of the term, as well as less dangerous to the players. Oriard, in his study of football in its many narrative forms, put this very succinctly as follows: "American football's originating act, the *fiat football* of the possession rule, in 1880 set in motion a series of consequent rule changes by which the modern game evolved over the next few decades ... The substitution of the scrimmage for the rugby scrummage, out of a simple desire to eliminate the element of change when putting the ball into play, began the development of an increasingly organized and rationalized sport, among its most distinctive qualities of strategy and team work" (1993: 143).

Utopian Social Relations in Games

Social organization of every kind is characterized by the presence of a hierarchy constituted according to one principle or another—age, gender, caste, estate, class, and so on. This can be a source of rampant alienation and dissatisfaction, and one of the ways in which these feelings have been overcome has been to provide theories explaining the presence of inequality—that is, ideologies. A strong element in these ideologies is the provision of a causal explanation for the unequal distribution of power and resources. Another element of these ideologies is the presentation of an ideal society in which inequalities are eliminated or diminished in their strength.

Christianity promises a world in which everyone is equal before God after death and comprising also a heaven where the last shall be first and some chosen few will sit at the right-hand side of God. Hinduism and Buddhism deconstruct the entire concept of a social organization of individual bodies and souls and promise a disappearance of all into nothingness—sooner or later. In addition, Hinduism also promises an amelioration of the effects of inequality by upgrading one at every incarnation, provided certain conditions are met, until nirvana is reached.

Clearly, hierarchy, and the evil effects thereof, and equality are central issues in the thought-ways of human kind. Secular approaches to the issue have created utopias in which hierarchies are abolished or recast according to various principles—merit verses inheritance, for example, or high value to society verses low value, and so on. De Tocqueville describes this nicely:

> Gradually the distinctions of rank are done away with; the barriers that once severed mankind are falling; property is divided, power is shared by man, the light of intelligence spreads, and the capacities of all classes tends towards equality. Society becomes democratic and the empire of democracy is slowly and peaceably introduced into institutions and customs. (1948: 9)

The transition was neither peaceful nor was it complete in the real world that de Tocqueville was describing and it was certainly slow since we are still trying to achieve such a democracy here as elsewhere. In games, however, such a democracy was given a mimesis and represented the doctrine of equality in an idealized form. This is true not only in regard to games today but to games in ancient times, too.

In ancient Greece, where competitive games played an important part in social, cultural, and political life, there were no team games. All such competitions were between individual athletes. In such events, unless a semblance of equality was created, *a priori* by one means or another, there would be no competition and the resulting event would be quite insignificant from the viewpoint of the spectators as well as of the athletes. The ideal of the equality of the athlete was central to the games—a feature constituted by making the "young men" compete against each other.

In many ways such a commitment to equality of the competitors was a continuation of the ideals contained in other areas of ancient Greek life. Edith Hall, classicist and student of Greek drama, has observed, "Of all the cultural legacies left by the ancient Greeks, the three which have had the most obvious impact on modern Western life are athletics, democracy and drama." She finds the common element in these forms of life to be the fact that they involved performance in an adversarial atmosphere in front of a large mass of often extremely noisy and critical spectators (2004).

This may well be true—but there is an additional element that is common to all three: each participant in these three forms of life was considered equal to the other in rights and duties. In none of these three forms were *a priori* privileges or aristocratic rights conferred on the human participants. An unknown figure could walk into a pestilence-ridden country and win a contest—the puzzle of the sphinx—and become King of Thebes. Indeed, the most striking feature, from one point of view, is the absence of too many rituals of domination and subordination in Greek dramas compared to, say, the historical plays of Shakespeare. Even gods and goddesses compete with mere mortals. Athena gets upset with Agamemnon and demands a forfeit of Iphigenia as if this were a poker game in the mythical Wild West: pay up or else...

Greek democracy, too, stressed the equal participation of at least its citizens in the deliberation that led to the making of political decisions. Women and slaves were not accorded this privilege—the principle of equality was observed on a restricted basis. Nevertheless, it must be observed that Greek women in the plays had both stature and power. Clytemnestra is not a docile and submissive woman; in the face of extreme provocation, she takes action to revenge herself against a husband who killed their daughter. Antigone, again, is not a submissive woman. She defies the king and faces a penalty unflinchingly. Not, certainly, an ideal of democratic equality; yet the theater represented active and assertive characters, both among the men and the women in equal measure.

This ideal was represented in the athletic events—though women were excluded. The games were idealized and systematized versions of the basic themes of social and cultural life of ancient Greece. The competitions were, no doubt, adversarial events before critical audiences, but the athletes participating in them were of relatively equal skill and age who were bound by the same rules of the game. This ideology is central to all contemporary games and, in fact, represents the fundamental feature of post-Enlightenment social and political democracy.

It is manifested in games in two forms: First, between players and teams, attempts are made to ensure that they are evenly "matched." In the event, of course, one player or one team is able to claim it is superior to the other. However, the margins of victory are usually within certain limits. Second, within teams, every player's role is presumed to be of equal importance as prescribed in the rules of the division of labor. Some of these players may be more skillful than others, but they are treated ideally as theoretically equal on the field of play.

To take the issue of equality between contestants first: Games are played between parties who are ostensibly equal in skill or strength or age or even gender. Experienced and well-trained players are never confronted with novices; heavyweights are not put up against lightweights; seniors are not allowed to face juveniles. Further, teams are arranged in such a way that all the best players are rarely concentrated on one team. "Seeding" is practiced in knock-out games, however, to ensure that the best players do not play the others in the early rounds and knock each other out.

The most obvious way this is managed is by the process of "handicapping"—practiced most systematically in golf. Long before it made its appearance in golf, the idea of handicapping, no doubt, was practiced in the ordinary games of everyday life between parents and children, and between older siblings and younger ones. Such games were both instruments of socialization as well as occasions for the demonstration of care and affection for the children. In playing a game with the less competent players, a gamester would hold back his or her strength, avoid taking advantage of the weaknesses or ignorance of the younger ones and even occasionally allow one of them to win. These procedures enable the younger ones to learn the game as it proceeds and give them a measure of self-esteem insofar as they are able to play the game with the more competent elders.

These practices of handicapping in informal confrontation between players—they need not occur only in the game between adults and children—are instruments that allow the game to be played at all: If the gamesters are so unevenly matched and do not practice handicapping, the game would not be, in fact, a game—indeed, there would not be a game in the game! Furthermore, the weaker party would not want to play the game again, if he or she is ensured only humiliation. To enable gaming to occur, there must be a certain level of equality between the parties, and if such equality does not obtain, steps must be taken to ensure that at least a degree of equality is created. In adult games, the system of handicapping is more formalized and systematic.

In no other field of human activity in the real world do its organizers and participants take such extraordinary steps to ensure that a contest is fair and evenly matched. In gaming utopias, such steps are a *sine qua non* of its very existence as a form of thought and activity.

The principle of equality is also maintained within a team in team games. Every player, however small his or her role in the overall strategy of play, may be considered equal in his or her participatory role. One cannot dispense with the goalkeeper in soccer or demote him or her to secondary status, just as one cannot do that with the placekicker in American football. "From each according to his ability"—to fulfill the goals of the team.

In playing games, an agent is playing one or more of the elements found in utopian literature—which are really features of humankind's "dreams," "aspirations," and "fantasies." These aspirations are really aspirations toward a less alienating, freer, and more open society than the ones in which the players find themselves. A citizen of a modern society is subject to the contingencies of an unequal division of labor and has to remain a "hunter, fisherman, a shepherd or a critical critic and must remain so if he does not want to lose his livelihood; while in communist society, where nobody has one exclusive sphere of activity but each can do one thing today and another tomorrow, to hunt in the morning, to fish in the afternoon, rear cattle in the evening, criticize after dinner, just as I have a mind, without ever becoming hunter, fisherman, shepherd or critic" (Marx and Engels, 1970: 53). Until such time as that, human agents have to content themselves with finding adventure in occasional playing at hunting or fishing, poker or bridge, tennis or badminton, golf, football or baseball; or with participating, vicariously, in the games that others play, and work in alienating jobs the rest of the time.

References

Abrahams, Roger. 1962. "Playing the Dozens." *Journal of American Folklore* 75 (297): 209–220.

Adler, Patricia, and Peter Adler. 1989. "The Gloried Self: The Aggrandizement and the Constriction of Self." *Social Psychology Quarterly* 52 (4): 299–310.

Alpers, Paul. 1972. "The Eclogue Tradition and the Nature of Pastoral." *College English* 34 (3): 352–371.

Alvarez, A. 1983. *The Biggest Game in Town.* Boston: Houghton Mifflin.

Anderson, Wanni Wibulswadi. 1980. *Children's Games in Rural Thailand.* Bangkok: Chulalongkorn University Publications.

Andrews, Keith. 1992. *The Skills of Cricket.* London: Crowood.

Anspach, Ralph. 1998. *The Million Dollar Monopoly Swindle.* Palo Alto, Calif.: American Printing.

Ashcraft, Richard. 1971. "Hobbes's Natural Man: A Study in Ideology Formation." *The Journal of Politics* 33 (4): 1076–1117.

Austin, J. L. 1970. *Philosophical Papers.* Oxford: Oxford University Press.

Bachelard, Gaston. 1964. *The Poetics of Space.* Boston: Beacon.

Bakhtin, Mikhail. 1981. *The Dialogic Imagination.* Austin: University of Texas Press.

———. 1984. *Rabelais and His World.* Bloomington: Indiana University Press.

———. 1986. *Speech Genres and Other Late Essays.* Austin: University of Texas Press.

———. 1990. *Art and Answerability.* Austin: University of Texas Press.

Bale, John. 1996. "Space, Place and Body Culture: Yi-Fu Tuan and a Geography of Sport." *Geografiska Annaler* 78B (3): 163–171.

Baltzell, Digby. 1995. *Sporting Gentlemen.* New York: The Free Press.

Barnett, Homer. 1938. "The Nature of the Potlatch." *American Anthropologist* 40 (3): 349–358.

Bellin, Andy. 2002. *Poker Nation.* New York: HarperCollins.

Bendix, Richard. 1962. *Max Weber: An Intellectual Portrait.* New York: Doubleday.

Benedict, Ruth. 1959 [1934]. *Patterns of Culture.* New York: Houghton Mifflin.

Berger, Peter, and Thomas Luckmann. 1968. *The Social Construction of Reality.* New York: Doubleday.

Best, David. 2002. "The Aesthetic in Sport." In Andrew Hollocheck (ed.), *Philosophy of Sport.* Upper Saddle River, N.J.: Prentice Hall.

Bharati, Agehananda. 1970. *The Tantric Tradition.* New York: Anchor Books.

Bissinger, H. G. 1990. *Friday Night Lights.* New York: Harper Perennial Books.

Blofeld, Henry. 2002. *Cricket and All That.* London: Hodder and Stoughton.

Bottomore, T. B. 1956. Karl Marx: *Selected Writings in Sociology and Philosophy.* New York: McGraw-Hill.

———. (ed.). 1963. *Karl Marx: Early Writings.* New York: McGraw-Hill.

Bourdieu, Pierre. 1979. *Outline of a Theory of Practice.* Cambridge: Cambridge University Press.

Breuer, Joseph, and Sigmund Freud. 1966. *Studies in Hysteria.* Boston: Beacon.

Browne, Basil. 1989. "Going on Tilt: Frequent Poker Players and Control." *Journal of Gambling Behavior* 5 (1): 3-21.

Burke, Kenneth. 1957. "Literature as Equipment for Living." In *Philosophy of Literary Form.* New York: Vintage Books.

———. 1959. "On Catharsis, or Resolution." *Kenyon Review* 3 (21): 337-374.

———. 1961. *The Rhetoric of Religion.* Boston: Beacon.

———. 1965. *Permanence and Change.* New York: Bubbs-Merrill.

———. 1967. "The Definition of Man." *Language as Symbolic Action.* Berkeley: University of California Press.

———. 1969a. *A Grammar of Motives.* Berkeley: University of California Press.

———. 1969b. *A Rhetoric of Motives.* Berkeley: University of California Press.

Buber, Martin. 1970. *I and Thou.* New York: McGraw-Hill.

Burns, Thomas. 1976. "Riddling: Occasion to Act." *Journal of American Folklore* 89 (352): 139-165.

Caillois, Roger. 1961. *Man, Play and Games.* Chicago: University of Chicago Press.

Cammann, Schyler. 1975. "The Systematic Study of Oriental Rugs: Techniques and Patterns." *Journal of the American Oriental Society* 95 (2): 248-260.

Campbell, Joseph. 1956. *The Hero with a Thousand Faces.* New York: Doubleday.

Cast, Alicia, and Peter Burke. 2002. "A Theory of Self-Esteem." *Social Forces* 80 (3): 1041-1068.

Chan, Johnny. 2004. Quoted in "Poker Pros: Now in TV's Glare, Rarely Pass Up a Game." *New York Times.* September 23, 2004, Section E-5.

Cherry, Christopher. 1975. "Games and Language." *Mind* 83 (336): 528-547.

Cohen, David. 1991. "Sexuality, Violence and the Athenian Law of Hubris." *Greece and Rome* 38 (Oct.): 171-188.

Concannon, Dale. 1995. *Golf: The Early Years.* New York: Smithmark.

Conroy, Pat. 2002. *My Losing Season.* New York: Bantam.

Craig, Hardin. 1950. "Morality Plays and Elizabethan Drama." *Shakespeare Quarterly* 1 (2): 64-72.

Crespi, Irving. 1956. "The Social Significance of Card Playing as Leisure Time Activity." *American Sociological Review* 21 (6): 717-721.

Crosset, Todd. 1995. *Outsiders in the Club House: The World of Women's Professional Golf.* Albany: State University of New York Press.

The Crusaders: Videotape of a High School Football Team's Season. 2002. Trenton, N.J.: Bosco Catholic High School.

Csikszentmihalyi, Mihaly, and Stith Bennett. 1971. "An Exploratory Model of Play." *American Anthropologist* 73 (1): 45-58.

Dargan, Amanda, and Steven Zietlin. 1990. *City Plan.* New Brunswick, N.J.: Rutgers University Press.

Dasgupta, Surendranath. 1962. *Indian Idealism*. Cambridge: Cambridge University Press.

De Bary, Theodore, Stephen Hay, Roy Weiler, Andrew Yarrow. 1958. *Sources of Indian Tradition*. New York: Columbia University Press.

Decker, Ronald, T. Depaulis, and Michael Dummett. 1996. *A Wicked Pack of Cards*. London: Duckworth.

———. 2002. *History of the Occult Tarot*. London: Duckworth.

Denzin, Norman. 1984. *On Understanding Emotions*. San Francisco: Jossey-Bass.

de Tocqueville, Alexis. 1948. *Democracy in America*. New York: Doubleday.

Dickie, James. 1968. "The Hispano-Arab Garden: Its Philosophy and Function." *Bulletin of the School of Oriental and African Studies* (University of London) 31 (2): 237–248.

Dover, Kenneth. 1974. *Greek Popular Morality in the Time of Plato and Aristotle*. Oxford: Basil Blackwell.

Dunning, Eric. 1999. *Sports Matters*. London: Routledge.

Durkheim, Emile. 1964. *The Division of Labor in Society*. New York: The Free Press.

Dyck, Noel, and E. P. Archetti. 2003. *Sport, Dance and Embodied Identity*. Oxford: Berg.

Eade, James. 1996. *Chess for Dummies*. Foster City, Calif.: IDG Books.

Elias, Norbert, and Eric Dunning. 1966. "Dynamics of Group Sports with Special Reference to Football." *British Journal of Sociology* 17 (4): 388–402.

———. 1986. *The Quest for Excitement: Sport and Leisure in the Civilizing Process*. London: Basil Blackwell.

Else, Gerald. 1970. *Aristotle's Poetics*. Ann Arbor: University of Michigan Press.

Empson, William. 1957. *Some Versions of Pastoral*. London: Chatto and Windus.

Erickson, Bonnie, and T. A. Nosanchuk, 1984. "The Allocation of Esteem and Disteem: A Test of Goode's Theory." *American Sociological Review* 49: 648–658.

Evans, David. 1976. "Riddling and the Structure of Context." *Journal of American Folklore* 89 (352): 166–188.

Fine, Gary Alan. 1987. *With the Boys: Little League Baseball and Preadolescent Culture*. Chicago: University of Chicago Press.

Fine, Gary Alan, and Kent Sandstrom. 1993. "Ideology in Action: A Pragmatic Approach to a Contested Concept." *Sociological Theory* 11 (1): 21–38.

Fischer, Bobby. 1972. *Bobby Fischer Teaches Chess*. New York: Bantam.

Fontenrose, Joseph. 1959. *Python: A Study of Delphic Myth and Its Origin*. Berkeley: University of California Press.

Foote, Nelson. 1951. "Identification as the Basis for a Theory of Motivation." *American Sociological Review* (Feb.): 14–21.

Forrest, A. J. 1957. *Village Cricket*. London: Robert Hale.

Fox, John Gerard. 1996. "Playing with Power: Ballcourts and Political Ritual in Southern Mesoamerica." *Current Anthropology* 37 (3): 483–509.

Frasca, Richard. 1990. *The Theater of the Mahabharata: Terukkuttu Performances in South India*. Honolulu: University of Hawaii Press.

———. 1998. "The Dice Game and the Disrobing (*Pakatai Tuyil*): A Terukkuttu Performance." *Asian Theater Journal* 15 (1): 1–44.

Freeman, Mike. 2002. "For Kickers and Fans Big Misses Linger." *New York Times*. December 8, 2002, Section 8, p. 1.

Fuchs, Stephen. 2001. *Against Essentialism: A Theory of Culture and Society.* Cambridge, Mass.: Harvard University Press.

Fuller, Peter. 1977. *The Champions.* New York: Urizen.

Gecas, Victor, and Michael Schwalbe. 1983. "Beyond the Looking Glass Self: Social Structure and Efficacy-Based Self-Esteem." *Social Psychology Quarterly* 46 (2): 77–88.

Geertz, Clifford. 1973. "Ideology as a Cultural System." In *The Interpretation of Cultures.* New York: Basic.

Giulianotti, Richard. 1999. *Football: A Sociology of the Global Game.* Cambridge: Polity.

Gleber, Anke. 1999. *The Art of Taking a Walk.* Princeton, N.J.: Princeton University Press.

Goffman, Erving. 1959. *The Presentation of Self in Everyday Life.* New York: Doubleday.

———. 1963. *Behavior in Public Places.* New York: The Free Press.

———. 1967. *Interaction Ritual.* New York: Doubleday.

———. 1969. *Strategic Interaction.* Philadelphia: University of Pennsylvania Press.

———. 1983. "Interaction Order." *American Sociological Review* 48 (1): 1–17.

Gold, Martin. 1976. *Delinquent Behavior in an American City.* Belmont, Calif.: Brookes Cole.

Greenblatt, Stephen. 1980. *Renaissance Self-Fashioning.* Chicago: University of Chicago Press.

Grice, Paul. 1989. *Studies in the Way of Words.* Cambridge: Cambridge University Press.

Gusfield, Joseph. 2000. *Performing Action.* New Brunswick, N.J.: Transaction.

Guttman, Alan. 1978. *From Ritual to Record.* New York: Columbia University Press.

Habermas, Jurgen. 1970a. "Toward a Theory of Communicative Competence." *Inquiry* 13 (3): 360–375.

———. 1970b. "On Systematically Distorted Communication." *Inquiry* 13 (3): 205–218.

Hall, Edith. 2004. Quoted in "When the Games Began." *New York Times.* March 9, 2004, Section F-4.

Hall, Edward. 1958. *The Silent Language.* New York: Doubleday.

Hamlyn's Complete Book of Card Games. 2001. London: Octopus Publishing Group.

Hamm, Mia. 1999. *Go for the Goal.* New York: HarperCollins.

Hammitszch, Horst. 1988. *Zen and the Art of the Tea Ceremony.* New York: St. Martin's.

Handelman, Don, and David Shulman. 1997. *God Inside Out: Siva's Game of Dice.* New York: Oxford University Press.

Harré, Rom, and W. Gerrod Parrott (eds.). 1996. *The Emotions.* London: Sage.

Hawking, Stephen. 1988. *A Brief History of Time.* New York: Bantam.

Herskovitz, Melville. 1952. *Economic Anthropology.* New York: Alfred Knopf.

Hiltebeitel, Alf. 1987. *The Ritual of Battle.* Chicago: University of Chicago Press.

Hobbes, Thomas. 1968 [1651]. *Leviathan.*

Hochschild, Arlie. 1983. *The Managed Heart: The Commercialization of Human Feeling.* Berkeley: University of California Press.

Holquist, Michael. 1968. "How to Play Utopia." *Yale French Studies* no. 41, Game, Play, Literature, pp. 106–123.

———. 1990. *Dialogism.* London: Routledge.

Huizinga, Johan. 1950. *Homo Ludens: A Study of the Play Element in Culture.* Boston: Beacon.

Hutchinson, D. 2002. *Legends of the Crease.* Sydney: Cadability Interactive Digital Solutions.

Hutton, Alice. 1979. *Cards Can't Lie: Prophetic, Educational and Playing Cards.* London: Jupiter.

Hyland, Drew. 1990. *Philosophy of Sport.* New York: Paragon.

Jacoby, James. 1987. *Jacoby on Bridge.* New York: Pocket Books.

James, C. L. R. 1983. *Beyond a Boundary.* New York: Pantheon.

Joas, Hans. 1996. *The Creativity of Action.* Chicago: University of Chicago Press.

Johari, Harish. 1975. *Leela.* New York: Coward, McCann and Geoghegan.

Josephson, Eric, and Mary Josephson. 1962. *Man Alone: Alienation in Modern Society.* New York: Dell.

Juhl, Jasper. 2003. "The Game, the Player, the World: Looking for a Heart of Gameness." In Marinka Copier and Joost Raessens (eds.), *Level-Up: Digital Games Research Conference Proceedings.* Utrecht: Universiteit Utrecht.

Kalberg, Stephen. 1980. "Max Weber's Type of Rationality: Cornerstones for the Analysis of Rationalization Processes in History." *American Journal of Sociology* 85 (5): 1145–1179.

Karp, David, G. P. Stone, and William Yoels. 1977. *Being Urban.* Lexington, Mass.: Heath.

Kermode, Frank. 2000. *The Sense of an Ending.* Oxford: Oxford University Press.

Kiernan, V. G. 1989. *The Duel in European History.* Oxford: Oxford University Press.

Kimmel, Michael. 1996. *Manhood in America.* New York: The Free Press.

Kumar, Krishan. 1987. *Utopia and Anti-Utopia in Modern Times.* New York: Blackwell.

Lefebvre, Henri. 1994. *The Production of Space.* Oxford: Blackwell.

Lévi-Strauss, Claude. 1966. *The Savage Mind.* Chicago: University of Chicago Press.

———. 1967. "The Structural Study of Myth." In *Structural Anthropology.* New York: Doubleday.

Lewis, Miles. 1987. "Architecture as Utopia." In Eugene Kamenka (ed.), *Utopias.* New York: Oxford University Press.

Luria, Alexander, and Lev Vygotsky. 1992. *Ape, Primitive Man and Child: Essays in the History of Behavior.* New York: Harvester.

MacDowell, Douglas. 1976. "'Hybris' in Athens." *Greece and Rome* 23 (4): 14–31.

Maguire, Joe. 1992. "Towards a Sociological Theory of Sport and the Emotions." In E. Dunning and C. Rojek (eds.), *Sport and Leisure in the Civilizing Process: A Critique and a Counter-Critique.* London: MacMillan.

Maines, David. 2001. *The Faultlines of Consciousness.* Hawthorne, N.Y.: Aldine de Gruyter.

Malcolm, Andrew. 1992. *Huddle: Fathers, Sons and Football.* New York: Simon and Schuster.

Malcolm, Dominic. 1999. "Cricket Spectator Disorder: Myths and Historical Evidence." *The Sports Historian* 19 (1): 1–26.

Malcolm, Norman. 1966. "Knowledge of Other Minds." In G. Pitcher (ed.), *Wittgenstein: The Philosophical Investigations: A Collection of Critical Essays.* New York: Doubleday.

Mangan, J. A. 1985. *The Games Ethic and Imperialism.* New York: Viking Penguin.

Mannheim, Karl. 1960. *Ideology and Utopia.* London: Routledge and Kegan Paul.

Manuel, Frank, and Fritzie Manuel. 1979. *Utopian Thought in the Western World.* Cambridge, Mass.: Harvard University Press.

Marples, M. 1954. *A History of Football.* London: Collins.

Martin, Patricia Yancy, and Robert Hummer. 1989. "Fraternities and Rape on Campus." *Gender and Society* 3 (4): 457–473.

Martindale, Don. 1960. *The Nature and Types of Sociological Theory.* Boston: Houghton Mifflin.

Marx, Karl, and F. Engels. 1970. *The German Ideology.* New York: International Publishers.

McCarthy, Doyle. 1984. "Towards a Sociology of the Physical World: George Herbert Mead on Physical Objects." *Studies in Symbolic Interaction* 5: 105–121.

———. 1996. *Knowledge as Culture.* London: Routledge.

McCleary, Kathleen. 2003. "On New Golf Courses, Nature Wins a Round." *New York Times.* June 6, 2003, Section F-1.

McKay, D. 1995. "A Sense of Place: The Meaning of Easter Road." Unpublished master's thesis, University of Edinburgh.

Mead, G. H. 1932. *The Philosophy of the Present.* Chicago: Open Court Publishing.

———. 1934. *Mind, Self and Society.* Chicago: University of Chicago Press.

———. 1938. *The Philosophy of the Act.* Chicago: University of Chicago Press.

———. 1962. Andrew Reck (ed.). *Selected Writings.* New York: Bobbs-Merrill.

Meisami, Julie Scott. 1985. "Allegorical Gardens in the Persian Poetic Tradition: Nezami, Rumi, Hafefz." *International Journal of Middle East Studies* 17 (2): 229–260.

Merleau-Ponty, Maurice. 1959. *The Structure of Behavior.* Boston: Beacon.

Morgenstern, Julian. 1966. *The Rites of Birth, Marriage, Death and Kindred Occasions Among the Semites.* Chicago: Quadrangle.

Mullins, Willard. 1972. "On the Concept of Ideology in Political Science." American Political Science Review 66 (2): 498–510.

Nelson, David. 1994. *An Anatomy of a Game.* Newark: University of Delaware Press.

Nicklaus, Jack, and Chris Millard. 2002. *Nicklaus by Design.* New York: Harry N. Abrams.

Noel, E. B., and J. O. M. Clark. 1924. *A History of Tennis.* Oxford: Oxford University Press.

Obeyesekere, Gananath. 2002. *Karma Imagined.* Berkeley: University of California Press.

O'Flaherty, Wendy. 1973. *Asceticism and Eroticism in the Mythology of Siva.* Oxford: Oxford University Press.

Ollman, Bertell. 1971. *Alienation: Marx's Conception of Man in Capitalist Society.* Cambridge: Cambridge University Press.

Oriard, Michael. 1991. *Sporting with the Gods.* Cambridge: Cambridge University Press.

———. 1993. *Reading Football: How the Popular Press Created an American Spectacle.* Chapel Hill: University of North Carolina Press.

Palmer, Arnold. 1999. *A Golfer's Life.* New York: Ballantine.

Panofsky, Erwin. 1982. *Meaning in the Visual Arts.* Chicago: University of Chicago Press.

Parsons, Talcott. 1961. "An Outline of the Social System." In Parsons, Talcott, E. Shils, K. D. Naegele, and J. R. Pitts (eds.). 1961. *Theories of Society.* New York: The Free Press.

Pasztory, Esther. 1972. "The Historical and Religious Significance of the Middle Classic Ballgame." In *Religion in Mesoamerica* 12: Mesa Redonda, Mexico. Sociedad Mexicana de Antropología: 441–455.

Pears, David. 1987. *The False Prison: A Study of the Development of Wittgenstein's Philosophy.* Oxford: Oxford University Press.

Peirce, Charles Sanders. 1955. *Philosophical Writings.* New York: Dover.

Perinbanayagam, R. S. 1982. *The Karmic Theater.* Amherst: University of Massachusetts Press.

Phillips, Caryl. 1999. *The Right Set.* New York: Vintage.

Plimpton, George. 1968. *Bogey Man.* New York: Harper and Row.

Postone, Moishe, Edward LiPuma, and Craig Calhoun. 1993. "Bourdieu and Social Theory." In Craig Calhoun, Edward LiPuma, and Joishe Postone (eds.), *Bourdieu: Critical Perspectives.* Chicago: University of Chicago Press.

Putney, Clifford. 2001. *Muscular Christianity: Manhood and Sports in Protestant America.* Cambridge, Mass.: Harvard University Press.

Rahula, Walpola. 1959. *What the Buddha Taught.* London: Gordon Frazer.

Rapport, Nigel. 1998. "The Hard Sell: Commercial Performances and the Narration of the Self." In Hughes-Freeland, Felicia (ed.), *Ritual, Performances and Media.* London: Routledge.

Ricoeur, Paul. 1984. *Time and Narrative.* Chicago: University of Chicago Press.

———. 1986. *Lectures on Ideology and Utopia.* New York: Columbia University Press.

Roberts, J. M., M. J. Arth, and R. R. Bush. 1959. "Games in Culture." *American Anthropologist* 61 (4): 597–605.

Rosenthal, Sandra. 1986. *Speculative Pragmatism.* Amherst: University of Massachusetts Press.

———. 2000. *Time, Continuity and Indeterminacy.* New York: State University of New York Press.

Rosman, Abraham, and Paula G. Rubel. 1972. "The Potlatch: a Structural Analysis." *American Anthropologist* 74 (3): 658–671.

Rubidge, Bradley. 1998. "Catharsis Through Admiration: Corneille Le Moyne and the Social Uses of Emotion." *Modern Philology* 95 (3): 316–334.

Ryan, Lawrence V. 1957. "Doctrine and Dramatic Structure in Everyman." *Speculum* 32 (4): 722–735.

Shackford, Martha Hale. 1904. "A Definition of the Pastoral Idyll." *PMLA* 19 (4): 583-592.

Sacks, Harvey. 1974. "An Analysis of the Course of a Joke's Telling in Conversation." In Richard Bauman and Joel Sherzer (eds.), *Explorations in the Ethnography of Speaking.* Cambridge: Cambridge University Press, 337-353.

Sacks, Harvey, E. Schegloff, and G. Jefferson. 1974. "A Simplest Systematics for the Organization of Turn-Taking for Conversation." *Language* 50 (4): 696-735.

Sauter, Wilmar. 2002. *The Theatrical Event.* Iowa City: University of Iowa Press.

Schacht, Steven. 1996. "Misogyny on and off the Pitch: The Gendered World of Male Rugby Players." *Gender and Society* 10 (5): 550-565.

Schaete, Linda, and David Freidel. 1991. "The Courts of Creation: Ballcourts, Ballgames, and Portals to the Maya Otherworld." In Vernon Scarborough and David Wilcox (eds.), *The Mesoamerican Ballgame.* Tucson: University of Arizona Press.

Schaff, Adam. 1963. *A Philosophy of Man.* New York: Monthly Review Press.

Schmidt, Raymond, and Wilbert Leonard II. 1986. "The Immortalization of the Self Through Sport." *American Journal of Sociology* 91 (5): 1088-1111.

Searle, Chris. 2001. *The Pitch of Life.* Manchester: Parrs Wood Press.

Searle, John. 1969. *Speech Acts.* Cambridge: Cambridge University Press.

Seymour, Harold. 1960. *Baseball: The Early Years.* New York: Oxford University Press.

Silverman, David J. 1998. *Harvey Sacks: Social Science and Conversation Analysis.* San Francisco: Sage.

Simmel, George. 1950. Kurt Wolff (ed.). *Essays in Sociology.* New York: The Free Press.

———. 1990. *The Philosophy of Money.* London: Routledge.

Sklansky, David. 1999. *The Theory of Poker.* Henderson, Nev.: Two Plus Two Publishing.

Snell, Bruno. 1953. *The Discovery of Mind.* Oxford: Basil Blackwell.

Sontag, Alan. 1977. *The Bridge Bum.* New York: William Morrow.

Spate, Virginia. 1987. "Arcady or Utopia? Figures in the Landscape in Late Nineteenth Century French Painting." In Eugene Kamenka (ed.), *Utopias.* New York: Oxford University Press.

Squires, Michael. 1970. "Far from the Madding Crowd as Modified Pastoral." *Nineteenth Century Fiction* 25 (3): 299-326.

Stcherbatsky, F. Th. 1962. *Buddhist Logic* (2 vols.). New York: Dover.

Steinberg, Marc. 1993. "Rethinking Ideology: A Dialogue with Fine and Sandstrom from a Dialogic Perspective." *Sociological Theory* 11 (3): 314-320.

Stirk, David. 1987. *Golf: The History of an Obsession.* London: Phaidon.

Stone, Gregory. 1971. "Sports: Play and Display." In E. Dunning (ed.), *The Sociology of Sport.* London: Frank Cass.

Suits, Bernard. 1967. "What Is a Game?" *Philosophy of Science* 34 (2): 148-156.

———. 1995. "The Elements of Sport." In W. J. Morgan and K. Meier (eds.), *Philosophic Inquiry in Sport.* Leeds: Human Kinetics.

Sullivan, Harry Stack. 1953. E. Perry (ed.). *Collected Works.* New York: W. W. Norton.

Tambiah, Stanley J. 1985. "A Performative Approach to Ritual." In *Culture, Thought and Social Action.* Cambridge, Mass.: Harvard University Press, pp. 123-158.

Tatz, Mark, and Jody Kent. 1977. *Rebirth: The Tibetan Game of Liberation.* New York: Doubleday.

Thomson, George. 1973. *Aeschylus and Athens.* London: Lawrence and Wishart.

Thrasher, Frederick. 1934. "Social Backgrounds and Informal Education." *Journal of Educational Sociology* 2 (4): 472–473.

Tuan, Yi-Fu. 1974. *Topophilia: A Study of Environmental Perception, Attitudes and Values*. Englewood Cliffs: Prentice Hall.

———. 1977. *Space and Place: The Perspective of Experience.* Minneapolis: University of Minnesota Press.

———. 1981. *Landscapes of Fear.* Minneapolis: University of Minnesota Press.

Tucci, Giusseppe. 1970. *The Theory and Practice of the Mandala.* New York: Sam Weiser.

Turner, Victor. 1974. *Dramas, Fields and Metaphors.* Ithaca, N.Y.: Cornell University Press.

Tygiel, Jules. 1983. *Baseball's Great Experiment: Jackie Robinson and His Legacy.* New York: Oxford University Press.

van Buitenen, J. A. B. 1973. *The Mahabharata* (2 vols.). Chicago: University of Chicago Press.

———. 1981. *The Bhagavadgita.* Chicago: University of Chicago Press.

Vygotsky, Lev. 1978. *Mind in Society.* Cambridge, Mass: Harvard University Press.

Wacquant, Loic. 1995. "The Pugilistic Point of View: How Boxers Think and Feel About Their Trade." *Theory and Society* 24 (4): 489–535.

———. 2004. *Body & Soul: Notebooks of an Apprentice Boxer.* New York: Oxford University Press.

Weber, Max. 1958a. *The Protestant Ethic and the Spirit of Capitalism.* New York: Scribner and Sons.

———. 1958b. *The Religion of India.* New York: The Free Press.

———. 1964. *The Sociology of Religion.* Boston: Beacon.

Wellman, Barry. 1983. "Network Analysis: Some Basic Principles." *Sociological Theory* 1 (1): 155–200.

White, Harrison. 1992. *Identity and Control.* Princeton, N.J.: Princeton University Press.

Wikan, Unni. 1990. *Managing Turbulent Hearts: A Balinese Formula for Living.* Chicago: University of Chicago Press.

Williams, Jack. 1999. *Cricket and England.* London: Frank Cass.

Williams, Oscar. 1952. *Immortal Poems of the English Language.* New York: Pocket Books.

Williams, Ron, and James Boyd. 1993. *Ritual Art and Knowledge.* Columbia: University of South Carolina Press.

Wilson, John. 1994. *Playing by the Rules: Sport, Society and the State.* Detroit, Mich.: Wayne State University Press.

Wittgenstein, Ludwig. 1958. *Philosophical Investigations.* London: Blackwell.

Wolf, Burton. 1976. "The Monopolization of Monopoly: The Landlord's Game." San Francisco: The Bay Guardian. Retrieved September 9, 2005, from *http://www.adena.com.*

Yachnin, Paul. 1982. "A Game of Chess and Chess Allegory." *Studies in English Literature* 22 (2): 317–330.

Ziff, Paul. 1974. "A Fine Forehand." *Journal of the Philosophy of Sport* 1 (2): 106–110.

Zurcher, Louis. 1970. "The 'Friendly' Poker Game: A Study of an Ephemeral Role." *Social Forces* 49 (2): 173–186.

Index

About the Author

Robert Perinbanayagam is a professor of sociology at Hunter College, City University of New York. He is the author most recently of *The Presence of Self,* which won the Charles Horton Cooley Award and the Theory Prize from the American Sociological Association.